# EVERYDAY
# ETHICS

## RELATED WORKS FROM GEORGETOWN UNIVERSITY PRESS

*Aquinas on Virtue: A Causal Reading*
Nicholas Austin

*A Culture of Engagement: Law, Religion, and Morality*
Cathleen Kaveny

*Ethics: The Fundamental Questions of Our Lives*
Wolfgang Huber, translated by Brian McNeil

*Kinship across Borders: A Christian Ethic of Immigration*
Kristin E. Heyer

# EVERYDAY ETHICS

## MORAL THEOLOGY and THE PRACTICES OF ORDINARY LIFE

MICHAEL LAMB
BRIAN A. WILLIAMS
EDITORS

Georgetown University Press / Washington, DC

The publisher is not responsible for third-party websites or their content. URL links were active at time of publication.

LIBRARY OF CONGRESS CATALOGING-IN-PUBLICATION DATA

Names: Lamb, Michael, 1982- editor. | Williams, Brian A., (Brian Alan), 1971–
    editor.
Title: Everyday Ethics : Moral Theology and the Practices of Ordinary Life/
    Michael Lamb and Brian A. Williams, editors.
Description: Washington, DC : Georgetown University Press, 2019. | This volume began as a
    conference on Everyday Ethics : A Future of Moral Theology? at the University of Oxford on
    May 26–27, 2016--Acknowledgments | Includes bibliographical references and index.
Identifiers: LCCN 2018059527 (print) | LCCN 2019015881 (ebook) | ISBN 9781626167087
    (ebook) | ISBN 9781626167070 (pbk.: alk. paper) | ISBN 9781626167063 (hardcover : alk.
    paper) Subjects: LCSH: Christian ethics--Congresses.
Classification: LCC BJ1189 (ebook) | LCC BJ1189 .E94 2019 (print) | DDC 241--dc23
LC record available at https://lccn.loc.gov/2018059527

♾ This book is printed on acid-free paper meeting the requirements of the American National Standard for Permanence in Paper for Printed Library Materials.

20 19      9 8 7 6 5 4 3 2  First printing

Printed in the United States of America.
Cover design by Pam Pease.

# CONTENTS

# ACKNOWLEDGMENTS

THIS VOLUME BEGAN as a conference titled "Everyday Ethics: A Future of Moral Theology?" at the University of Oxford on May 26–27, 2016. We are especially grateful to Nigel Biggar, Ginny Dunn, the McDonald Centre for Theology, Ethics, and Public Life, and Al and Peter McDonald of the McDonald Agape Foundation for supporting the idea for this conference and working to make it possible. We are also grateful to a number of cosponsors, including Christ Church, Oxford; the Faculty of Theology and Religion at the University of Oxford; New City Commons and the Institute for Advanced Studies in Culture at the University of Virginia; the Oxford Character Project; Oxford University Press; and the Templeton World Charity Foundation. A generous grant from the John Fell Fund at the University of Oxford provided essential support for the conference and edited volume. We are also grateful for support from the Templeton Honors College at Eastern University and Wake Forest University.

We owe special thanks to Michael Banner for the work that inspired the conference and edited volume and for his gracious support throughout the process of organizing both. We also owe a heartfelt thanks to the contributors whose insightful essays populate this volume: Michael Banner, Luke Bretherton, Brian Brock, Morgan Clarke, Molly Farneth, Craig Gay, Eric Gregory, Jennifer Herdt, Philip Lorish, Charles Mathewes, Patrick McKearney, Rachel Muers, Stephanie Mota Thurston, and Justin Welby. A number of respondents at the conference helped to refine the arguments in this volume and enriched the interdisciplinary conversation, including Sabina Alkire, David Clough, Sir Andrew Dilnot, Victoria Nash, Chad Wellmon, Joshua Yates, and Ruth Yeoman. Two anonymous reviewers offered helpful feedback that improved the volume significantly. Other friends and colleagues were valuable conversation partners in conceiving and supporting the conference and subsequent volume. We especially thank Jonathan Brant, Emily Gum, Joshua Hordern, Philip Lorish, James Orr, Martyn Percy, and Greg Thompson. We also thank Cameron Silverglate for his help formatting the volume and preparing it for publication.

Finally, we are grateful to Georgetown University Press for believing in this volume and bringing it to publication. It has been a joy to work with Hope LeGro, Glenn Saltzman, and their committed team. Their dedication to publishing significant works in religion and ethics is a testament to the important role that Georgetown University Press plays in enriching the study and practice of everyday ethics.

# INTRODUCTION

## CONTEXTUALIZING EVERYDAY ETHICS:
## MORAL THEOLOGY MEETS ANTHROPOLOGY
## AND THE SOCIAL SCIENCES

### MICHAEL LAMB AND BRIAN A. WILLIAMS

WHEN MANY PEOPLE THINK OF ETHICS, they tend to focus on "hard cases": moral dilemmas that involve a seemingly intractable conflict between competing values, beliefs, or commitments. Such moral quandaries captivate the popular imagination, populating news cycles, advice columns, and introductory college courses and textbooks. Scholars and students consider, for example, whether it is ethical to tell a lie that might have good consequences or whether it is right to take another's life for a just cause. Others debate whether a government can violate religious convictions or whether genetic enhancements are morally permissible. Hard cases are useful conceptual and pedagogical tools that enable us to analyze moral conflicts, identify general principles, and apply principles to practical issues in ways that prompt moral reflection and deliberation. But a potential danger lurks in this approach: an exclusive focus on hard cases can reduce ethics to dramatic and rare moments of decision, which are often quite detached from most people's lived experiences. This reduction obscures the ethics of ordinary practices and the ways that our communities and cultures shape (and are shaped by) our actions, character, and commitments.[1] A focus on extraordinary dilemmas ignores "the ethics of everyday life."[2]

Over the last decade and a half, scholars in theology and religion have sought to reorient attention to these dimensions of ordinary life by looking to anthropology and the social sciences to inform their normative theorizing and moral imagination.[3] By drawing on ethnographic analyses of particular communities and thick descriptions of everyday practices, they have sought to explicate the norms that govern these communities and identify the virtues, practices, and traditions that constitute their shared ethical life. At the same time, many anthropologists and social scientists have turned to ethics and religion as objects for empirical analysis, examining moral and religious traditions not simply as systems of beliefs but as collections of practices, norms, and rituals that shape ordinary life. This "ethical turn" in anthropology has highlighted the insights that emerge from the theoretical analysis of empirical data and ethnographic observation.[4]

Such interdisciplinary exchange has proven generative on both sides, sparking new lines of inquiry and opening up emerging fields of academic study. But such disciplinary boundary-crossing also raises difficult normative and methodological questions for scholars working across these fields: What can moral theologians learn from anthropology and the social sciences? Do moral theologians benefit primarily from anthropology's ethnographic method or also from the substantive insights gleaned from social scientific analysis? How can an "ethnographic turn" assist moral theologians in attending more sensitively and constructively to the embodied ethics of everyday life, and what might such a turn neglect or obscure?

Similarly, anthropologists and social scientists might question what they can learn from normative inquiry and conceptual analysis in moral theology: What opportunities, risks, or limitations accompany this encounter? How should scholars working across these disciplines reconcile emergent tensions between theoretical reflection, normative inquiry, and empirical analysis? To what extent should normative judgments be acknowledged, ventured, or withheld, and by whom and for what purpose? And how do our social, institutional, and disciplinary locations implicate us in certain ways of seeing, thinking, and judging, including how we conceptualize "ethics" or even the "everyday"? These questions animate the methodological reflections and practical applications in this volume.

Our investigation takes its starting point from the recent work of Michael Banner, who proposes a new direction for moral theology. In *The Ethics of Everyday Life: Moral Theology, Social Anthropology, and the Imagination of the Human*, he argues that the discipline of moral theology or Christian ethics as generally practiced in classrooms and textbooks is "insufficiently interested in the social."[5] Preoccupied with hard cases and abstract conclusions about good and bad acts, especially in the realm of bioethics, it has become complacently unconcerned with narrating "psychologically and socio-culturally realistic" accounts of people's quotidian moral decisions and actions.[6] According to Banner, this represents a failure of self-understanding and practice on the part of moral theology. While it should attend to difficult questions, moral theology should also fulfill its pastoral and therapeutic responsibilities to proclaim "good news" that liberates people's daily moral lives. This task requires moral theology to narrate a plausible account of how the good, right, and appropriate may be embodied in the various stages and phases of normal, everyday lives. As Banner explains, a moral theology obsessed with hard cases "has the capacity neither to support the imagination and practice of the good, nor to engage critically and therapeutically with the imagination and practice of the bad."[7] Thus, he suggests, "the task of moral theology, properly conceived, . . . must be not only to judge, but to understand and characterize the lives out of which our actions, good or bad, plausibly, persuasively, or even compellingly arise."[8] A moral theology detached from social context and lived experience fails to serve people as it should.[9]

To offer an "ethics not of hard cases, but of the life course," Banner argues that moral theology should engage deliberately and constructively with social anthropology, a discipline whose cultural sensitivity and thick descriptions could enable moral theologians to narrate a fuller and more textured account of everyday life in all its "psychological and sociocultural depth."[10] In *The Ethics of Everyday Life*, Banner models this method by drawing on ethnographic analysis to illuminate major "moments in the life course"—conception, birth, suffering, death, and burial.[11] In addition to being moments through which every life passes, these particular events interest Banner for two reasons. First, they are likely to "feature in any outline syllabus for a course in social anthropology," but their understanding and practice are often fiercely contested.[12] In these contestations, the meaning of human life is at stake. How a culture thinks about and practices these moments largely reveals and determines how it thinks about human existence more generally. Therefore, Banner calls moral theology to attend to these contested practices with the kind of nuanced care he sees within the discipline of social anthropology. Banner's hypothesis (and one he tests and models throughout his book) is that this approach keeps moral and theological reflection rooted in the lives of actual communities and individuals and, in turn, informs ethical analysis with the textured depth and detail of concrete, lived experience.[13]

Second, as a Christian theologian, Banner recognizes that these major life moments reflect the events in Christ's life that find their way into the Christian creeds. The Apostles' Creed, for example, states that Christ was "conceived by the Holy Spirit, born of the Virgin Mary, suffered under Pontius Pilate, was crucified, died, and was buried." The Bampton Lectures, from which *The Ethics of Everyday Life* originated, explicitly ask speakers to comment on a set of topics that include "the Articles of the Christian Faith, as comprehended in the Apostles' and Nicene Creeds."[14] In his 2013 lectures, Banner accepts this charge by focusing on the moments of Christ's life recounted in the creeds: moments that have been sculpted, painted, preached, poeticized, and prayed from the beginning of the Christian church and that have come to shape a broad Christian vision of human being and living in diverse temporal and cultural settings.[15] "Through these countless engagements with the life of Christ," Banner argues, "that life has been brought to diverse imaginative realizations and in those realizations different architectures of the human and of human subjectivity have been explored, staged, elaborated and commended."[16] The variegated Christian imagination of human being that has emerged, he suggests, might benefit from conversations with social anthropology and other moral imaginaries of human being that were not begotten from the Christian tradition.

The significance of Banner's approach and the challenge it presents have been recognized by scholars across the disciplines. In April 2015, anthropologists and sociologists from the Society for the Anthropology of Religion organized a symposium on Banner's book at their biennial meeting in San Diego, California.[17] A year later, in May 2016, New City Commons and The McDonald Centre for Theology, Ethics, and Public Life hosted an international conference at the University of Oxford (from which this volume emerges) that invited theologians, anthropologists, philosophers, and social scientists to critically engage Banner's proposal and consider how it could be extended to areas of everyday ethics that his book does not address. A few months later, in September 2016, Banner's book was cited as the inspiration for a conference on theological anthropology at the University of Leuven, where he was the keynote speaker. And in October 2016, the Kirby Laing Institute for Christian Ethics at the University of Cambridge convened a symposium devoted to analyzing Banner's approach. This serious scholarly interest across multiple fields, institutions, and continents reflects what Charles Mathewes describes in chapter 12 as the "epoch-marking" character of Banner's work. For Mathewes, *The Ethics of Everyday Life* serves as "a kind of capstone to the past few decades' methodological reflection in theological ethics and an exemplary text for what moral theology, once it has learned from those methodological reflections, can do."[18]

Although Banner's work is distinctive, it is not entirely new. As several contributors to this volume note, Banner's approach echoes disciplinary trends in moral philosophy and religious ethics during the late twentieth and early twenty-first centuries.[19] In 1958, G. E. M. Anscombe's seminal article "Modern Moral Philosophy" helped to initiate the recovery of virtue ethics in moral philosophy. Challenging legalistic theories of Kantianism and utilitarianism that focus on acts, obligations, and duties abstracted from particular characters, contexts, and communities, Anscombe suggested that philosophers should stop doing moral philosophy until they develop "an adequate philosophy of psychology," including "an account of human nature, human action, the type of characteristic a virtue is, and above all of human 'flourishing.'"[20] Several scholars took up Anscombe's call. In 1971, Edmund Pincoffs targeted a dominant strand of "quandary ethics" that reduces ethical analysis to justifying and applying abstract principles to discrete "moral problems" rather than considering the social contexts of individual agents and the virtues, communities, and forms of moral education they need to flourish.[21] A decade later, Alasdair MacIntyre's *After Virtue* did more than any book to recover the centrality of virtues, practices, and narratives in the moral life.[22] Due to the influential work of Anscombe, Pincoffs, and

MacIntyre, among others, moral philosophers have come to see virtue ethics as a viable alternative to Kantian and consequentialist theories of ethics.[23]

While the revival of virtue ethics in the last fifty years has redirected attention to everyday forms of character and community in ways that resonate with Banner's approach,[24] some recent manifestations of virtue ethics in moral philosophy tend to reflect the kinds of analytical abstraction that underwrote early critiques of its alternatives. Many contemporary theories of virtue ethics remain fairly technical and abstract, focusing, for example, on theoretical disputes about justificatory standards for right action or metaethical claims about how virtue relates to other moral considerations without devoting significant attention to how virtue is cultivated within a life. Even some philosophers who devote their work to justifying, identifying, or individuating virtues do not often consider the everyday practices needed to cultivate and sustain character in ordinary social and political communities.[25]

Scholars of religious ethics have avoided some of these limits by grounding their conceptions of virtue, character, and narrative within particular traditions and communities, offering thick descriptions of concrete practices that avoid the analytical abstraction characterizing some recent work in philosophy.[26] Stanley Hauerwas's account of Christian virtues and their role in forming (and being formed by) the church has been among the most influential in Christian ethics.[27] In a similar vein, a number of scholars in theology, ethics, and congregational studies have explored how ethnography can inform their understanding of ecclesiology, making "ecclesiology and ethnography" a growing interdisciplinary field.[28]

Other scholars have sought to expand the scope of ethics beyond the bounds of religious institutions by making an ethnographic turn to wider communities of concern. Luke Bretherton and Jeffrey Stout, for example, have drawn on their ethnographic analyses of broad-based community organizations to show how religious citizens and institutions have built grassroots coalitions to address urgent moral and political issues.[29] Similarly, Melissa Snarr has highlighted how local coalitions of religious activists have partnered with labor unions and civic organizations to build moral agency and political support for the living wage movement.[30] Meanwhile, a number of feminist, liberationist, *mujerista*, and womanist theologians from diverse traditions across the globe have redirected ethical attention and social criticism to ordinary political, social, and economic practices and structures, while other scholars have drawn on ethnographic analyses of particular communities to illuminate the moral diversity and theological complexity of lived experience.[31] These ethnographic turns in religious ethics resonate deeply with Banner's ethnographic approach to moral theology.[32]

Interestingly, similar trends have characterized the last decade of scholarship in anthropology and the social sciences. Indeed, Banner's foray into ethnography was originally inspired by social anthropologists who made moral and religious communities the subjects of their analysis.[33] As a moral theologian on the UK's Human Tissue Authority, Banner was particularly informed by Lesley Sharp's description of the moral relations between organ donors and recipients in her book *Strange Harvest*.[34] As Banner delved deeper into the field, he came to appreciate anthropology's "social intelligence" and capacity "to fathom and map moral worlds" that are highly relevant to moral theology but often ignored or misunderstood.[35] In looking to anthropology, Banner found numerous conversation partners.[36] Over the last decade, an increasing number of influential anthropologists and social scientists have focused their research on analyzing morally normed social dynamics and developing anthropological methods to study ethical practices and moral communities.[37] Recent work by Paul Brodwin, Juliet du Boulay, Didier Fassin, James Faubion, James Laidlaw, Michael Lambek, and Joel Robbins, among many others, illustrates this turn toward everyday ethics within social anthropology.[38]

The purpose of this volume is to explore what can be learned from this interdisciplinary exchange, with a particular focus on what moral theology can learn from anthropology and the social sciences. By starting with Banner's methodological proposal and considering how it might be analyzed, applied, and extended, this collection seeks to extend Banner's basic approach to other areas and open new vistas on how we understand the methods, practices, and challenges of everyday ethics.

## An Overview

The volume proceeds in three parts. The essays in part I provide a careful and critical engagement with Banner's methodological approach from various disciplinary perspectives. In chapter 1, Molly Farneth, a scholar of religious and philosophical ethics, situates Banner's work within recent trends in religious studies. While Farneth endorses Banner's attention to character formation and the relationships and rituals in which it is embedded, she notes a tension in Banner's vision of moral theology: although he acknowledges diversity within the Christian tradition, he often refers to "the Christian imagination" in the singular, without explicitly acknowledging the plurality of Christian imaginations. To illustrate, Farneth identifies two divergent Christian enactments of the Stations of the Cross: Mel Gibson's film *The Passion of the Christ* and an event organized by a Philadelphia faith-based group that enacts Christ's suffering as a way to prevent gun violence. By distinguishing the effects of these diverse imaginings, Farneth emphasizes that rituals are not only expressive and formative practices that forge solidarity but also "sites of contestation over which sorts of people and societies we want to bring about."

In chapter 2, Stephanie Mota Thurston situates Banner's account more broadly within the tradition of post–Vatican II Christian social ethics in the United States. Thurston agrees that much of the dominant discourse in ethics, particularly professional ethics, focuses heavily on "hard cases" and relies on forms of moral philosophy often disassociated from morality as an everyday social practice. However, she argues that certain strands within the Christian tradition have already been utilizing methods that seek to depict the elaborate textures of everyday life. Drawing on the work of Katie Cannon and Ada María Isasi-Díaz, Thurston puts Banner's project in conversation with the past three decades of womanist ethics and *mujerista* theology. Thurston focuses on two of Banner's central claims: his methodological claim about the need for moral theology to engage more deeply with social anthropology, and his practical claim that this methodological realignment will assist moral theology in its "therapeutic" task. In these two areas, Thurston sees fertile ground for deeper engagement with diverse strands of thought within the Christian tradition.

In chapter 3, social anthropologist Morgan Clarke endorses Banner's use of ethnographic accounts to supply rich descriptions of the "ordinary" for ethical reflection, which enables moral theologians to tease out the implicit beliefs embedded in many social practices and provides material for the kind of normative ethical reflection they hope to accomplish. Yet Clarke also pushes moral theologians to clarify what constitutes the "ordinary" and "everyday" and to consider whether these categories can accommodate the explicit rules, laws, and beliefs that saturate the daily practices and habits of diverse traditions. Clarke suggests that, for Banner, the "everyday" refers more to the method of ethnography (the close observation of ordinary people and practices) than to the subject of ethics, which, like the examples of organ transplants Banner analyzes, might be quite extraordinary. Situating Banner's work within larger shifts in the anthropology of ethics and exploring structures of institutionalization and professionalization, which are also central to Herdt and Gregory in chapters 5 and 6, Clarke draws on his ethnographic work in Islam to argue that Banner's scope should be broadened to include the rules, decisions, and structures of professions and institutions, including Banner's own discipline of Christian ethics.

In chapter 4, Brian Brock offers a perspective from moral theology. He contrasts Banner's methodological project with other attempts to overcome the tension between academic theology and the embodied life of the church. Unlike recent attempts that simply combine ecclesiology and ethnography or justify theology to the social sciences, Brock argues that Banner remains deeply theological while being practically engaged and politically radical. This integrated approach frees Banner from continuous reflection on method and allows him to move more immediately to densely textured insights into the "ethical life worlds" in which people enact moral decisions. After situating Banner's approach alongside earlier turns to the everyday in European thought, Brock compares Banner's method with the three tiers Gerald

McKenny identifies in contemporary ethical responses to emerging medical technology. Brock argues that Banner encompasses multiple tiers by offering fine-grained reflection on the effects of particular techniques in order to inquire into the "practices, activities, and states that are worthwhile for human beings to pursue." Brock concludes by contrasting Banner's ethnographic turn and Stanley Hauerwas's narrative theology to illuminate the distinctive features of their approaches.

The essays in part II extend Banner's basic methodological approach to other areas of everyday ethics that are absent from his original work. As mentioned above, Banner concentrates on major moments in a life course, in particular the "paradigmatically human" moments that define every human life, including the life of Christ as recounted in the Christian creeds.[39] Such a focus provides a useful heuristic for a Christian theologian, particularly one charged in the Bampton Lectures with commenting on those creeds. These moments also align with Banner's field of expertise, bioethics, which is particularly suitable to analyses of conception, birth, suffering, death, and burial. To move beyond bioethical analysis of extraordinary moments, part II considers how Banner's methodological approach might be applied to other, perhaps more everyday, practices.

In chapter 5, Jennifer Herdt considers practices of education. Situating Banner's work within the mid-twentieth-century retrieval of socially embedded virtue ethics and postliberal attention to culture, Herdt affirms Banner's "cultural turn" as a beneficial way to interpret the world and act more responsibly within it. But echoing other contributors, she registers three caveats: (1) social anthropology should be used alongside other disciplines that also offer thick descriptions of lived social realities, (2) scholars should recognize that the Christian tradition generates multiple moral imaginaries rather than a singular one, and (3) everyday ethics should be recast as a form of "engaged social criticism." Herdt next considers how anthropologically informed social criticism might help us understand two contemporary models of education: one embodied in the disciplinary specialization, expert knowledge, and institution-building of the modern research university and one enacted in the critical thinking, communal deliberation, and social activism of the Highlander Folk School. Herdt argues that both models attend to the moral formation of persons within ongoing traditions of practice and need not be seen as antithetical to each other or to the Christian tradition. She concludes by noting recent developments in the US college admissions process that acknowledge education as moral formation in a way that is compatible with Christian visions of service and love.

One of Herdt's central claims is that specialization and institutionalization are not necessarily incompatible with the Christian faith. Eric Gregory presses this point further in chapter 6. Drawing on recent ethnographic analyses of contemporary humanitarianism, Gregory considers what social anthropology can teach moral theologians about humanitarian aid, a practice often perceived to be central to the Christian life but rarely studied in Christian ethics. While Gregory affirms anthropologists' patient attention to the "lived realities of humanitarian work" and their criticisms of humanitarianism's potential to facilitate complicity in structures of domination, he also worries that anthropology's often totalizing critique can authorize a "romance of powerlessness" that discourages the pursuit of justice through the institutional structures needed to address poverty, domination, and inequality on a global scale. According to Gregory, institutionalization, professionalization, and organizational efficiency, like any human technology, can be dehumanizing, but they need not be. They can also be "tools for human flourishing" and "forms of the human spirit that participate in divine transcendence." Gregory offers an alternative to the anti-institutionalism that characterizes some moral theology and social anthropology, encouraging scholars in both fields to recognize "love's fleshly work" in mundane spheres.

In chapter 7, Craig Gay critically analyzes the technological mind-set that increasingly conditions how persons view themselves and the world. While certain aspects of modern technology should be celebrated, Gay argues that a large and growing body of evidence suggests that modern technology—in particular, automatic machine technology—is not necessarily conducive to "ordinary, embodied human thriving," especially in the realms of everyday work and relationships. He suggests that people have adopted a "mechanical" outlook that justifies the mastery of human and non-human nature in terms of productivity and profitability. Given the Christian commitment to incarnation and resurrection, Gay concludes that Christians in particular should not acquiesce in the face of technology's diminution of embodied human existence.

In chapter 8, Philip Lorish follows Gay's concern with economically driven technology by offering a critical assessment of the recent economic shift from "managerial capitalism" toward "flexible capitalism." Modeling how ethnographic insights can inform moral theology, Lorish draws on careful studies of cultural trends and personal conversations with entrepreneurs and workers in Silicon Valley to illustrate the emergence of the contingent worker economy and analyze how three core concepts—collaboration, disruption, and optimization—have transformed our conceptions of work and our relations to employers, colleagues, and neighbors. In light of these radical changes, Lorish argues that moral theologians can benefit from the observational and descriptive skills provided by the social sciences, along with their ability to track social norms and practices through time. But he contends that the changing landscape of technology and work will also require moral theologians to venture prospective judgments—to give "counsel" on how best to respond to the future. Lorish cautiously offers such counsel in his conclusion, where he ventures four provisional judgments to guide moral theologians as they consider the effects of new technologies on human persons and communities, the opportunities and obligations of neighbor love, and the role of the state in a shared economy.

In chapter 9, Justin Welby, the archbishop of Canterbury, continues the focus on technology and work by analyzing the economic practices of borrowing and spending. Drawing on his personal experience as an executive in the oil industry, the chair of the UK's Parliamentary Commission on Banking Standards, and the leader of the Church of England, Welby argues that if moral theology is to offer a salutary economic ethic that nurtures a just financial system, it must understand the nature of the market and the "billions of everyday people" whose decisions make up the global economy. For Welby, this task involves analyzing the complex interplay between risk and reward, spending and hoarding, money and power. It also involves understanding two factors within the financial market that inhibit the development of a more just economy: moralizing regulation and impersonal technology. The first, he argues, is based on inadequate conceptions of human nature, while the second actively suppresses the personal encounters that once regulated and humanized financial transactions. Challenging these two assumptions, Welby encourages scholars to consult theology, social anthropology, and economics in order to develop a more just global economy.

Rachel Muers considers the everyday ethics of eating in chapter 10, offering an ethical, theological, and methodological analysis of food sharing. Focusing in particular on the "boundaries" and "joining points" of practices, Muers explores the practice of food sharing across various contexts. To frame the discussion, she examines Jerome's defense of Christian asceticism amid the stark diversity of the world's diets and offers a close reading of food sharing in specific passages of scripture. She then uses anthropological research and case studies to examine food sharing in diverse social and historical contexts, including natural settings between non-human animals, social settings in the East End of London in 1913, and contemporary settings of the Real Junk Food Project. By identifying how food sharing reflects our physically embodied and culturally embedded sociality, Muers shows how this practice can exemplify a joining together that neither ignores the embodied particulars of the joining parties nor allows those particulars to prohibit genuine communion. For Muers, the complexity of food-sharing practices emphasized by anthropological analysis illustrates how careful attention to everyday practices can not only inform the content of moral theology but provoke much-needed reflection on how it is done.

Part III returns to larger methodological questions to explore what the ethnographic turn might mean for the future of moral theology. In chapter 11, Luke Bretherton situates Banner's turn to ethnography within a long tradition of Anglican social thought that looks to culture as a starting point for Christian ethics. While ethnography can enhance and inform Christian theology's emphasis on embodied and relational forms of life, Bretherton highlights three conundrums that this cultural turn presents for moral theology: (1) a tension between recognizing the radical otherness of divine transcendence and looking to history and culture as immanent sites of divine encounter; (2) a tension between seeing either conflict or harmony as the basis of social, political, and economic relations in a fallen world; and (3) a tension between thickly describing everyday practices and challenging idolatrous structures that dominate or distort our way of being in the world. If ethnography is to inform moral reflection, Bretherton argues, theologians must adequately address these tensions between Christ and culture. To offer a constructive way forward, Bretherton draws on his own ethnographic study of broad-based community organizing and interfaith relations to recast the fundamental tasks of Christian ethics.

In chapter 12, Charles Mathewes situates Banner's work among its methodological forebears and argues that it has special relevance to how the contemporary church engages religiously and philosophically plural cultures. According to Mathewes, the church can choose between two basic paths. The now popular "Benedict Option" encourages Christians to reject a corrupt modern culture and focus inwardly on the church, emphasizing personal formation and ecclesial community in ways that often only superficially and unnecessarily oppose the complex culture beyond its bounds. Mathewes, by contrast, prefers what he calls the "Francis Option," which recognizes that while the church is not "of" the world, it is still "in" and "for" it. He argues that anthropology and the social sciences can help the church and its moral theologians by encouraging openness toward the broader culture, increasing awareness of social complexity, and supplying conversation partners and allies. At the same time, Mathewes suggests that moral theology can offer anthropologists and social scientists important conceptual resources for analyzing the tensions of modern life. He focuses on two: the character of human agency and the challenge of pluralism. Incorporating insights from several contributors in this volume, Mathewes concludes that a constructive yet critical engagement with anthropology and the social sciences can help moral theology develop a "moral ethnography" and "sacramental ethics" that celebrates the "transfiguration" of the everyday.

In the concluding chapter, Michael Banner offers a retrospective look at his own work in light of the critical engagement and practical applications offered by contributors to this volume. Tying together themes from the preceding essays, Banner deconstructs his own work with refreshing candor, highlighting its limits and blind spots and clarifying his original purposes as they have been tested through ongoing interdisciplinary engagement. Though he acknowledges that he is not the first moral theologian to call attention to the everyday and the insights of social anthropology, he maintains that the discipline has yet to take this call to heart. In order to fulfill its purpose, Banner concludes, Christian ethics "needs to have the humility and patience to engage ethical lives attentively and openly, with a willingness to allow these lived ethical worlds to disclose themselves to us."

Finally, Patrick McKearney offers a bibliographic essay that surveys the current exchange between moral theology, anthropology, and the social sciences. A social anthropologist who studies theology and religion, McKearney situates these ideas and approaches within their larger disciplinary contexts, identifies important texts and authors from each field, and explores the central questions and tensions that emerge in this interdisciplinary dialogue. He concludes by considering two themes—suffering and tragedy—that highlight alternative approaches to integrating insights from theology and anthropology. McKearney's essay provides an invaluable resource for scholars, students, and citizens interested in understanding everyday ethics and exploring prospects for interdisciplinary research and reflection.

## Conclusion

Ultimately, this volume aims to direct attention toward everyday ethics and explore what scholars can learn through critical and constructive engagement across disciplinary boundaries. We recognize that this effort has several limitations. First, since our aim is to assess what moral theology can learn from anthropology and the social sciences, most of our contributors are moral theologians rather than anthropologists or social scientists. But as the contributions from Clarke and McKearney show, we also value insights from these fields and hope this volume will deepen this interdisciplinary conversation while showing how scholars from other disciplines can engage ethnographic work. Second, since the volume takes its starting point from Michael Banner's book, most of our contributors approach these issues from the perspective of Christian moral theology rather than from other religious traditions. Yet as Clarke demonstrates through his helpful engagement with Islam in chapter 3 and McKearney shows through his survey of scholarship in this emerging field, scholars and practitioners working in other traditions—both within and beyond Christianity—have valuable perspectives to offer. Third, this volume does not offer ethnographic case studies of particular communities. Rather, it focuses on particular practices that may be shared by diverse communities, even if they are enacted in different ways. Finally, this scholarly attention to everyday practices is neither exhaustive nor conclusive. Many other ordinary practices are also worthy of consideration, and, as Farneth, Thurston, Herdt, and Muers highlight, many of these practices involve diverse imaginings and contested enactments. Our hope is that this volume opens the space for that contestation and encourages both scholars and citizens to think more intentionally about the ethics of their everyday lives.

## Notes

1. For an influential critique, see Edmund Pincoffs, "Quandary Ethics," *Mind* 80, no. 320 (1971): 552–71; and Edmund Pincoffs, *Quandaries and Virtues: Against Reductivism in Ethics* (Lawrence:

University of Kansas Press, 1986). For similar critiques in religious ethics, see Stanley Hauerwas, *The Peaceable Kingdom: A Primer in Christian Ethics* (Notre Dame, IN: University of Notre Dame Press, 1983), esp. 4, 116–34; and Richard B. Miller, "On Making a Cultural Turn in Religious Ethics," *Journal of Religious Ethics* 33, no. 3 (September 2005): 409–33, esp. 410–13.

2. Michael Banner, *The Ethics of Everyday Life: Moral Theology, Social Anthropology, and the Imagination of the Human* (Oxford: Oxford University Press, 2014).

3. See Patrick McKearney's appendix in this volume. For analyses of the "cultural turn" in religious ethics and the need for fieldwork to craft an "ethics of ordinary life," see, for example, Ted A. Smith, "Redeeming Critique: Resignations to the Cultural Turn in Christian Theology and Ethics," *Journal of the Society of Christian Ethics* 24, no. 2 (2004): 89–113; Miller, "On Making a Cultural Turn"; and Todd David Whitmore, "Crossing the Road: The Case for Ethnographic Fieldwork in Christian Ethics," *Journal of the Society of Christian Ethics* 27, no. 2 (2007): 273–94. For an insightful and sustained treatment of ethnographic methods and examples of their use in Christian ethics, see Christian Scharen and Aana Marie Vigen, eds., *Ethnography as Christian Theology and Ethics* (London: Continuum, 2011).

4. See, e.g., Michael Lambek, introduction to *Ordinary Ethics: Anthropology, Language, and Action*, ed. Michael Lambek (New York: Fordham University Press, 2010); Didier Fassin, "The Ethical Turn in Anthropology: Promises and Uncertainties," *Journal of Ethnographic Theory* 4, no. 1 (2014): 429–35.

5. Banner, *Ethics of Everyday Life*, 7.

6. Banner, 24, 203, quoting Joel Robbins, "Where in the World Are Values? Exemplarity, Morality and the Social Process," in *Recovering the Human Subject: Freedom, Creativity and Decision*, ed. James Laidlaw, Barbara Bodenhorn, and Martin Holbraad (Cambridge: Cambridge University Press, 2018), 174.

7. Banner, *Ethics of Everyday Life*, 12.

8. Banner, 12.

9. Banner, 7–8, 12–13, 202–5.

10. Banner, 4, 23.

11. Banner, 23. In consecutive chapters, Banner considers in vitro fertilization (chap. 2); infertility and adoption (chap. 3); suffering and the politics of compassion (chap. 4); hospice, euthanasia, and Alzheimer's (chap. 5); burial and mourning (chap. 6); and memory and forgiveness (chap. 7).

12. Banner, *Ethics of Everyday Life*, 2; cf. 35, 202.

13. Banner, 23.

14. Banner, 2; Michael Banner, "What Moral Theology (and Moral Philosophy) Needs from Social Anthropology," *Cambridge Journal of Anthropology* 33, no. 2 (2015): 111–15.

15. See Banner, *Ethics of Everyday Life*, 2; and Banner, "What Moral Theology," 114.

16. Banner, "What Moral Theology," 114.

17. Published as "Anthropology and Moral Philosophy: A Symposium on Michael Banner's *The Ethics of Everyday Life*," *The Cambridge Journal of Anthropology* 33, no. 2 (Autumn 2015): 111–39, with contributions from Michael Banner, Lesley A. Sharp, Richard Madsen, John H. Evans, J. Derrick Lemons, and Thomas J. Csordas.

18. See Charles Mathewes, chapter 12 in this volume.

19. See, for example, Molly Farneth, chapter 1; Stephanie Mota Thurston, chapter 2: Brian Brock, chapter 4; Jennifer Herdt, chapter 5; Rachel Muers, chapter 10; Luke Bretherton, chapter 11; and Mathewes, chapter 12.

20. G. E. M. Anscombe, "Modern Moral Philosophy," *Philosophy* 33 (1958): 1–19, reprinted in Roger Crisp and Michael Slote, eds., *Virtue Ethics* (Oxford: Oxford University Press, 1997), 26–44, at 26, 43–44.

21. Pincoffs, "Quandary Ethics."

22. Alasdair MacIntyre, *After Virtue: A Study in Moral Theory* (Notre Dame, IN: Notre Dame University Press, 1981).

23. For a collection of influential essays on virtue ethics, see Crisp and Slote, *Virtue Ethics*.

24. Banner tends to downplay the compatibility of contemporary virtue ethics, in part, because he associates it with MacIntyre's *After Virtue*. Banner argues that MacIntyre's "sweeping charge that modernity is morally amnesiac is not one which suggests a great openness to the need to attend to, and the possibility of learning from, moral practice" (*Ethics of Everyday Life*, 23n43). However, as numerous scholars affirm, one need not accept MacIntyre's decline narrative of modernity to recognize a role for virtues and practices in the moral life. See, for example, Jeffrey Stout, *Democracy and Tradition* (Princeton, NJ: Princeton University Press, 2004), 118–39.

25. As one virtue theorist writes, "It is curious that many of us philosophers who talk about what the virtues are so rarely stop to consider how the virtues come to be." See Daniel C. Russell, "Aristotle on Cultivating Virtue," in *Cultivating Virtue: Perspectives from Philosophy, Theology, and Psychology*, ed. Nancy Snow (Oxford: Oxford University Press, 2015), 17. Richard Miller makes a similar point about much work in contemporary religious ethics: "Often what goes by virtue theory pays little attention to the wider cultural forces that contribute to the formation of our dispositions" ("On Making the Cultural Turn," 426). In the last few years, however, a number of virtue ethicists have begun to devote attention to how virtue is formed. See, for example, Snow, *Cultivating Virtue*; Julia Annas, *Intelligent Virtue* (New York: Oxford University Press, 2011); Kristján Kristjánsson, *Aristotelian Character Education* (London: Routledge, 2015); and Christian B. Miller, *The Character Gap: How Good Are We?* (New York: Oxford University Press, 2018).

26. See Herdt, chapter 5 in this volume.

27. See, for example, Stanley Hauerwas, *Vision and Virtue: Essays in Christian Ethical Reflection* (Notre Dame, IN: Fides Publishers, 1974); Stanley Hauerwas, *A Community of Character: Toward a Constructive Christian Social Ethic* (Notre Dame, IN: University of Notre Dame Press, 1981); Hauerwas, *The Peaceable Kingdom*; Stanley Hauerwas, *The Hauerwas Reader*, edited by John Berkman and Michael Cartwright (Durham, NC: Duke University Press, 2001).

28. See, e.g., Pete Ward, ed., *Perspectives on Ecclesiology and Ethnography* (Grand Rapids, MI: Eerdmans, 2012); and Christian B. Scharen, ed., *Explorations in Ecclesiology and Ethnography* (Grand Rapids, MI: Eerdmans, 2012). Ward offers a helpful survey of six book-length studies that apply these qualitative methods in Pete Ward, "Attention and Conversation," in Ward, *Perspectives on Ecclesiology and Ethnography*, 36–49.

29. Luke Bretherton, *Christianity and Contemporary Politics: The Conditions and Possibilities of Faithful Witness* (Oxford: Wiley-Blackwell, 2010); Luke Bretherton, *Resurrecting Democracy: Faith, Citizenship, and the Politics of a Common Life* (Cambridge: Cambridge University Press, 2015); and Jeffrey Stout, *Blessed Are the Organized: Grassroots Democracy in America* (Princeton, NJ: Princeton University Press, 2010).

30. C. Melissa Snarr, *All You That Labor: Religion and Ethics in the Living Wage Movement* (New York: New York University Press, 2011).

31. See Thurston, chapter 2 in this volume, and the essays in Scharen and Vigen, *Ethnography as Christian Theology and Ethics*. See also, for example, María Pilar Aquino, Daisy L. Machado, and Jeanette Rodriguez, *A Reader in Latina Feminist Theology: Religion and Justice* (Austin: University of Texas Press, 2002); The Mud Flower Collective, *God's Fierce Whimsy: Christian Feminism and Theological Education* (New York: Pilgrim Press, 1985); Katie G. Cannon, *Katie's Canon: Womanism and the Soul of the Black Community* (New York: Continuum, 1995); Katie Geneva Cannon, Emilie M. Townes, and Angela D. Sims, *Womanist Theological Ethics: A Reader* (Louisville, KY: Westminster John Knox, 2011); Miguel A. De La Torre, *Doing Christian Ethics from the Margins*, 2nd ed. (Maryknoll, NY: Orbis, 2014); Stacey M. Floyd-Thomas, *Mining the Motherlode: Methods in Womanist Ethics* (Cleveland, OH: Pilgrim Press, 2006); Marla F. Frederick, *Between Sundays: Black Women and Everyday Struggles of Faith* (Berkeley, CA: University of California Press, 2003); Ada María Isasi-Díaz, *En La Lucha / In the Struggle: A Hispanic Women's Liberation Theology* (Minneapolis, MN: Fortress Press, 1993); and Ada María Isasi-Díaz, *La Lucha Continues: Mujerista Theology* (Maryknoll, NY: Orbis, 2004).

32. For an analysis of other influential works, see Patrick McKearney's appendix in this volume.

For a useful analysis of the history and method of ethnography with special attention to its relevance for Christian theology and ethics, see Scharen and Vigen, *Ethnography as Christian Theology and Ethics*, 3–74.

33. For Banner's description of the genesis of his project, see Banner, "What Moral Theology."

34. Lesley A. Sharp, *Strange Harvest: Organ Transplants, Denatured Bodies, and the Transformed Self* (Berkeley: University of California Press, 2006). For an analysis of other relevant and influential works, see McKearney's appendix in this volume.

35. Banner, "What Moral Theology," 113–14.

36. For Banner's description of the social anthropologists most influential on his work, see *Ethics of Everyday Life*, 26n54.

37. See McKearney's appendix in this volume.

38. See, e.g., Paul Brodwin, *Everyday Ethics: Voices from the Front Lines of Community Psychiatry* (Berkeley: University of California Press, 2013); Juliet du Boulay, *Cosmos, Life, and Liturgy in a Greek Orthodox Village* (Limni, Greece: Denise Harvey, 2009); James Faubion, *An Anthropology of Ethics* (Cambridge: Cambridge University Press, 2011); Didier Fassin, ed., *A Companion to Moral Anthropology* (Oxford: Wiley-Blackwell, 2012); James Laidlaw, *The Subject of Virtue: An Anthropology of Ethics and Freedom* (Cambridge: Cambridge University Press, 2013); Lambek, *Ordinary Ethics*; and Joel Robbins, *Becoming Sinners: Christianity and Moral Torment in a Papua New Guinea Society* (Berkeley: University of California Press, 2004). While work in the anthropology of ethics and religion has increased in recent years, it is not altogether new. See Thomas J. Csordas, "Reading Michael Banner on Moral Theology and Social Anthropology," *Cambridge Journal of Anthropology* 33, no. 2 (2015): 130. For an excellent analysis of how thick description in the anthropology of ethics might inform the judgment of religious ethicists, see Patrick McKearney, "The Genre of Judgment: Description and Difficulty in the Anthropology of Ethics," *Journal of Religious Ethics* 44, no. 3 (2016): 544–73.

39. Banner, *Ethics of Everyday Life*, 2, 35, 202. Although Banner sometimes describes his subject in terms of life "stages," Csordas notes that Banner focuses more on "specific moments of life transition" rather than longer periods of the life course ("Reading Michael Banner," 129).

# PART I

# EVALUATING BANNER'S PROPOSAL

═══════════════

## INTERDISCIPLINARY PERSPECTIVES ON MEANING AND METHOD

# 1

# TOWARD AN ETHICS OF
# SOCIAL PRACTICE

## Molly Farneth

Michael Banner's *The Ethics of Everyday Life* proposes that moral theology attend to ordinary social practices, explain how these practices create and maintain the norms that constitute a shared ethical life, and then offer a theological understanding of and response to them. It is a worthy proposal that resonates with work already under way in religious studies. Religious ethicists, in particular, should welcome its attempt to bring ethnographic and normative inquiry together.

The importance of rituals and other social practices in religious and ethical formation is a common theme in contemporary religious studies, but it also echoes through a tradition of theologians and philosophers stretching back to antiquity. When moral theologians and religious ethicists recover this theme, they enter debates that have been going on for a long time: debates about how character is formed, deformed, and transformed; debates over the social functions and effects of rituals; and perhaps most importantly, debates over what sorts of people and communities we should aspire to become through them.

These debates assume what Banner rightly asserts—namely, that social practices shape people of one kind or another. The contestation is largely about what kind of people, and thus what kind of communities, we have reason to want. The cultivation of compassionate subjectivities, which Banner commends, is important. It also prompts us to consider what other virtues well-formed people should have. We need to grapple with such questions if we are going to take Banner's proposal seriously as scholars of our traditions and as critics of our societies.

In what follows, I illustrate how these questions arise for religious ethics when, in the spirit of Banner's proposal, we look closely at one of his examples, the following of the Stations of the Cross.[1] Banner argues that the Stations of the Cross and other forms of meditation on the Passion are ethically and politically significant because of how they imagine the suffering of Christ and the cultivation of compassion in the face of such suffering. But, we must ask, compassion for whom? Accompanied by what other affective and behavioral habits and dispositions? With what social structure, roles, and powers as their context? If ethics is to take the social practical turn, we will need to be clear about how these questions should be answered in light of the diversity of contemporary practices modeled on the Stations of the Cross—and the diversity of effects that these and similar practices might produce in people and societies.

## Banner's Social Practical Turn

Before turning to the Stations of the Cross, let me first outline Banner's methodological proposal and say a few words about its concern with rituals and other social practices that inculcate habits, dispositions, and virtues. Banner argues that moral theology is overly preoccupied with "hard cases." "So practiced," he writes, "moral theology is insufficiently interested in the social; specifically, it lacks a concern for the plausible narration of moral lives, and this lack of concern has doleful consequences for its apologetic, or . . . its therapeutic or evangelical responsibilities and potential."[2] In this, Banner echoes moral theologians such as Stanley Hauerwas, whose work turns to the character and conditions of moral lives, understood within a Christian narrative.[3] The so-called narrative turn has been one of the most important developments in recent Christian ethics.

Banner combines this *narrative* turn with what we might call the *social practical* turn—an ethics that considers the relationships, social practices, and organizational structures in which moral lives are shaped and lived. Banner proposes that moral theology and ethics, in conversation with social anthropology, ought to make those relationships, practices, and structures visible. "Anthropology's concern with the reproduction of the social," he writes, "is a concern with the everyday, the routine, and the normal—and thus may serve to remind moral theology of where its work might, at the very least, begin."[4] Banner directs his readers' attention toward "everyday life," and he draws on the work of social anthropologists first to show how the categories that shape our lives—categories such as kinship, childhood, compassion, aging, and mourning—are constructed and maintained and then to offer theological guidance for an ethics of everyday life.

The turn from an ethics of hard cases, or what the philosopher Edmund Pincoffs called "quandary ethics," toward an ethics of everyday life involves a significant shift in what ethicists analyze.[5] Quandary ethics, as Pincoffs characterized it, focuses on "a quandary which arises because I fall into a certain situation. The situation is such that it can be described in perfectly general terms, without any reference to me as an individual."[6] Quandary ethics abstracts from the characteristics of the moral agent and his or her social and historical context. It also tends to focus on extraordinary cases that most people will never confront, such as the famous trolley problem and the ticking time bomb scenario. An ethics of everyday life, by contrast, must be concerned with character, its formation, and its transformation, on the one hand, and with the social roles, relationships, and institutions in which moral agents are embedded, on the other.[7] It must attend to the social matrices in which moral agents are formed and live their lives. Banner aims to show how social anthropology—and, in particular, ethnography—can contribute to and inform normative inquiry in these matters.

The social practices that constitute our everyday lives are sites of continual innovation and change. One often implicit challenge for an ethics of everyday life is to make clear which forms of relationship and practice *ought* to be cultivated and why. This normative question adds the distinctly ethical dimension to anthropological accounts that focus on ethnographic observation and thick description of everyday communities and practices.

On the second page of the book, Banner notes the vast diversity of Christian reflections on the life of Christ. I will quote him at some length here to give a sense of the diversity he describes:

> Christ's life has been imagined, represented, enacted, expounded, and interrogated, not only through the drama of the liturgy and the liturgical year, but also through sermons, prayers, through biblical commentary, exegesis, and contemplation, in doctrinal, moral and philosophical theology, in art of all kinds . . . , in devotional writings, mystery plays, poems, and other forms of literature, in hymns, oratorios, cantatas, spirituals, and every other type of musical work—and so on. Through these *highly diverse and virtually countless* engagements with the life of Christ, that life has been brought to an imaginative realization and in that realization a particular architecture of the human and of human subjectivity (with certain emotions, attitudes, and perceptions), has been explored, staged, elaborated, and commended.[8]

The diversity of forms that these Christian imaginations of the life of Christ have taken and, presumably, the diversity of effects that those imaginations have on those who have "explored, staged, elaborated, and commended" them is striking. But by the end of the introduction, Banner has begun to refer to the Christian imagination in the singular. The book's main question, he writes, is this: "How does *the Christian imagination* of conception, birth, suffering, death, and burial bear on the human life course, and envisage and sustain *a Christian form of human being?*"[9] Surely the answer to Banner's question must be multiform. But his use of the singular here—"the Christian imagination" and "a Christian form of human being"— leaves me wondering about *which* imagination is normative in Banner's account of the ethics of everyday life and what principled grounds he employs in making that determination.[10]

## What Kinds of Selves and Societies?

To see the implications of this diversity for the ethics of everyday life, we might turn to one of Banner's own examples, meditation on the Passion, which was not an important focus of Christian thought or practice until the late medieval period. Banner argues that the emergence of practices that focused on Christ's suffering enabled new ways of experiencing and responding to that suffering—empathically, in sorrow, compassion, and love.

Among these practices is the following of the Stations of the Cross, a form of devotion that developed as a way of bearing witness to Jesus's suffering and death. In the traditional form of the practice, the worshipper proceeds along fourteen stations, each of which depicts a moment in Jesus's procession from his condemnation in Jerusalem to his crucifixion to the placement of his body in the tomb. Worshippers stop at each station for prayer, contemplation, and visualization. On Good Friday, this practice often takes the form of a public processional. One person will carry a cross, recalling Jesus's own bearing of the cross. Banner quotes historian of Christianity Rachel Fulton, arguing that the Stations of the Cross "schooled religiously sensitive women and men in the potentialities of emotion, specifically love, for transcending the physical, experiential distance between individual bodies—above all, bodies in pain."[11] Banner suggests that through the enactment of the Stations of the Cross, medieval Christians cultivated compassion for the suffering Christ.

The Stations of the Cross, Banner argues, is what Foucault calls a "technology of the self."[12] It is a bodily practice through which worshippers train their thoughts and actions in order to cultivate an empathic response to the suffering of another—to *feel* Christ's suffering, to share in it, and to respond in sorrow, compassion, and love. Reenacting the Stations of the Cross is not only a symbolic remembrance; it is also a bodily practice that enables particular ways of being in the world.

This is one situation in which the diversity of Christian imaginations and enactments of the life of Christ complicates matters. Banner asks, "How do we take up or take on Christ's suffering and those in whom he suffers?"[13] Contemporary forms of meditation on and reenactment of the Passion, some inspired by the Stations of the Cross, respond to this question in different ways. Some focus on the cultivation of compassion for the suffering Christ, while others also intend to cultivate compassion for sufferers other than Christ. This is not an insignificant distinction. It is worth keeping in mind that meditation on Christ's suffering in Good Friday liturgies and Passion plays was long associated with outbursts of anti-Semitic violence in Europe.[14] It is often unclear whether or how the cultivation of compassion for the suffering Christ might translate into compassion for others, and it is clear that it sometimes does not. Furthermore, while some practices that focus on Christ's suffering are intended to cultivate compassion alone, others are concerned with generating or expressing other relevant habits, dispositions, and commitments—such as solidarity and justice—in the face of violence, harm, and domination.

Consider two contemporary variations on the traditional devotional practice. The first is Mel Gibson's 2004 film, *The Passion of the Christ*, which depicts, in violent detail, Christ's movement from condemnation to crucifixion. For his filmic representation of the Passion, Gibson was influenced not only by Gospel accounts but also by medieval depictions of the Stations of the Cross and the visions of the German Augustinian nun Anne Catherine Emmerich.[15] Like the Stations of the Cross, the film is not a "mere recollecting of these events."[16] Its viewers become spectators to the torture and torment of Christ, voyeurs in the spectacle of his suffering through Gibson's relentless and horrifying images of violence. Compelling viewers to meditate on that violence at length, Gibson sought to create not only a cinematic event but also a religious experience. As Richard Alleva notes in *Commonweal*, "Gibson has elected to make a ritualistic work rather than a dramatic one, a cinematic equivalent of following the stations of the cross on Good Friday."[17] Like the Stations of the Cross, the film is intended to provoke love and grief in the face of Christ's pain.

But what kind of Christians does Gibson intend to shape through that experience? With viewers' gaze fixed on Christ's tortured and suffering body—and without attention to Christ's teachings about, say, the "least of these"—it is not clear that Gibson intends for viewers to feel compassion toward sufferers other than Christ. And some have argued that the experience of watching the film may not be suited to the cultivation of compassion at all. In an insightful essay on how the film situates its viewers relative to the violence it portrays, Amy Hollywood suggests that "[the viewers'] position is more passive and more voyeuristic than that of those actively engaged in the process of meditation and, so, at least potentially more sadistic than compassionate."[18] With the incorporation of *The Passion of the Christ* into religious educational curricula and worship services, the question of what kinds of Christians and communities the film is intended to shape is not a merely academic one.

The second example is an interreligious event called the Stations of the Cross Gun Violence Prevention Walk organized by a local faith-based gun violence prevention group in the Germantown neighborhood of Philadelphia. On Good Friday in 2016, two hundred people, including clergy of multiple religious traditions, gathered in front of a Methodist church. The front lawn of the church looked like a cemetery: it was covered in crosses, each of which bore the name, age, and death date of someone killed by gun violence in Philadelphia in the previous year. There were 238 crosses, 238 deaths. The people who gathered picked up crosses, bore them on their bodies, and began to walk. They walked a one-and-a-half-mile loop, stopping at sites of recent gun violence for prayer and contemplation led by the family members of those killed by gun violence and by clergy of multiple religious traditions.

These are both technologies of the self, modeled on the Stations of the Cross and intended to provoke and promote particular affective responses and habits. But Foucault's notion of technologies of the self is, on its own, ethically neutral. To say that the Stations of the Cross is a technology of the self does not give us, as ethicists or as agents, much insight into the virtues or vices that it cultivates, the norms it legitimizes, or the forms of relationship and community it enables. Clearly, the two technologies I have mentioned work on practitioners in different ways and to different ends. Does the quasi-ritual of watching *The Passion of the Christ* cultivate a compassionate subject, one capable of suffering with Christ in another? And is compassion the only relevant response to suffering? With what other affects and dispositions is this compassion conjoined? And what would a society populated with the selves produced by this technology be like? The same questions can be asked, and should be asked, of the Stations of the Cross Gun Violence Prevention Walk.

The contrast between the way these two practices would have us "take up or take on Christ's suffering and those in whom he suffers" is stark.[19] Whereas viewers of *The Passion of the Christ* are situated as spectators to the violence borne by Christ, participants in the Stations of the Cross Gun Violence Prevention Walk are partakers in the remembrance of his suffering and the suffering of others. They mark it with their own bodies, bearing the crosses that symbolize those killed by gun violence, reclaiming sites of violence as sites of mourning, remembrance, and resolve. Whereas in Gibson's film the connection between the suffering of Christ and the suffering of those "in whom he suffers" is unclear, in the second example, these suffering others—people killed by gun violence, their loved ones, and their communities—are the focus of participants' compassion. But the ritual is intended to cultivate more than compassion in the face of suffering. It is also intended to express anger at the injustice of that suffering, grievance toward those who fail to enact gun control legislation, and solidarity in the face of suffering. The Stations of the Cross Gun Violence Prevention Walk combines Christian compassion with concern about injustice and domination.

## Ethical Contestation and Everyday Life

To the extent that Banner has a principle of selection for the everyday Christian practices that he highlights or commends in *The Ethics of Everyday Life*, it seems to be their connection to the cultivation of compassion. But his emphasis on cultivating compassion for those who suffer leaves him grappling with Didier Fassin's charge that humanitarianism characterized by compassion for the suffering other (which Fassin takes to be a product of Christianity) reduces the various wrongs and harms inflicted on people to mere misfortune.[20] As Fassin puts the point, "Inequality is replaced by exclusion, domination is transformed into misfortune, injustice is articulated as suffering, violence is expressed in terms of trauma."[21] Humanitarian reason, or the "politics of compassion," Fassin argues, is inattentive to the power relations that create and sustain inequality, domination, injustice, and violence. Banner is troubled by Fassin's charge, although he suggests that it might be possible to "imagine and practice a better humanitarianism" rooted in "the continued appropriation of the suffering of Christ, by means of various technologies of the self."[22] Banner's hope is that the imagination of the life and death of Christ can yield a response to Fassin that produces a form of compassion that does not collapse into voyeurism or mere pity.[23] This is a good thing to hope for, but to realize it, more needs to be said about how we ought to assess the various imaginations and practices that shape Christian selves.

Banner writes that "rites and rituals, at least living rites and rituals, are not self-contained or empty—they are enactments of an imagined sociality in schematic and idealized form, and as they are enacted they exert pressure on what is the case for the sake of what should and might be."[24] I think that is exactly right. Rituals express the commitments, attitudes, and passions of a group, and they cultivate the habits, dispositions, and identities of its members. Rituals can forge solidarity; they can also enforce the boundaries and define the roles of a social structure.

For those reasons, we must keep at the forefront the fact that rites are sites of contestation over which sorts of people and societies we want to bring about. This contestation occurs among practitioners who adapt existing rituals and reimagine their meanings in order to reform or change the norms and social structures that are imagined or enacted through those rituals. This includes the individuals and groups who have drawn on traditional practices of meditating on the Passion to enact and enable new forms of religious experience and subjectivities. Such contestation also occurs among ethicists, who reflect on those rituals with normative concerns in mind. Ethicists of everyday life ought to be interested, as Banner is, in how rituals and other social practices shape the shared ethical life of a community, both consciously and unconsciously, for good and for ill. And, I think, ethicists must also attend to the diversity of, and contestation over, rituals in these processes. It is unclear what Banner thinks about this second issue. When he writes, toward the end of the book, that generating the right response to suffering, harm, and grievance "is not a matter of Christians inventing new rites, but of living in accordance with rites of remembrance that we already have and that seek to colonize our life and times and re-member Christ,"[25] I want to know more about what Banner thinks about ritual innovation, contestation, and reform, particularly when these are aimed at reimagining norms and social structures, challenging oppression, and forging relationships in which accountability and mutual recognition go hand in hand. The methodological question that I raised earlier, about Banner's grounds for highlighting certain practices and not others as exemplifying and cultivating "a Christian form of human being," is inseparable from normative questions about the substance of Christian ethics. Christian imaginations of the life of Christ have served not only to cultivate compassion for sufferers—as nearly all of Banner's own examples suggest—but also, in some cases, to constrict practitioners' sense of who deserves compassion and, in other cases, to foster appropriate anger in the face of injustice and domination along with resolve in the struggle for a just peace. These are very different sorts of everyday ethics, and if we wish to fulfill the spirit of Banner's constructive proposal, we would do well to name the differences.

## Notes

1. See Michael Banner, *The Ethics of Everyday Life: Moral Theology, Social Anthropology, and the Imagination of the Human* (Oxford: Oxford University Press, 2014), 82–106.

2. Banner, 7.

3. For instance, Stanley Hauerwas and William Willimon write, "It is important to recognize that all ethics, even non-Christian ethics, arise out of a tradition that depicts the way the world works, what is real, what is worth having, worth believing. Tradition is a function and a product of community. So all ethics, even non-Christian ethics, make sense only when embodied in sets of social practices that constitute a community." See Stanley Hauerwas and William H. Willimon, *Resident Aliens: Life in the Christian Colony* (Nashville, TN: Abingdon Press, 2014), 79.

4. Banner, *Ethics of Everyday Life*, 27.

5. Edmund Pincoffs, "Quandary Ethics," in *Revisions: Changing Perspectives in Moral Philosophy*, ed. Stanley Hauerwas and Alasdair MacIntyre (Notre Dame, IN: University of Notre Dame, 1983). See also Edmund Pincoffs, *Quandaries and Virtues: Against Reductivism in Ethics* (Lawrence: University Press of Kansas, 1986).

6. Pincoffs, "Quandary Ethics," 104.

7. My own view of social ethics is developed along Hegelian lines in Molly Farneth, *Hegel's Social Ethics: Religion, Conflict, and Rituals of Reconciliation* (Princeton, NJ: Princeton University Press, 2017).

8. Banner, *Ethics of Everyday Life*, 2 (emphasis added).

9. Banner, 5 (emphasis added).

10. Jennifer Herdt raises a similar question in chapter 5 of this volume.

11. Quoted in Banner, *Ethics of Everyday Life*, 89.

12. See Banner's discussion of Foucault in Banner, 100–101.

13. Banner, 106.

14. Vincent J. Miller, "Theology, Devotion, Culture," in *Mel Gibson's Bible: Religion, Popular Culture, and the Passion of the Christ*, ed. Timothy K. Beal and Tod Linafelt (Chicago: University of Chicago Press, 2005), 42. For a historical account of anti-Semitism in the Passion play, see Gordon R. Mork, "Christ's Passion on Stage: The Traditional Melodrama of Deicide," *Journal of Religion & Society*, S1 (2004): 1–9.

15. On Gibson's influences, see Peter J. Boyer, "The Jesus War," *New Yorker*, September 15, 2003, 58–71; and Mark D. Jordan and Kent L. Brintnall, "Mel Gibson, Bride of Christ," in Beal and Linafelt, *Mel Gibson's Bible*, 81–90. On the devotional practices that provide context for the film,

see Miller, "Theology, Devotion, Culture." On the medieval aesthetics of Gibson's film, see Alison Griffiths, "The Revered Gaze: The Medieval Imaginary of Mel Gibson's *The Passion of the Christ*," *Cinema Journal* 46, no. 2 (Winter 2007).

16. Banner, *Ethics of Everyday Life*, 89.

17. Richard Alleva, "Mel Gibson's *The Passion of the Christ*," *Commonweal* (April 9, 2004).

18. Amy Hollywood, "Kill Jesus," in Beal and Linafelt, *Mel Gibson's Bible*, 164.

19. Banner, *Ethics of Everyday Life*, 106.

20. See Banner's engagement with Fassin in Banner, 93.

21. Didier Fassin, *Humanitarian Reason: A Moral History of the Present* (Berkeley: University of California Press, 2011), 6, quoted in Banner, *Ethics of Everyday Life*, 96.

22. Banner, *Ethics of Everyday Life*, 106.

23. For one attempt to articulate a Christian vision of humanitarianism that is sensitive to injustice and domination, see Gregory, chapter 6 in this volume.

24. Banner, *Ethics of Everyday Life*, 134. He cites the Eucharist as an example—although, of course, the meaning and effects of that rite have been and continue to be issues of significant contention among Christians.

25. Banner, 197.

# 2

# ENGAGING THE EVERYDAY IN WOMANIST ETHICS AND *MUJERISTA* THEOLOGY

STEPHANIE MOTA THURSTON

IN THE 1980S, feminist scholars in religion, ethics, and theology began to press the academy in the United States to reimagine its aims, methods, sources, and epistemological stances.[1] Part of what emerged from these collaborative efforts was a recognition that embodiment, experience, narrative, and relationality were critical components of theology. Many of these insights laid the groundwork for the contemporary ethnographic turn in religious studies and theology, a turn that we see reflected in Michael Banner's *The Ethics of Everyday Life*.[2] Banner's primary disciplinary critique is leveled against dominant forms of moral theology and Christian ethics, particularly textbook and popular versions of professional ethics, that focus on "hard cases" and ignore the textured realities of everyday life. That these instantiations of Christian ethics are dominated by hard cases and moral dilemmas is surely an apt description. That they are capable of little more than judging licitness is surely an apt critique.

Nevertheless, some of Banner's readers who are familiar with the broad contours of post–Vatican II Christian social ethics may find that his description of the state of the field leaves out an important development. During this period, Christian social ethics, at least in North and South America, has increasingly shifted from an engagement with philosophy to an engagement with social sciences, cultural theory, and anthropology. Indeed, decades before the broader field would begin to marginally recognize this ethnographic turn, womanist ethicists and *mujerista* theologians turned their attention to the everyday lives and contexts of particular communities—to the texture of the ordinary, to *lo cotidiano*. Writing in tribute to Ada María Isasi-Díaz after her recent death, Michelle Gonzalez Maldonado recalls, "I remember years ago sitting at a conference watching Ada María being criticized for her use of ethnography and her refusal to make essentialist claims about all Latinas. I think back at this moment with a smile on my face because her critics could not have been more wrong. Today, we see more and more the ethnographic turn within the study of religion."[3] Now that there has decidedly been an ethnographic turn, we must not overlook the early contributions that were made nearly four decades ago from the margins of the field.

In light of these contributions, this chapter encourages readers to view Banner's important work as a contribution to a rich corpus on the everyday, the roots of which, I contend, are exemplified in the early works of womanist ethicist Katie Cannon and *mujerista* theologian Ada María Isasi-Díaz. Importantly, in the opening pages of *The Ethics of Everyday Life*, Banner notes that his introductory chapter will merely "hazard" some reasons as to why the discipline of moral theology "does not embrace and practice everyday ethics as it should."[4] For Banner, the "diagnosis of the deficiency is not essential to the argument of the book."[5] In other words, if readers were to find his description of the various disciplines either incomplete or inaccurate, this would not undermine his central argument and overall constructive project. Surely, the constructive chapters in Banner's monograph stand as compelling illustrations of the anthropological engagement that his introductory chapter commends. However, a deeper engagement with marginalized strands of the tradition that have been attending to the everyday for decades, and that ushered in this ethnographic turn, could be a further boon to the broader field as it continues to explore what is at stake in attending to the everyday.

This chapter, then, has two aims. First, I aim to situate Banner's account more broadly within the tradition of post–Vatican II Christian social ethics, specifically in the US context. More specifically, I highlight the work of Katie Cannon and Ada María Isasi-Díaz and note those who have followed them in developing, expanding, and sharpening womanist and *mujerista* thought. I focus primarily on methodological developments within Christian ethics, where I see the most fruitful overlaps between Banner's work and the womanist and *mujerista* traditions. My second aim is to consider some of the ways in which each thinker articulates the sources and tasks of moral theology and ethics. In the concluding section, I pose questions that gesture toward what I take to be two important areas for future conversation among these diverse perspectives—namely, the *sources* and *tasks* of Christian moral theology and ethics.

## *Lo Cotidiano* or "the Everyday"

In Michael Banner's introductory chapter of *The Ethics of Everyday Life*, he implores moral theology to abandon its dominant form, an ethics of "hard cases," and develop its own "everyday ethics."[6] For Banner, the development of an everyday ethics requires a disciplinary realignment among moral theology, moral philosophy, and social anthropology. In its dominant form, the "hard cases tradition" fails to provide a "well-developed or considered narrative context to explain [the] character and existence" of the good *or* the bad.[7] In other words, moral theology "lacks a concern for the plausible narration of moral lives."[8]

Since moral theologians need narratives that are socially, culturally, and psychologically grounded, Banner argues that social anthropology is the only discipline among the three that is suited for this task precisely because it is the only one truly concerned with "morality." Banner describes morality as an "everyday practice which exists on the ground—the practice of appraising ourselves and others against notions of the good, or the right, or the fitting."[9] Because moral theology in its dominant form lacks "'psychologically and socioculturally realistic' narratives," its moral pronouncements are empty.[10] Banner thus argues for a moral theology "which can fathom what we may casually refer to as the 'unfathomable' choices and wishes of contemporary life."[11] In short, moral theology must first be able to understand complex human desires and the forms of human being within which those desires are shaped, cultivated, and emergent. In Banner's assessment, moral theology needs to engage more fully with social anthropology for this work.

In this context, Katie Cannon and Ada María Isasi-Díaz are appropriate figures to consult since they, albeit in different ways, exemplify early strands within the discipline that do attend to morality as a deeply contextual everyday social practice. As I understand Banner's argument, it is social anthropology's ethnographic method that can best assist moral theology in its construction of an everyday ethics. The anthropologist's ability to generate a "thick description" from her prolonged fieldwork is central to the ethnographic task.[12] So too are the theories of human life, culture, and society that emerge. So, while Cannon and Isasi-Díaz draw from different disciplines and methods—Cannon turning to the Black women's literary tradition and Isasi-Díaz turning to ethnography—the common thread that runs between their work is attention to the everyday moral lives of women in their particular communities.

In her 1984 essay "Moral Wisdom in the Black Women's Literary Tradition," Cannon argues that the Black women's literary tradition could and should be used to "interpret and explain the community's socio-cultural patterns from which ethical values can be gleaned."[13] Cannon points her readers back to the early eighteenth century, arguing that this literary tradition preserves authentic depictions of Black women's everyday context, their lives, and the moral agency they develop under conditions of oppression. Importantly, Cannon's use of the literary tradition encompasses more than written literature. An epigraph from Sherley Anne Williams in the opening essay of *Katie's Canon* explains, "And when we (to use Alice Walker's lovely phrase) go in search of our mothers' gardens, it's not really to learn who trampled on them or how or even why—we usually know that already. Rather, it's to learn what our mothers planted there, what they thought as they sowed, and how they survived the blighting of so many fruits."[14]

Cannon received this inheritance in her North Carolina home—a "folklore sanctuary" where her mother told the stories of her ancestors. For Cannon, "these narratives are the soil where my inheritance from my mother's garden grew."[15] These stories transmit not only depictions of the everyday lives of her ancestors but also the moral wisdom that enables survival and persistence in the midst of domination.

The cultural inheritance of folklore, spirituals, and prayers can be traced back to the everyday practices of her enslaved ancestors. The folklore created by enslaved Africans and orally passed from generation to generation was a "strategy for coping with oppression," as "coded messages would communicate what they considered good, worthy, and meaningful."[16] Under conditions of total domination, these values had to be masked, so it was through folklore that enslaved Africans were able "to indict slavery and to question the society in which it flourished."[17] Through folklore, themes of freedom, resistance, and moral agency were communicated and upheld. By "objectifying their own lives in folktales," Cannon argues, "Afro-American slaves were able to assert the dignity of their own persons."[18] Given that this cultural inheritance likely resonates with other Black women descended from slaves in the United States, Cannon's choice to plumb the Black women's literary tradition as a source of moral wisdom is all the more compelling.

While this literary tradition is rooted in the folklore, spirituals, and prayers of enslaved Africans from the antebellum South, Cannon argues that the "work of Black women writers can be trusted as seriously mirroring Black reality" as that reality moved through Reconstruction, Jim Crow, informal segregation, the civil rights movement, and resegregation.[19] Taken as a whole, "the Black women's literary tradition delineates the many ways that ordinary Black women have fashioned value patterns and ethical procedures in their own terms, as well as mastering, transcending, radicalizing, and sometimes destroying pervasive, negative orientations imposed by the mores of the larger society."[20]

In her 1984 essay, Cannon describes her method as having a number of goals. She eschews the aim of trying to create a universal, normative ethic but rather emphasizes the importance of description and understanding. She illustrates not only how this literary analysis helps us understand the richness and nuance of Black women's moral struggle for survival and their "various coping mechanisms," but also how it challenges the dominant moral discourses that do not account for agents living under conditions of tyranny.[21]

The literary figure who most captured Cannon's attention was "novelist, journalist, folklorist, anthropologist, and critic" Zora Neale Hurston.[22] In her chapter "Resources for a Constructive Ethic: The Life and Work of Zora Neale Hurston,"

Cannon lauds Hurston for her contribution to the "concrete depiction of Black life."[23] Central to Cannon's reading is Hurston's ability to depict the intricate ways in which Black women struggled to "prevail against the odds with integrity."[24] Hurston's anthropological training enabled her to depict the moral wisdom and agency of Black women concretely, in a particular time and place.

While Cannon dove into the Black women's literary tradition to generate a contextually grounded "thick description" of her community's everyday ethics, Ada María Isasi-Díaz employed ethnographic methods to generate her account. Isasi-Díaz began her work and research with grassroots Hispanic women in the United States in the early 1980s, initially calling her theology a Hispanic women's liberation theology. In her subsequent work she took up the label of *mujerista* theology. In earlier work, she describes her method as "dialogue," but by her 1993 publication of *En La Lucha: Elaborating a Mujerista Theology*, she locates her method specifically within ethnography.[25]

Isasi-Díaz explains that in order to understand the "significance of our everyday world, how we understand and describe our bodily and material existence as Hispanic Women," it is necessary to understand the meaning and implications of ethnicity and the socioeconomic reality in which Hispanic women find themselves.[26] Her first chapter is dedicated to this contextualizing task. Isasi-Díaz identifies ethnography as the research method she uses to "gather the voices and lived-experiences" of Hispanic women.[27] She describes the process of gathering these narratives through ethnographic interviews that are "much more a conversation, a dialogue," where she aims more to learn *from* the women rather than merely gather data *about* them.[28] For this reason, Isasi-Díaz freely mixes methods during her one-on-one and group interviews. These methods include case studies, free story interviews, focused interviews, and life histories. Isasi-Díaz presents lengthy transcribed responses from her interviews alongside her interpretations. Including large portions of the Hispanic women's responses allows readers to get a sense of the diversity of experiences, values, and contexts that make up their everyday lives. Yet Isasi-Díaz's more interpretive claims, informed by her interaction with the women and the broader socioeconomic context, help to generate key moral themes and understandings. She describes this method as "translating the accounts into one another."[29]

Isasi-Díaz explains that a key feature of the interview was to provide an opportunity for Hispanic women to reflect on their decision-making processes in order to "investigate how they exercise their moral agency, thus creating meaning in and through their lives."[30] As the title of her text suggests, the struggle for survival is an overarching theme that emerges from her ethnographic interviews and analysis. This struggle for survival includes the women's own struggle and the struggle for their families, particularly their children. For these women, *la lucha* is also a struggle for their culture and language—for "our deep sense of community, our valuing of the elderly and the children, the religiosity of our culture, the importance of honor as an expression of the worth and value of every single person."[31]

Another significant feature of Isasi-Díaz's work, and Latina/o theology more broadly, is *lo cotidiano*, or the everyday. Christopher Tirres traces the emergence of this concept to feminist critical theory in the 1960s and 1970s in Eastern Europe and Latin America.[32] For Isasi-Díaz, however, *lo cotidiano* is not merely a descriptive concept in a strictly ethnographic sense. Rather, *lo cotidiano*

> constitutes the immediate space of our lives, the first horizon in which we have our experiences, experiences that in turn are constitutive elements of our reality. . . .
> *Lo cotidiano* situates us within our experiences. It has to do with the practices and beliefs that we have inherited, with our habitual judgements, including the tactics we use to deal with the everyday. However, by *lo cotidiano* we do not refer to the a-critical reproduction or repetition of all that we have been taught or to which we have been habituated. On the contrary, we understand by *lo cotidiano* that which is reproduced or repeated consciously by the majority of people in the world as part of their struggles for survival and liberation.[33]

For Isasi-Díaz, *lo cotidiano* is closely linked to common sense and the kind of prudence and folk wisdom that grassroots Latinas employ during their daily struggle for their well-being, for the well-being of their family, and for survival.[34] Given the central place that *lo cotidiano* plays in Isasi-Díaz's theology, it is no wonder that she, despite criticism from the academy, insists on ethnographic and narrative methods as a way to hear, understand, depict, and learn from the moral wisdom of grassroots Latinas.

The work of Cannon and Isasi-Díaz illustrates how two important strands within Christian moral theology and ethics developed rich, localized depictions of the everyday by engaging with literary traditions and ethnography. In the nearly four decades that have followed their early contributions, these strands within the field of Christian ethics have been developed, refined, and expanded. Banner's call for an everyday ethics capable of providing a "plausible narration of moral lives," I believe, can find nourishing roots in these strands of the discipline.[35]

## Moral Theology's Tasks and Sources—Future Conversations

In the introduction to *En La Lucha*, Ada María Isasi-Díaz situates *mujerista* theology within the historical context of Catholic moral theology. During the sixteenth through the eighteenth centuries, she claims, Catholic moral theology "denigrated into a 'science of guilt and sin' [and] remained almost exclusively preoccupied with the training of priests as judges until the Vatican II Council."[36] In her assessment, many Hispanic women, specifically Catholic Hispanic women, struggle against the "legalistic understanding of the nature and role of conscience" imposed through the sacrament of penance in the Catholic Church.[37] The task of *mujerista* theology, then, is to be a liberative praxis. One of its main goals is to "enhance the development of the moral agency of Hispanic Women."[38] Given this context, it becomes clearer how her dialogical ethnographic method was itself a liberative theological praxis. Isasi-Díaz's theological method creates the space for Hispanic women both to *recognize* themselves as moral agents and to *cultivate* deliberative moral agency.

Through the years that Isasi-Díaz worked with, befriended, and interviewed Hispanic women across the United States, she collected the moral and religious understandings of her interlocutors. Importantly, she believes "that those religious understandings are part of the ongoing revelation of God, present in the midst of the community of faith and giving strength to Hispanic Women's struggle for liberation."[39] Isasi-Díaz clarifies that the struggle for liberation and survival means more than "barely living." Rather, "survival has to do with the struggle *to be* fully" and to have "the power to decide about one's history and one's vocation or historical mission."[40] *Mujerista* theology seeks liberation and wholeness for Hispanic women in the United States by affirming their moral agency and liberating their conscience as a medium for God's ongoing revelation.

While Isasi-Díaz's theological critique engages institutional Catholic moral theology and practice, Cannon's womanist critique engages certain forms of mainline Protestant ethics. In her readings of theological ethics, "the assumptions of the dominant ethical systems implied that the doing of Christian ethics in the Black community was either immoral or amoral."[41] Values that depend on the "existence of freedom and a wide range of choices" are insufficient amid conditions of oppression.[42] Assumptions about the conditions of life within which moral action takes place obscure the moral agency of the most marginalized among us. As Cannon explains, "the real-lived texture of Black life requires moral agency that may run contrary to the ethical boundaries of mainline Protestantism [as] Blacks may use action guides which have never been considered within the scope of traditional codes of faithful living."[43] A womanist framework, then, is a response to these assumptions that aims to promote as well as liberate the wholeness of Black women.

Cannon introduces her essays in *Katie's Canon* with a poignant metaphor for the womanist methodological framework that shapes her engagement with the Black women's literary tradition: "My grandmother, Rosa Cornelia White Lytle, was the gatekeeper in the land of 'counterpain.' She was always available with salves, hot towels, and liniments to cure physical aches and spiritual ills. As a charismatic healer, Grandma Rosie's practice consisted of diagnosis, treatment, and prevention in the maintenance of overall wholeness . . . . In 1983, 'Womanism' became the new gatekeeper in my land of counterpain."[44] Cannon employs this womanist framework not only to critique oppressive inherited traditions and systems of domination but also to illumine the moral wisdom in her community that can liberate and make them whole.

In the Black women's literary tradition, Cannon found a moral wisdom that is "extremely useful in defying oppressive rules or standards of 'law and order' that unjustly degrade Blacks [and] helps Blacks purge themselves of self-hate, thus asserting their own validity."[45] Later, Cannon explains how the rich description of the Black community's central values can serve to "free Black folks from the often deadly grasp of parochial stereotypes."[46] In both of these claims, Cannon illustrates how her methodological commitments illuminate an everyday ethics, a moral wisdom, that both liberates and affirms the dignity of Black Americans, especially Black women.

For some of us working in moral theology and Christian ethics, Cannon and Isasi-Díaz are our foremothers, and our continued ethnographic work and literary analysis builds on their insights. Their work gave us the space to think about the everyday struggles of our communities and the courage to understand ethics and theology as a liberative praxis for women on the margins of society. One of the most compelling aspects of Banner's *Ethics of Everyday Life* is how he too insists that the dominant form of moral theology is failing at its proper task. Banner does not use the language of liberation to describe moral theology's task, yet I see strong resonances between the liberationist aims we see in Cannon and Isasi-Díaz and what Banner describes as the therapeutic or pastoral aims of moral theology.

For Banner, the "task of moral theology, properly conceived . . . must be not only to judge, but to understand and characterize the lives out of which our actions, good or bad, plausibly, persuasively, or even compellingly arise."[47] What undergirds much of Banner's critique of dominant forms of moral theology is its inability to attend to its proper tasks and responsibilities. He laments the form of moral theology that is equipped only to name the good and denounce the bad without grasping the "deep character and logic of different forms of life."[48] The construction of a culturally and contextually informed everyday ethics is necessary for what Banner calls moral theology's "therapeutic" task.[49] Moral philosophy, in his assessment, is ill-equipped to assist moral theology in these tasks. Therefore, moral theology should turn to social anthropology, a discipline he believes is better suited to help moral theologians develop an everyday ethics.

Banner hopes that a moral theology properly attentive to morality as an everyday social practice can first "set out an everyday ethics which would sustain and support the Christian imagination of the human."[50] Then, and only then, is moral theology in a position to "address pastorally and therapeutically other ethical imaginaries and forms of life."[51] Moral theology should provide a socially compelling Christian imagination of human being, as opposed merely to judgments about what is right or wrong in the face of "hard cases." If moral theology can make this shift, it can fulfill its pastoral, therapeutic, and evangelical task. Though some readers in the US context may bristle at the word *evangelical*, Banner simply means that moral theology should be good news in the face of our daily struggles and hardships.

Cannon, Isasi-Díaz, and Banner all critique forms of moral theology and Christian ethics that are failing at their task. They each envision a kind of moral theology capable of doing more than judging—a moral theology that heals, liberates, saves. Cannon likens womanist ethics to "salves, hot towels, and liniments."[52] As a gatekeeper to one's "counterpain," womanist Christian ethics ought to liberate and foster wholeness and dignity for Black women in America. Isasi-Díaz's ethnographic method is itself a liberative praxis. Liberation and salvation for Latinas requires cultivating and acknowledging their moral agency and "having what one needs to live and be able to strive towards human fulfilment."[53] Finally, Banner calls for an everyday ethics that can respond therapeutically, pastorally, and as good news in our everyday lives. Banner's chapters each illustrate how moral theology can be therapeutically responsive to individuals through conception, birth, suffering, death, and burial.

Isasi-Díaz's *mujerista* theology is, in part, a response to specific oppressive sacramental practices and a Catholic moral theology narrowly focused on the judgment of sin. It attends to the ways in which these practices bear on particular women in a particular place and time. Its liberative task is specific and contextual, and its aim is to promote full and flourishing lives for these women. Similarly, Cannon's womanist ethics is a response to specific forms of mainline Protestant theological ethics whose virtues and values may not be accessible to Black women living amid structures of racial, gender, and socioeconomic oppression. It attends to these particular women, to their everyday struggles, joys, and strategies for surviving with dignity. Its liberative task is also specific and contextual and seeks to identify and affirm the ways Black women "prevail against the odds with moral integrity."[54] This, of course, is not to say that only Catholic Latinas in the United States can find liberation in *mujerista* theology or that only Black women in the United States can find a salve in womanist Christian ethics. Rather, their focus on particular communities illustrates a rejection of a singular Christian ethic that can speak compellingly to all individuals in all communities and all contexts.

More importantly, their attention to *lo cotidiano*, or the everyday lives of these women, is, in part, a search for moral wisdom. Cannon and Isasi-Díaz are clear that the everyday is a *source* for their normative moral theology and ethics. Cannon, for example, finds moral wisdom in the Black women's oral tradition as well as in the sermons and female characters in Zora Neal Hurston's literary works.[55] Isasi-Díaz seeks to learn *from* the Latinas she interviews. For both, the moral wisdom that emerges from ordinary women struggling to survive and thrive with dignity and integrity is often a critique of oppressive forms of *Christian* theology and ethics, and this seems to be the case because the tasks of womanist and *mujerista*/Latina theology are fundamentally liberative.

As I understand Banner, the source of the Christian imagination of human being is the life of Christ, specifically the creedal moments of Christ's life. Whatever is meant by Christ's life, however, must be interpreted through biblical texts, liturgical practices, and creedal, doctrinal, and cultural traditions. When Banner describes *the* Christian imagination that will be poised to engage critically and therapeutically with other ethical imaginations, it can at times seem as though he is suggesting that there is but one Christian imagination of human being, as Molly Farneth emphasizes in chapter 1. Even if that is not the claim, I am left wondering who is doing the imagining and how we should understand competing imaginations of human being found *among* Christians, say, with regard to in vitro fertilization or assistive reproductive technologies.[56] In other words, *whose* Christian imagination is doing the therapeutic work?

One of the many contributions that feminist and liberationist theologians have made to the broader field is the realization that the particularities of the theologian and the community with whom and for whom she is writing will invariably shape her interpretation of Christ's life—of his conception, birth, healing, ministry, suffering, death, and resurrection. They will also shape her interpretation of the Christian scriptures and traditions. For moral theologians who center Christ's life, then, the most pressing questions I am left with are "*Whose* Christ?" and "For *whom*?"[57]

In this chapter, I have attempted to demonstrate the most significant ways in which Banner's proposals for the future of moral theology intersect with the early works of Cannon and Isasi-Díaz. All three attend to the everyday, criticize forms of theology that merely judge right and wrong action, and advocate for a moral theology and ethics capable of liberation or healing. As the womanist and Latina strands have developed over the past several decades, certainly not all contemporary womanist and Latina moral theologians/ethicists employ ethnography or attend as closely to the everyday as I contend Cannon and Isasi-Díaz do. Nonetheless, I would encourage future dialogue among contemporary womanist and Latina moral theologians/ethicists and moral theologians less familiar with these strands but who are invested in the "ethnographic turn."

Questions about the sources and tasks of moral theology and ethics seem to be the most compelling areas for future dialogue. Regarding the sources of moral theology, Cannon and Isasi-Díaz emphasize how the everyday is a source for a liberative moral theology and ethics, while Banner emphasizes Christ's life as the source of a therapeutic, pastoral, and evangelical moral theology. While these are not totalizing claims, they raise significant questions: Is Christ's life normative for our moral lives, and if so, in what ways? Whose Christ is funding which Christian imagination of human being? And what forms of community does that imagination envision? Do moral exemplars in the Christian Scriptures and traditions or even saints play a normative role in an everyday ethics?[58] Regarding the tasks of moral theology, I see resonances between the womanist and Latina theologians' liberative task and Banner's therapeutic, pastoral, and evangelical tasks, but are these tasks so similar after all? Are the distinctions significant in important ways? And if so, which task or set of tasks is most appropriate for various contexts? Future conversations around questions such as these are surely just one way in which Banner's valuable work might find conversation partners in the work of womanist and Latina theologians who continue to attend to the everyday.

## Notes

1. The Mud Flower Collective, *God's Fierce Whimsy: Christian Feminism and Theological Education* (New York: Pilgrim Press, 1985). The Mud Flower Collective was a diverse group of women in theological education who gathered in 1982 to collaboratively reflect on the state of theological education by both offering and modeling a new vision for theological education. One of the results was the 1985 publication of *God's Fierce Whimsy*. Contributors included Katie Cannon, Beverly Harrison, Carter Heyward, Ada María Isasi-Díaz, Bess Johnson, Mary Pellauer, and Nancy Richardson.

2. Michael C. Banner, *The Ethics of Everyday Life: Moral Theology, Social Anthropology, and the Imagination of the Human* (Oxford: Oxford University Press, 2014). For a recent account of this ethnographic turn, see also Christian Scharen and Aana Marie Vigen, eds., *Ethnography as Christian Theology and Ethics* (New York: Continuum, 2011), especially chapter 2.

3. Michelle Gonzalez Maldonado, "Ada María Isasi-Díaz Encountered God in the Messiness of Life," *National Catholic Reporter*, December 12, 2016, https://www.ncronline.org/blogs/ncr-today/ada-mar-isasi-d-az-encountered-god-messiness-life.

4. Banner, *Ethics of Everyday Life*, 4.

5. Banner, 4.

6. Banner, 3–4.

7. Banner, 12.

8. Banner, 7.

9. Banner, 7.

10. Banner, 12.

11. Banner, 16.

12. See Clifford Geertz, *The Interpretation of Cultures: Selected Essays* (New York: Basic Books, 1973), especially chapter 1 for defining "thick description." See also Efram Sera-Shriar, *The Making of British Anthropology, 1813–1871*, Science and Culture in the Nineteenth Century, no. 18 (London, VT: Pickering & Chatto, 2013) for an insightful understanding of the development of the discipline into its more contemporary forms of prolonged in situ observation.

13. Reprinted as chapter 4 in Katie G. Cannon, *Katie's Canon: Womanism and the Soul of the Black Community* (New York: Continuum, 1995), 59.

14. Cannon, 27.

15. Cannon, 28.

16. Cannon, 33.

17. Cannon, 34.

18. Cannon, 34.

19. Cannon, 61.

20. Cannon, 62.

21. Cannon, 60.

22. Cannon, 77.

23. Cannon, 77.

24. Cannon, 79.

25. See Ada María Isasi-Díaz and Yolanda Tarango, *Hispanic Women: Prophetic Voice in the Church / Mujer Hispana: Voz Profética En La Iglesia* (1988; repr., Scranton, PA: University of Scranton Press, 2006).

26. Ada María Isasi-Díaz, *En La Lucha / In the Struggle: A Hispanic Women's Liberation Theology* (Minneapolis, MN: Fortress Press, 1993), 62.

27. Isasi-Díaz, 62.

28. Isasi-Díaz, 66.

29. Isasi-Díaz, 69.

30. Isasi-Díaz, 76.

31. Isasi-Díaz, 21.

32. Christopher D. Tirres, "Conscientization from within *lo Cotidiano*: Expanding the Work of Ada María Isasi-Díaz," *Feminist Theology* 22, no. 3 (2014): 312–23.

33. Ada María Isasi-Díaz, *La Lucha Continues: Mujerista Theology* (Maryknoll, NY: Orbis, 2004), 95.

34. Isasi-Díaz, 99.

35. For some contemporary womanist theology that incorporates ethnographic research, see Marla F. Frederick, *Between Sundays: Black Women and Everyday Struggles of Faith* (Berkeley: University of California Press, 2003); and Linda E. Thomas, *Under the Canopy: Ritual Process and Spiritual Resilience in South Africa* (Columbia: University of South Carolina Press, 1999). For recent scholarship on methods in womanist theology, see Stacey M. Floyd-Thomas, *Mining the Motherlode: Methods in Womanist Ethics* (Cleveland, OH: Pilgrim Press, 2006), which offers an overview of Black women's literary tradition, sociology, and historiography as sources for constructive womanist ethics; and Linda E. Thomas, "The Social Sciences and Rituals of Resilience in African and African American Communities," in *The Cambridge Companion to Black Theology*, ed. Dwight N. Hopkins and Edward P. Antonio (New York: Cambridge University Press, 2012). For recent scholarship on methods in Latina theology, see María Teresa Dávila, "A Latina Methodology for Christian Ethics: The Role of Social Sciences in the Study of Praxis of the Option for the Poor in the United States," in *Faith, Feminism, and Scholarship: The Next Generation*, ed. Melanie L. Harris and Kate M. Ott (New York: Palgrave Macmillan, 2011); and Elizabeth Conde-Frazier, "Participatory Action Research: Practical Theology for Social Justice," *Religious Education* 101, no. 3 (September 1, 2006): 321–29. For some contemporary Latina theology that incorporates literature or *cuentas*, see Teresa Delgado, "Prophesy Freedom: Puerto Rican Women's Literature as a Source for Latina Theology," in *A Reader in Latina Feminist Theology: Religion and Justice*, ed. María Pilar Aquino, Daisy L. Machado, and Jeanette Rodriguez (Austin: University of Texas Press, 2002); Gail Pérez, "Ana Castillo as *Santera*: Reconstructing Popular Religious Praxis," in Aquino, Machado, and Rodriguez, *Reader in Latina Feminist Theology*; and Ivone Gebara, *Out of the Depths: Women's Experience of Evil and Salvation* (Minneapolis, MN: Fortress Press, 2002).

36. Isasi-Díaz, *En La Lucha*, 4.

37. Isasi-Díaz, 147.

38. Isasi-Díaz, 141.

39. Isasi-Díaz, 1.

40. Isasi-Díaz, 16.

41. Katie G. Cannon, *Black Womanist Ethics*, American Academy of Religion Academy Series, no. 60 (Atlanta, GA: Scholars Press, 1988), 2.

42. Cannon, 2.

43. Cannon, 2.

44. Cannon, *Katie's Canon*, 23.

45. Cannon, 59.

46. Cannon, 62.

47. Banner, *Ethics of Everyday Life*, 12.

48. Banner, 12.

49. See Banner, 12–13.

50. Banner, 23.

51. Banner, 23.

52. Cannon, *Katie's Canon*, 23.

53. Isasi-Díaz, *En La Lucha*, 35.

54. Cannon, *Black Womanist Ethics*, 2.

55. See especially chapters 6 and 7 in Cannon, *Katie's Canon*.

56. See Banner's chapter 2, "Conceiving Conception: On IVF, Virgin Births, and the Troubling of Kinship," in Banner, *Ethics of Everyday Life*.

57. I would like to thank M. T. Dávila for suggesting this language to describe the questions I am raising.

58. Thomas G. Evans's current ethnographic work is one important example of what is often called popular religion. In his master's thesis, he explores how Santo Toribio became the unofficial saint of migrants. Evans details how Santo Toribio "helps mitigate the criminal nature of this act by showing God's approval and blessing. He places the pain and social distortion of border crossing in Roman Catholic contexts of holiness and divine intervention." Evans's ethnography illustrates how some of the Catholic laity in Mexico and on the US border have constructed an everyday ethics around migration in which the normative force is not Christ's life but that of a saint whom they interpret quite differently than the official Catholic Church. This example, alongside Banner's constructive chapters, would be a fruitful place for a discussion about the sources of moral theology and everyday ethics. See Thomas G. Evans, "Santo Toribio: The Rise of a Saint" (MA thesis, University of Denver, 2011), ii.

# 3

# SOCIAL ANTHROPOLOGY, ETHNOGRAPHY, AND THE ORDINARY

## Morgan Clarke

MICHAEL BANNER PROPOSES that "moral theology can and should be reconceived through an engagement with social anthropology." Indeed, he argues that, as things stand, social anthropology alone is properly equipped to understand morality, as well as social phenomena like aging and dementia, in a broad rather than academically specialized sense.[1] As a social anthropologist, I can hardly demur. My own research and teaching is in a number of fields closely related to the themes of Banner's book: the anthropology of religion (Islam); bioethics, medical anthropology, and the new kinship studies; and the new anthropology of ethics. So I keenly appreciate Banner's particular respect for anthropology. But I also have some thoughts of my own about the anthropological ideas that he draws on. If these comments thus at points seem contrary, I nevertheless hope they do not distract from a general round of anthropological applause.

First, I think it worth noting that by *social anthropology* Banner means especially its characteristic emphasis on long-term fieldwork and the richly textured ethnographic accounts of social life that it can produce. He does not, I think, have in mind high anthropological "theory," such as attempts to "explain religion" or ritual. That is perhaps for the best, as most such theories have proved rather unsuccessful, foundering on the diversity and irreducibility of exactly that rich ethnography. For other anthropologists, theory means more critical theory, and Banner demonstrates considerable sympathy for the critical stance of much anthropology, not least medical anthropology. Another tradition I sense Banner might be in sympathy with is one that sees theory as a matter of writing through the lens of ethnography. That is, good ethnography depends on being able to spell out fully the implications of the ideas of the people being studied in ways relevant to one's audience. "The theoretical conclusions will then be found to be implicit in an exact and detailed description."[2] As a consequence, if I may quote my own teacher, "Wherever fieldwork is done . . . one is listening for the unsaid" so as to work out "what must be the case to get from this point in what was said to that?"[3] It is thus with an admirably anthropological sensibility that Banner senses something of a deaf ear in Francis, Kellaher, and Neophytou's ethnography of contemporary English mourning, for instance, when they let their own assumptions—that if people talk to the dead, they must in some sense imagine them still to be alive—fill in the gaps.[4]

Banner approves, then, of the project of teasing out the implicit and the corresponding identification of one's subject as "ordinary" or "everyday life."[5] One might adduce the parallel project of ordinary language philosophy, one of whose leading lights, J. L. Austin, famously called for fieldwork in philosophy.[6] Less happily, to my mind, Banner draws inspiration from the turn within anthropology toward "ordinary ethics"—in Michael Lambek's words, quoted by Banner, "ethics that is relatively tacit, grounded in agreement rather than rule, in practice rather than knowledge or belief, and happening without calling undue attention to itself."[7] Just as Banner is making a move within the field of moral theology, so Lambek is making a move of his own—analogous but different—within a burgeoning new subfield of the anthropology of ethics, which needs a little further discussion.

This venture has been an attempt within anthropology to regain a vision of ethics as something distinctive within the human experience rather than as effectively a synonym for culture generally. As Banner notes, one important shift within this emergent field was to identify the parochialism of seeing morality and ethics as a "code of conduct" and to move toward other visions, such as those of virtue ethics and the later Foucault's interest in practices of the self, that is, the ways in which people try to achieve desired subjectivities.[8] Many of the key early examples taken up were those of people with projects of religious commitment. For example, one better understands why millions of Egyptian women took up "the veil" toward the end of the twentieth century in terms of their projects to make themselves good Muslims rather than as mere false consciousness.[9] But then came a backlash within anthropology: this focus on religious virtuosos is unrealistic, critics argued. Most people do not have such committed and coherent life projects, so we should focus instead on "ordinary Muslims" (or Christians, for that matter) and "everyday religion." For Lambek, studying ordinary ethics entails a shift away from studying religious ethics altogether. "Through religion," he argues, "the ordinary is transcended and ethics intellectualized, materialized, or transcendentalized."[10]

The relationship between Christianity and the ordinary is, incidentally, not clear to me in Banner's book. At some points, Christianity is part of people's ordinary lives. Banner offers much praise, for example, of Juliet du Boulay's account of Orthodox Christianity in a Greek village.[11] At other points, Christianity seems completely at odds with the ordinary, as in Banner's comments on Christianity's revolutionary denial of the primacy of biological relatedness in kinship. At still others, he seems to suggest that an otherworldly Christianity must be infused into everyday practice, as in his discussion of suffering, or when he cites George Dix on the historical transformation of worship "as consummating the 'whole life of man' and not as 'the contradiction of daily life,'"[12] or in his discussion of the Mérode Altarpiece, with its juxtaposition of ordinary life and the extraordinary annunciation.[13] But if, as Lambek would have it, what is religious is not ordinary, then would a study that insists on an exclusive focus on the ordinary not therefore require a sifting out of the religious from the rest of life? That might seem to be the implication of Lambek's position, although I think it a mistake, perhaps more of a theological move than a sociological one.[14]

This points us further to the slipperiness of the notion of the ordinary. As Timothy Jenkins says, we often invoke the everyday "for want of a better term."[15] It is a notoriously difficult one to pin down, as a survey of the canonical discussions of Lefebvre, Barthes, Certeau, or Perec might demonstrate.[16] This French critical tradition sought in part to reclaim the humdrum, the banal, and the routine from their neglect and denigration (by religion and capitalism), through resistance and resilience, for sure, but more especially—and inspired by anthropology's ethnographic methods—through heightened attention. But paradoxically, the more one scrutinizes and celebrates the everyday, the less everyday it becomes. "If we go too far, the everyday ceases to be itself: it becomes the exceptional, the exotic, the marvellous."[17]

Banner asks us to focus on key life moments: conception, birth, suffering, death, burial. They happen to all of us (except burial perhaps), but are they ordinary and everyday occurrences? That is a matter of perspective. Banner tells us the key ethnography that inspired him to explore anthropology further was Lesley Sharp's wonderful account of organ transplantation in the United States.[18] But is organ transplantation really an everyday phenomenon? Surely not. What Banner finds inspirational is, I think, not so much the ordinary itself—whatever that might be—but the ethnographic method that Sharp follows, talking to non-specialists involved in the transplant enterprise and trying to tease out the assumptions in their reactions toward it. One can have ethnographic accounts of extraordinary phenomena; it is a matter more of method than subject. Where ordinary language philosophy was in part a radical call to fieldwork in a discipline that had eschewed it, "ordinary ethics," to my mind, just collapses back into ordinary anthropology.

The ordinary really makes sense only in opposition to something else, and, to be fair, Banner is clear about the opposition he wishes to make: between everyday ethics—ethics in practice for its subjects, who need not be specialists, as best captured through ethnographic analysis—and the sort of ethics of "hard cases" that he sees as typical of moral theology or bioethics, which is exotic, abstracted, intellectualized, and parochial. This is a familiar move within medical anthropology and sociology,[19] and it has gained enough momentum to have won some hurt rejoinders from the bioethicists. As Leigh Turner argues, "We need social analysis that moves beyond depicting bioethicists as so superficial that they might well be labelled sinners and social scientists as so discerning and attuned to the suffering of the vulnerable that they might be regarded as saints."[20]

Anthropology's critique of the abstracted, formalistic nature of bioethics is of a piece with a wider anthropological impatience with talk of schematic rules. Recall Lambek's interest in "ethics that is relatively tacit, grounded in agreement rather than rule, in practice rather than knowledge or belief." Likewise, Pierre Bourdieu famously dismissed the "fallacies of the rule" as a guide to human behavior.[21] I could easily multiply the examples, but I mention them here to suggest that Banner thinks along similar lines. He traces the roots of dissatisfaction with moral theology back to its beginnings in the practice of confession and its accompanying penitential handbooks with their juridical calculus of a tariff of penances. By the twentieth century, "It had become unbiblical, legalistic, individualistic . . . mere casuistry."[22] Legalism seems the very antithesis of the everyday.

But this could also seem to be more theology than sociology. Our everyday lives are actually saturated with talk and use of rules. That is not just a matter of the constraints of state law or the toils of bureaucracy, although those are genuinely ubiquitous. Children's bedtimes or television watching can be as much a source of legalistic discussion as the hard cases of bioethics. Our most trivial and secular projects of the self—dieting, rationing smoking, exercise—are replete with forms just as "ruly" as religious ones. Indeed, the use of rules is one of the great technologies of the self.[23] Banner himself cites the popularity of the medieval *Ars moriendi* genre, which provided detailed instructions for how to die well, and he even laments the lack of such suitable "scripts" in our own times.[24]

In this light, Banner's dismissal of the practices of the confessional is, from my non-partisan perspective, striking. Islam has analogous institutions, and it has been a great advance to understand them as modes of personal, pedagogical engagement rather than as solely academic and legal. It is through such hands-on engagement with Muslims in need that an Islamic religious authority can be seen as a "real shaykh," although the generality of rules can make them unforgiving in particular cases.[25] That tension between rule and life no doubt also led to the rich exceptionalism and development of the Christian casuistical literature. It is this side of the casuistical tradition, one founded in real-life engagement, that led Albert Jonsen and Stephen Toulmin down exactly the opposite path to Banner in their seminal *The Abuse of Casuistry:*[26] to see the resurrection of casuistry—rather than its final killing-off—as the answer to the seemingly insoluble problems of bioethics. For Jonsen and

Toulmin, the casuist and confessor are more akin to a doctor, diagnosing individual cases through practical experience, than the armchair philosopher (and, by extension, bioethicist), groping for general rules through cogitation alone.

Impatient with the notion of the confessional as an effective site of everyday religious pedagogy, Banner is also, I would hazard, not too impressed by doctors' claim to authority. He broadly follows medical anthropology's overwhelmingly critical stance toward biomedicine, of a piece with anthropology's wider cynicism toward the supposed cultural poverty of Western capitalist modernity. We live in "a social world which is experienced as somewhat bleak," subject to the "harsh logic" of a "harsh world," Banner says.[27] While this is sadly no doubt true of many people's lives in our troubled times, I am not sure that it constitutes a rounded ethnographic appreciation of life in the contemporary UK. But further, to characterize the medicalization of birth, for instance, as a "de-meaning" process, while comprehensible, glosses over its institution of a different, distinctive set of meanings. Ideally, one would have a proper appreciation of them and their reasons too. After all, even paperwork can make for a fascinating ethnography.[28]

Banner asks with a justified sense of outrage how the various professionals associated with the Alder Hey scandal could have acted as they did, with such blank incomprehension of the motivations of everyday people. His response is to urge greater attention on the part of professionals to everyday motivations. Quite right, but another would be to try, in parallel, to understand why professionals think and act the way they do. I suspect that Banner shares anthropology's rejection of "rationality" as the ultimate criterion for the intelligibility of human action. But I also think that the phenomenon of fundamentalist rationalism, if I can put it like that, as exemplified in Banner's account by John Harris's response to the Alder Hey debates, needs due attention in itself.[29] Formality, bureaucratic rationality, and legalism are all part of our everyday experience of complex society. One cannot simply leave them out. Perhaps Banner needs to hear the bioethicist's confession after all.

What, finally, is the relationship that Banner has in mind between the ethnography of everyday life, the moral theology that he hopes to reform, and the everyday ethics that he wishes to see it develop? Moral theology is to redirect its interests toward shaping "an everyday ethics which would support and sustain a Christian form of human being."[30] Here the anthropologist and the theologian have, I think, parted ways. In this dialectic, religion again seems to lie in some sense outside the everyday, in that a knowledge of the ordinary is to facilitate its more effective Christianization. As to what constitutes the right sort of Christianity, Banner seems confident he knows. The anthropological vocation requires one to be open to, and shaped by, the other. As a hopeful bystander, I would wish that Banner lets himself become enough of an anthropologist to allow our profane, contemporary everyday to shape him a little in return.

# Notes

1. Michael Banner, *The Ethics of Everyday Life: Moral Theology, Social Anthropology, and the Imagination of the Human* (Oxford: Oxford University Press, 2014), 7, 125, 202.

2. Edward Evans-Pritchard, "Some Reminiscences and Reflections on Fieldwork," *Journal of the Anthropological Society of Oxford* 4, no. 2 (1973): 3.

3. Paul Dresch, "Wilderness of Mirrors: Truth and Vulnerability in Middle Eastern Fieldwork," in *Anthropologists in a Wider World: Essays on Field Research*, ed. Paul Dresch, Wendy James, and David Parkin (Oxford: Berghahn Books), 122–23.

4. Banner, *Ethics of Everyday Life*, 166–72, discussing Doris Francis, Leonie Kellaher, and Georgina Neophytou, *The Secret Cemetery* (Oxford: Berg, 2005).

5. On which, see Timothy Jenkins, "Fieldwork and the Perception of Everyday Life," *Man (N.S.)* 29, no. 2 (1994): 433–55.

6. J. L. Austin, "A Plea for Excuses: The Presidential Address," *Proceedings of the Aristotelian Society (N.S.)* 57 (1956–1957): 9.

7. Michael Lambek, introduction to *Ordinary Ethics: Anthropology, Language, and Action*, ed. Michael Lambek (New York: Fordham University Press, 2010), 2, cited by Banner, *Ethics of Everyday Life*, 201.

8. Banner, *Ethics of Everyday Life*, 26. Banner picks up the latter trope in order to venture a more persuasive account of Christianity's interest in suffering than that offered by some academic commentary (99–101). For a good guide to the new anthropology of ethics, see James Laidlaw, *The Subject of Virtue: An Anthropology of Ethics and Freedom* (Cambridge: Cambridge University Press, 2014).

9. Saba Mahmood, *Politics of Piety: The Islamic Revival and the Feminist Subject* (Princeton, NJ: Princeton University Press, 2004).

10. Lambek, introduction to *Ordinary Ethics*, 3. On the former point, see, e.g., Samuli Schielke, "Second Thoughts about the Anthropology of Islam, or How to Make Sense of Grand Schemes in Everyday Life," *Working Papers*, no. 2 (Berlin: Zentrum Moderner Orient, 2010).

11. Juliet du Boulay, *Cosmos, Life, and Liturgy in a Greek Orthodox Village* (Limni, Greece: Denise Harvey, 2009).

12. George Dix, *The Shape of the Liturgy* (London: Dacre Press, 1945).

13. Banner, *Ethics of Everyday Life*, 28, 29–34, 41–47, 54–59, 177–79.

14. See Morgan Clarke, "Cough Sweets and Angels: The Ordinary Ethics of the Extraordinary in Sufi Practice in Lebanon," *Journal of the Royal Anthropological Institute (N.S.)* 20, no. 3 (2014): 407–25.

15. Jenkins, "Fieldwork," 444.

16. Michael Sheringham, *Everyday Life: Theories and Practices from Surrealism to the Present* (Oxford: Oxford University Press, 2006).

17. Sheringham, 23, 398.

18. Lesley Sharp, *Strange Harvest: Organ Transplants, Denatured Bodies, and the Transformed Self* (Berkeley: University of California Press, 2006).

19. See, e.g., Arthur Kleinman, "Anthropology of Bioethics," in *Writing at the Margin: Discourse between Anthropology and Medicine* (Berkeley: University of California Press, 1997), 41–67.

20. Leigh Turner, "Anthropological and Sociological Critiques of Bioethics," *Bioethical Inquiry* 6, no. 1 (2009): 88.

21. Pierre Bourdieu, *Outline of a Theory of Practice*, trans. Richard Nice (Cambridge: Cambridge University Press, 1977), 22.

22. Banner, *Ethics of Everyday Life*, 10–11.

23. See Morgan Clarke, "Legalism and the Care of the Self: Shari'ah Discourse in Contemporary Lebanon," in *Legalism: Rules and Categories*, ed. Paul Dresch and Judith Scheele (Oxford: Oxford University Press, 2015), 231–57.

24. Banner, *Ethics of Everyday Life*, 111–13.

25. Hussein Agrama, "Ethics, Tradition, Authority: Toward an Anthropology of the Fatwa," *American Ethnologist* 37, no. 1 (2010): 2–18; Morgan Clarke, "The Judge as Tragic Hero: Judicial Ethics in Lebanon's Shariʻa Courts," *American Ethnologist* 39, no. 1 (2012): 106–21.

26. Albert Jonsen and Stephen Toulmin, *The Abuse of Casuistry: A History of Moral Reasoning* (Berkeley: University of California Press, 1988).

27. Banner, *Ethics of Everyday Life*, 71.

28. See, e.g., Matthew Hull, *Government of Paper: The Materiality of Bureaucracy in Urban Pakistan*, (Berkeley: University of California Press, 2012).

29. Banner, *Ethics of Everyday Life*, 22.

30. Banner, 34.

# 4

# "THE EVERYDAY" AGAINST THE "AND" IN "THEOLOGY AND SOCIAL SCIENCE"

## BRIAN BROCK

*THE ETHICS OF EVERYDAY LIFE* is a book of profound insight. But its insightfulness becomes apparent only if the reader moves beyond the author's several hints that what we are being offered is a novel ethical method. Good theology has never been generated by a method, but it valorizes itself in speaking insightfully about the world Christians and their contemporaries inhabit. The claim that Michael Banner has offered us some fine moral theology rests not on the method he offers but rather on his penetrating insights as he investigates a wide range of ethically significant "life worlds." My use of the awkward language of "ethical life worlds" is not an invocation of states of mind and intention but of social domains such as the hospital, the hospice, the care home for the elderly, or the fertility clinic.

I take my clue for this counterreading from a phrase offered by Banner himself, which nicely encapsulates the book as a whole: "Perspicacious presentation of the warp and weft of everyday life refers us to the richness of a religious imagination, which by means of rituals and routines, serves to shape the forms and patterns of daily existence with their particular modes of knowing, feeling and acting."[1] In this chapter, I will suggest why Banner's intuition that thick descriptions of life worlds are necessary to situate any serious ethical thinking makes his approach genuinely insightful and ethically productive. It is a framing of Christian ethics that offers substantively *theological* access to a wide range of contested questions in complex and largely neglected ethical domains relating to technologies, cultural changes, and institutional structures. And it achieves this without collapsing into utilitarian calculations that leave theology with nothing to do or effervescing into such high-level conceptualities that little new insight into the most important moral problems of the contemporary world can emerge.

Such counterreadings place the burden of proof on the expositor. I will first tease out the reasons why Banner should not be read as fitting within contemporary attempts to draw together academic theology and social scientific research. He differs from this contemporary theological work by neither incorporating the "results" of empirical research into his theology nor granting empirical researchers methodological autonomy. He is best understood as being engaged in a specifically contoured theological conversation with social scientific researchers. Substantiating these claims will require excavating some of the links between his approach and the everyday ethics that emerged from 1960s French Marxism. A second section will sketch the theological presumptions that fund this approach. A final section will display how such a reading lets the material discussions that make up the bulk of *The Ethics of Everyday Life* shine, focused as it is on material ethical questions of profound import to citizens of modern Western societies. By presenting Banner as less methodologically radical than he presents himself (part one), I will suggest that he achieves a more theologically coherent relation to the social sciences (part two) that issues in a theological ethics able to address the intimate domains of human life usually ignored by academic ethicists (part three).

## Traveling with Everyday Radicals

The easiest misreading of Banner's project is an understandable one: assuming he is a latecomer to the academic growth industry called "ecclesiology and ethnography."[2] This loose affiliation of theologians has come together for the laudable purpose of countering the estrangement of theological discourse from the everyday life of the church. One of its proponents has recently criticized Oliver O'Donovan's work in a manner that sounds distinctly like Banner's criticism of Christian ethics as a whole:

> Ethnographic description is not the same as critique. Rather, it is a vital adjunct to interpreting the times and a way of self-reflexively bringing under the microscope with some degree of rigor the problem O'Donovan names as our intuitive sympathies for our context. This is in contrast to the primary form Christian ethics takes in the late modern period, notably, intellectual history and philosophical analysis, which are too prone to bracket their own social location from the analysis and too often sit so far above the fray that they forget [to understand the ethicists, work as intimately bound up with our participation in the church and the world] . . . . [T]he addition of an ethnographic moment . . . is a poultice against mystifications and generalisations based on anecdote, against confusing a worldly teleology for eschatology, and against an amnesia that we are worshippers first and academics second.[3]

My aim is to distinguish the approach of *The Ethics of Everyday Life* from this more popular approach in order to show that the resemblance is superficial. Banner is not proposing the introduction of an "ethnographic moment" into theological method in order to keep Christian ethicists honest. Nor is he seeking to bring together two discrete disciplines called theology and social science, whose agenda is signaled by the *and* conjoining the terms *ecclesiology* and *ethnography*.

The most obvious signal that Banner is taking a different route toward a not dissimilar end lies in the book's title, more specifically, the language of "everyday life." The assumptions Banner makes about the shaping of life and perception by language usage draws on a broad set of modern Marxist traditions that have funded most contemporary critical cultural studies. Marx's most famous line (from his "Theses on Feuerbach") was "The philosophers have only interpreted the world, in various ways; the point is to change it." This maxim has been most influentially taken up by a group of German Marxists who came to be called the Frankfurt School. For them, "To reinterpret daily life is to change it."[4] It can be generally said that the social scientific methodologies dominant in English-speaking universities take their premises either from logical positivism or the critical Marxism of the German Frankfurt school.

What is less well known is Marx's dictum developed in other directions. In the 1950–1960s Western Marxists were seeking to define themselves against the Stalinist poisoning of the label *Marxist*. The French developments are most interesting for our purposes, as here the term *everyday life* came to describe a discrete sociocritical methodology. The French Marxist Henri Lefebvre creatively reappropriated Marx's account of alienation for a postconsumerist society under the heading "critical analysis of everyday life" in his three-volume analysis of modern consumer society.[5] Not unlike Alasdair MacIntyre's Marx-inspired starting point, Lefebvre saw that the problem of modern alienation occurs in the thick of daily life. Any resistance to modern alienation must be born in daily life. This alienation, as well as any form of resistance, could be grasped only by attending to the relation of language to material practices.[6]

This emphasis on the language of everyday life thus had a twofold purpose. The first was to move Marxism beyond negative slogans ("Death to the Exploiters") toward positive formulations such as "Life First!"[7] That trajectory was later codified in a Freudian Marxist tradition that understood its central task to be the critique of the subjective barriers to revolutionary change. These thinkers presumed that the psychological barriers associated with alienation had not been fully appreciated by Marx, who assumed that once people had been made aware of their alienation they would be sufficiently cured of it. To repair this missing psychological component of alienation, these revisionist Marxists moved away from seeking to revise practice by way of centralized promulgation of general pronouncements made by experts (as in Stalinism) toward preparation for revolution by breaking the bonds constraining the perception of alienated and isolated individuals. The crucial shift is from pursuing a centrally organized response that attempted to remove the habits that entrapped the population in false realities and toward a diffused approach that attempted to give each individual in the populace the intellectual tools to break through the psychological barriers entrapping them in their self-alienation.

The ethical and emancipatory message of Marxism was thus addressed to individual readers. The task was conceived as helping readers gain a fresh view of the forms of action that capitalist societies declare off-limits. Lefebvre highlighted the central insight of this tradition:

> The consumer does not desire. He submits. . . . He obeys the suggestions and the orders given to him by advertising, sales agencies or the demands of social prestige. . . . [T]hese "orders" from outside become subtly abstract fragments or absurdly concrete "motivations." Desires no longer correspond to genuine needs; they are artificial. . . . [E]veryday life has literally been "colonized." It has been brought to an extreme point of alienation, in other words, profound dissatisfaction, in the name of the latest technology of "consumer society."[8]

Far from being something applicable as a "critical poultice," these thinkers see sociological research as a means of undermining the fiction of conceptual neutrality and, in so doing, politicizing citizens. "Marx transforms epistemology into sociology," as one adherent of this approach explains.[9]

At root, this approach is fired by a faith that a different world is not only possible but already afoot. Unlike the thinkers of the Frankfurt School as well as Alasdair MacIntyre, Lefebvre's account is not fundamentally a decay narrative. It is a sympathetic hunt for that which is not alienated, the smaller ways in which resistance to the status quo is already being hammered out. To approach daily life as a hopeful search for alternatives to the regnant order, one scholar points out, situates the task of the critic as setting free "the latent wealth, to bring out the implicit, unexplored content of daily life, valorising it."[10]

Because such investigations are pursued among people rendered fragile by alienation, they must be oriented not only by appropriate questions but also a sensitive investigative stance: "Studying daily life (its details) at a given moment bypasses the concept, simulates apprehension of the concrete, goes no further than what is immediate [and so] . . . must proceed with caution, restraint, respect. It must respect lived experience, rather than belabouring it as the domain of ignorance and error, rather than absorbing it into positive knowledge as vanquished ignorance."[11] This is why, I would suggest, Lefebvre sounds at pivotal points more like Banner the theologian than most academic anthropologists:

> Everyday discourse . . . has a stable content . . . which is bound up not (as the classical thesis has it) with an unchanging human nature, but with the fact that social

relations have for a long time, if not always, been relations of force, authority and power, dependency, inequality in power and wealth. Such relations are tolerable only when they are masked. Daily life and its ambiguity, simultaneously effect and cause, conceal these relations between parents and children, men and women, bosses and workers, governors and governed. For its part critical knowledge removes the screens and unveils the meaning of metaphors. It demonstrates that what makes the functioning of society possible is neither self-interest on its own, nor violence, nor the imaginary, but the ethics inherent in discourse. At the heart of daily life and its speech we find ethical values, which are supports of social life in that they make it tolerable.[12]

In other words, and using biblical terminology that he occasionally deploys, in seeking out these pockets of resistance to the denuding patterns of our world, Banner is "plundering the [wealth of the] Egyptians." Taking his orientation from a theological narrative, he is looking for counterpractices that are significantly richer and more humane than those which characterize many domains of modern Western culture that he understands to threaten genuinely flourishing human life. As he does so he finds that anthropologists can help Christians and others imagine ways of thinking and enacting forms of life that the moral common sense of modernity apparently rules out of court. But only a certain kind of anthropology will do—and only when attended to by a certain kind of theology.

Christian ethicists today who are more committed to the status quo or who are unaware of this revolutionary discourse can easily overlook the ways Banner's project is a fellow traveler with the Marxist tradition's political project of imaginative and practical resistance to the laws of liberal capitalism. "Revolutionary change may involve the exhilaration of throwing off imaginative shackles, of suddenly realizing that impossible things are not impossible at all, but it also means most people will have to get over some of this deeply habituated laziness and start engaging interpretative (imaginative) labor for a very long time to make those realities stick."[13] Though in The Ethics of Everyday Life Banner eschews the language of revolution here used by David Graeber,[14] Banner's intention and approach remains extremely close to this intellectual powerhouse of the Occupy Movement. Without proposing that Banner is explicitly associating himself with this contemporary neo-Marxist tradition, it is clear that any suggestion that his book is a tired retread of the "turn to sociology" is a misunderstanding based on ignorance of his conceptual and political debts to contemporary leftist thought.[15]

That Banner is a fellow traveler with this leftist tradition is also highlighted by attending to the multiple convergences of the social issues with which he is concerned and the types of responses he suggests. Graeber, for instance, laments the inhumanity of modern bureaucratic capitalism by meditating on how the inanity of institutionalized forms and rules both disempowered his aging mother and cost him immense amounts of time and frustration as he tried to secure her care. For Graeber, the inability of the capitalistic social order to provide anything like a human-scaled care for its ailing members is especially diagnostic of how heartless and bureaucratic neoliberalism can be and how this springs from a lazy refusal to imagine our world otherwise.

If Graeber's social analysis of the bureaucratic society was catalyzed by a grueling stretch caring for his ailing mother, Banner's *Ethics of Everyday Life* grows from a very similar sort of experience, a moment of empathy for the grief-stricken parents of the children whose tissues were taken without permission in the course of what came to be called the Alder Hey scandal.[16] That the representatives of both government and medical establishments were so confused, inarticulate, and dismissive of these parents' grief lit a holy ire in Banner. Formative moments of transition in human lives were not being (and worse, could not be) taken seriously in the concrete. And modern construals of the remit of ethical thinking were at least partially to blame in presuming the parents' grief to be ethically irrelevant. This concern with the denuding quality of modern moral perception, combined with an acute sense that moderns have given up finer moral sensitivities held by some of our forebears, is explicitly lined at this point with the approach of Alasdair MacIntyre.[17] But for the reasons already surveyed, Banner diverges from MacIntyre by moving from observations about the poverty of contemporary liberal ethical frameworks to formulating trajectories and connections with Christian thought that might foster new experiments in practice and language so that the "dead zones" of the contemporary moral imagination can be recolonized.

Banner's contention that modern analytical philosophy has contributed to the creation of imaginative "dead zones" derives not from MacIntyre but from Ludwig Wittgenstein. Though not signaled on the surface of the text, Wittgenstein funds the underlying faith that resistance is already afoot and that people's real-life problems very often can never be erased by conceptual or linguistic sleight of hand. Wittgenstein augments the neo-Marxist insight that alienation is more deeply embedded than a mere change of habit can remedy. The poverty of modern ethical theory is sustainable only by systematically evading engagement with people's real-life problems. Banner is clear that this affliction was evident among the politicians and medics involved in the Alder Hey case. In Wittgenstein's terms, "Some philosophers (or whatever you like to call them) suffer from what may be called 'loss of problems.' Then everything seems quite simple to them, no deep problems seem to exist any more, the world becomes broad and flat and loses all depth, and what they write becomes immeasurably shallow and trivial."[18]

In drawing insights from neo-Marxism and Wittgenstein together in this way, Banner has fashioned a mode of Christian political engagement that diverges from much contemporary public theology by intentionally eschewing the interminable debates about *whether* and *how* Christians might speak in public about the pain, frustrations, and confusions experienced by a secular public, and instead attempting to *do so*. The effort that is spent defining the field of theology and explaining how it can be synchronized with the demands of social scientific research is largely bypassed by Banner, who, resting secure in his grasp of concrete exemplifications of alienation, moves directly to an ad hoc engagement with a wide range of social scientific researchers who may have little or no personal interest in theology.

## Orienting Empirical Questions Theologically

Banner is enabled to take this less frequently traveled methodological route on the basis of a Christian theology that assumes the embedding of cultural worlds in a created realm whose alpha and omega is Jesus Christ. Given that it is by no means clear that ordinary Christians should imitate the God-man who came to this world to save us all, Banner's move is a subtle one: he asks us to think about what was going on as Christians through the ages *imagined* what Christ's life and death might mean for their own. In *The Ethics of Everyday Life*, Banner persistently asks how Jesus's life and death were imaginatively translated into a model for the living and dying of Christians in diverse sets of cultural and life circumstances.

This first subtle positioning is teamed with a second: the proposal that Christians today ought to take much more seriously *all* the media in which Christians have imagined Jesus's reshaping of everyday lives. Not only theologians but also Christian artists, poets, musicians, politicians, and laypeople through the ages have imagined what Christ's life meant for their own. The traces of these imaginative grapplings with Jesus's countercolonization of everyday sensibilities are visible in all sorts of texts and artifacts from material culture.[19] In all these fora, Christians were pointing toward ways of living that the authorities and cultural forces in which they were immersed claimed to be impossible. Like his Marxist fellow travelers, Banner's text does not attempt to make universal pronouncements but offers a wide range of worked examples to provoke individual readers to fresh imaginations of the ways of living open to them in their own contexts.

Humans are material beings who hope. Their living is always a living in faith.[20] I have suggested that this line of thinking situates Banner in the vicinity of the Marxist tradition with its concern with alienation, the assumption that the way things are is not the way they have to be. Those who think that the status quo is good enough can rightfully be called alienated in their refusal to countenance the thought that their lives could always be more thoughtfully lived. This suggests that Banner's deepest challenge to contemporary theology is pressing a question about how what we believe, and who we take to be our "we," situates our listening to and intervention in the lives of others. The anthropologist and theologian stand on the *same* ground precisely in the work of attempting to formulate their research question—a task that is inextricably shaped by what each one hopes for and believes in. If this is indeed where Banner the Christian and theologian stands as each listens to and responds to the world, it becomes clear why his prioritization of practical over theoretical knowledge—which amounts to a resistance to all metaphysics that take up the attitude of a spectator—is in the end an entailment of a fundamentally Christological account of reality.[21]

Banner performs this theology in his extended reflections on Augustine's life and work, which function as the theological backbone of the book. Without explicitly stating his strategy at this point, Banner clearly takes Augustine's life to exemplify an imagination fired by contemplating the life of Jesus Christ in a particular social location. Banner's insistence that Christianity's imagination not be limited to a set of theological beliefs or narrowly doctrinal texts leads him to range widely across the whole corpus of Augustine's letters, sermons, and theological tracts, situating them in their historical context. This is done so deftly and succinctly that only their recurrence at pivotal points signals that these engagements are playing an orienting role in the progress of the book. Like Banner himself, Banner's Augustine is also a member of the establishment and yet is constantly agitating for others to take roads they believe are impossible, like the judge Augustine entreats to pardon a convicted criminal. We have here a political Augustinianism that is important today because of the depth of the Augustine being presented as well as the critical distance being maintained as this portrait is painted from the political and ideological lords of our age.

Having suggested that Banner's engagement with the grief of the Alder Hey parents is the meeting point of all the sight lines of *The Ethics of Everyday Life*, it can now be stated more explicitly how Banner diverges from social anthropology. His question is not how the parents' grief impacts him or reshapes his own identity (which it clearly has). He simply takes it as a reality that the grief of the Alder Hey parents, and the refusal of doctors and politicians to take it seriously, expose contemporary moral callousness. It self-evidently levies a moral claim that needs no theological defense. His empathetic connection with this grief has propelled him into the anthropological literature in search of thinkers who do not suffer from what may be called "loss of problems."

Thus, despite Banner's rhetoric of a call to a new disciplinary alliance with cultural anthropology, it is clear that what he is proposing is not a simple valorization by the theologian of the status quo in the main streams of contemporary Anglophone academic anthropology. Practitioners of that discipline, for instance, are constantly preoccupied with overcoming the positivist observer-observed dichotomy, which they often attack in a range of ingenious ways. Yet as they do so, they never relinquish the basic desire to bring phenomena "out there" in the world of human culture into a descriptive account captured on the written page. Banner's divergence from his conversation partner James Faubion highlights the crucial point of methodological divergence. Faubion's texts are highly determined by the desire responsibly to overcome the tendency of anthropologists to objectify those whom they are attempting to describe.[22] Banner never attempts to "merge" his point of view with those whose lives he is describing in the manner of Faubion and his guild, nor, it seems, is he particularly worried that professional anthropologists sometimes objectify those they observe. He is apparently unencumbered by the bad conscience that besets social scientists, which they constantly labor to meet by diffusing the observer-object problem. How can this be?

Banner lives within the Christian tradition, which has its own distinctive grammar, anchored in cask-strength, first-order theological language. That language comprehends human wisdom and configures it in distinctive ways. This premise alone renders his project a good deal more sophisticated in aim and practice than approaches that simply bring together two academic disciplines assumed to be methodologically discrete. It also represents his most radical divergence from the status quo in contemporary Christian ethics, dominated as it is today by post-Troeltschian approaches aiming to decontaminate the ethics of contemporary Christians either by updating them for an enlightened age or by showing how Christians can be counted on to support the ethical progressivism espoused by Western elites of any faith or none. Banner's contribution to the ethics and ecclesiology discussion is ultimately his insistence on pressing the question of how empirical research questions are formed. For him, the positioning of the theologian as a witness to suffering calls for a Christ-centered reengagement of imagination. Social scientific research may aid in the fleshing out of context-sensitive Christian imagination, but it can never generate it. This is an irreducibly theological responsibility, as ethnography has no place to stand outside the reality confessed by the Christian "we," the church. This is no denial that believers and unbelievers share the world of everyday life, nor that shared moral concerns can emerge. But it is a theology that seeks a more supple way to understand and inhabit it together.

## Examining Ethical Life Worlds

I have spent a far greater proportion of this chapter on metacommentary on Banner's method than Banner himself does in *The Ethics of Everyday Life*. One important gain of his decision not to invest significant efforts defending his method is the freedom it gives him to advance incisive and densely textured material insights concerning a range of contemporary moral perplexities in a concise and theologically compelling fashion. The contribution of Banner's work to the discipline of Christian ethics is best seen by highlighting what is methodologically distinctive about his angle of approach to the material questions engaged in the body of the work.

I will focus my comments on Banner's discussion of material questions by looking at chapters 2 and 3, which orbit around the contemporary Western relation to the beginning of human life, shaped as it is by a range of relatively new artificial reproductive techniques, from in vitro fertilization to prenatal testing. The premise of these chapters is that the ethical literature has been "narrowly concerned with the licitness or illicitness of various means of becoming pregnant, and has thus typically neglected more fundamental questions about whether and how technology, the use of which may or may not be licit in principle, should figure within Christian life, thought, and practice."[23]

It is a criticism of ethical approaches to the prenatal field that has been mapped in more detail by Gerald McKenny, who surveys the dominant ethical frameworks philosophers and theologians have deployed to frame the ethical problems that emerge in this life domain.[24] Very few contemporary approaches, he begins, succeed in framing these technologies in a manner that fosters robustly critical and constructive ethical engagement. But their failures do yield useful methodological insights. McKenny groups the dominant ethical approaches into three basic categories.

At the most obvious first level, the so-called new technologies can be considered simply as new devices and techniques that facilitate new ways of reaching new, but more often familiar, ends. Beginning from this definition, much of the medical ethics literature contents itself with a narrow set of questions about whether proposed new techniques should be deployed. Various risk-cost-benefit equations have been developed to generate conclusions about whether a given technology is "ethical." But since substantial investments have already been made in developing new techniques and devices by the time such questions are asked, the chances of serious critical engagement are vanishingly small—a warning borne out by the most cursory survey of the literature in which this approach is taken.

A second level of analysis vastly complexifies the moral equation by considering the seemingly endless effects that deploying new techniques and devices puts in motion. Such wider-scope investigations inevitably reveal how quickly and deeply new techniques, by altering practices, reshape human practices and self-understandings. To take two obvious examples, modern life-support equipment and advanced directives resituate people's sense of what it means to die, just as modern reproductive technologies change how parenting is understood. The seemingly endless proliferation of effects is proof enough for many that ethical assessments of such technologies can do no more than focus on first-level analyses of the boons and benefits offered by specific techniques or devices, narrowly conceived. To others, this problem suggests the opposite solution: take one further step back in order to gain a wider perspective on the patterns that may be glimpsed in the apparently disordered domain of second-level effects.

Those taking this latter approach have focused on a third level of technological developments, beginning from the observation that modern Westerners seem to have developed a characteristic form of technological activity best considered as its own distinct way of relating to the world. Some regard this distinctive way of life as problematic in itself because Western humanity now seems to be approaching the whole material world as a "standing reserve" to be harnessed for ends that humans designate—including human beings themselves. Such a position represents a reaction to the dominant narrative that emerged in the early modern period in which technology came to be understood as the activity of modern secular humanity to demystify the material world. We are the humanity that has electricity, fluoride toothpaste, and antibiotics, these thinkers suggest, and enjoying these practical benefits entails some sort of commitment to technical progress as a good.

The polarization of such accounts into utopian and dystopian versions need not detain us here. The real problem, McKenny points out, is that these third-level accounts rarely offer sharp enough instruments to tease apart the practical questions raised by particular technological developments. Substantial work remains to be done to concretize what a global tale about the rise of "Western technological humanity" tells us about whether we should resist or embrace any given proposed technique or device. Though this third-level analysis is much more attractive to many theologians in being close to their own idioms, if it is to be deployed in practice, some descent will have to be made into second- or first-level analyses of the techniques in question.

The dominant response to this dilemma in Christian ethics, here falling into line with secular philosophical medical ethics, has been to rest content with first-level analyses. The apparent elegance of the utilitarian calculation of risks and costs can be augmented by bringing in supplementary questions about whether pursuing a given technological development will draw resources away from the pressing needs of others, confer unfair competitive advantage for some, reinforce problematic social norms, and so on. But in taking this route, McKenny protests, "theology fades into the background. There may be theological reasons for favoring one theory of justice over another or weighing one kind of harm over another, but these reasons will generally serve as a preamble to discussions conducted in the standardized terms of policy discourse. The result is that theology is marginalized in most debates about the concrete implications of technology."[25]

McKenny is dissatisfied with this outcome. Surely there must be a middle way between theologically robust but abstract analyses and those that are detailed but theologically vacuous. In his survey of the literature, he finds two thinkers who have successfully descended from the third to the second level of analysis, a domain typically left to the social scientists. "Theological and pastoral reflection on modern medicine—I have in mind here the work of Stanley Hauerwas and William F. May—criticizes the attitudes and practices regarding suffering and death in modern medicine from the standpoint of alternative attitudes and practices that modern medicine is said to have displaced."[26] These thinkers succeed in being both theological and engaged with details by shifting the focus of ethical engagement from particular techniques and devices, as in the first-level analysis, to questions about the practices, activities, and states that are worthwhile for human beings to pursue. Only after this first step has been accomplished are questions asked about how particular changes in techniques or institutions might foster or erode flourishing forms of human life.

McKenny's map of contemporary ethical methods allows us to see one of the main contributions of Banner's book by showing how rare it is that ethicists brave the complexities of second-level analysis. Banner's work represents a new approach to this second level of analysis that McKenny commends but does not himself perform. The distinctiveness of Banner's approach that McKenny's analysis has allowed us to see can be further drawn out by way of contrast with the not dissimilar work of Stanley Hauerwas, which McKenny has praised.

In *Naming the Silences: God, Medicine and the Problem of Suffering*, Hauerwas works hard to offer the reader a fine-grained depiction of the aporias of modern life, a form of life deeply shaped by the technologies unthinkingly embraced. Hauerwas focuses his prosecution of this point by considering the hard case of the pediatric oncology ward, a cultural domain whose most distinctive feature is the loss of any role played by communities of support for grieving sufferers. Modern medical care has developed an armory of techniques of historically unparalleled power deployed by technicians with unparalleled knowledge of the body's workings. The whole package, however, is tied together by the implicit promise that if we will submit to it wholly, it will save us from death. The problem created by the "war on cancer" is that it becomes unintelligible to care for the "lost causes" who will not beat their cancer. In such unintelligible life-situations, "the best we can do is comfort one another in the loneliness and the silences created by our suffering."[27] Banner's project follows the same strategy in drawing attention to a spectrum of contemporary human suffering hidden by modern techniques and the quests they sustain, such as the "chasing of the blood tie" by infertile parents.

The role played by the social sciences in Hauerwas's attempt to give texture to the spaces of human life differs from Banner's approach in subtle but important ways. Hauerwas's book opens with a lengthy summary of a novel offering an imaginative entry into the death of a child and the questions this provokes in the heart of her ambiguously Christian father. Social scientific observations are subsequently introduced to substantiate the senses in which this imaginative rendering accurately portrays the ethical life world of the oncology unit, in which all the coordinates for what will be counted as a good and bad—or better, an intelligible or unintelligible—action are already set in advance.[28] Hauerwas contrasts this narrative with a Christian narrative that he suggests presents death and suffering as far more coherent and intelligible. It is the novel that sets the terms of the critical analysis, with the social science serving to support this imaginative presentation of the ethical context.

This twofold approach allows Hauerwas's claim that our "only hope lies in whether we can place alongside the story of . . . pointless suffering . . . a story of suffering that helps us know that we are not thereby abandoned."[29] It is the suffering of Jesus Christ, mediated through a church, that allows Christians to patiently persevere and remain present with others when faced with pointless suffering and imminent death. Such Christ-shaped willingness to join in suffering renders morally and theologically intelligible the everyday lived reality of childhood cancer that medicine, with all its techniques and linguistic comportment, has rendered unintelligible.

With these moves, Hauerwas renders some of the pressing questions of our age accessible to theological analysis and very helpfully displays how third-level general theological claims gain purchase on second-level analyses of contentious devices or techniques. However, in common with many third-level analyses, he seems much less interested in ethical questions about contentious technologies and more in how Christians might live in a world already configured by these technologies.

I am sure Banner would agree with the premise of Hauerwas's case: Christian ethics must always begin anew with the world in which we find ourselves by trying to make sense of how to go on. This fundamental agreement extends further to the basic construal of the task of the Christian ethicist, which is to draw attention to the humanly important aspects of life that have been obscured or lost in modern ways of living.

This suggests that the only substantial divergence between Banner and Hauerwas is a tactical one regarding the way in which the "measure of Christ's human being" is invoked for the shaping of emancipatory Christian perception and imagination. Banner seems much more interested in a rich and sustained investigation of traditional Christian practices, not only to indicate what is displaced by the practices of the modern world but also to flesh out more precisely and across several human life-stage points where this displacement has occurred. The final sentence of Banner's book helpfully illustrates his proximity to and divergence from Hauerwas's *Naming the Silences* as well as the proximity of both to the Marxist tradition of everyday ethics. "The task of an everyday Christian ethics is, in its own lesser part, to imagine, recount, and thereby hopefully sustain the practice and enactment of human being after the measure of Christ's human being."[30]

Banner uses anthropological descriptions to help readers understand the relevance of reimagining the available options in contemporary life worlds. The various artifacts left to us by Christians of previous generations can help to catalyze Christian thinking about modern life worlds that are also usefully described by social scientists. But there is no sequence to this procedure. The innovation in Banner's strategy is not in his reliance on social anthropology per se but in the way he draws it into his theological engagement with other human beings in order to give flesh to the "ethical life worlds" in which people imagine, and Christologically reimagine, the paths that are open to them as they face all sorts of questions: how to cope with infertility, whether to put their parents in a care home, or what to say when the remains of one's stillborn child have not been returned.

## Notes

1. Michael Banner, *The Ethics of Everyday Life: Moral Theology, Social Anthropology, and the Imagination of the Human* (Oxford: Oxford University Press, 2014), 28.

2. The network of those interested in this approach has recently founded *Ecclesial Practices: Journal of Ecclesiology and Ethnography* as well as the Eerdmans monograph series Studies in Ecclesiology and Ethnography.

3. Luke Bretherton, review of *Self, World and Time: Ethics as Theology*, vol. 1, *An Induction*, by Oliver O'Donovan, *Studies in Christian Ethics* 27, no. 3 (2014): 366–67.

4. Stuart Jeffries, *Grand Hotel Abyss: The Lives of the Frankfurt School* (London: Verso, 2016), chap. 3.

5. The three volumes were Henri Lefebvre, *Critique de la vie quotidienne I: Introduction* (Paris: Grasset, 1947); *Critique de la vie quotidienne II: Fondements d'une sociologie de la quotidienneté* (Paris: L'Arche Editeur, 1961); and *Critique de la vie quotidienne III: De la modernité au modernisme (pour une métaphilosophie du quotidian)* (Paris: L'Arche Editeur, 1981). All three volumes appear together in translation in Henri Lefebvre, *Critique of Everyday Life: The One-Volume Edition*, trans. John Moore (London: Verso, 2014).

6. The most relevant texts are the first two volumes of Lefebvre's *Critique de la vie quotidienne* (appearing in 1947 and 1961), which deeply shaped later influential texts like Roul Vaneigem, *The Revolution of Everyday Life*, trans. Donald Nicholson-Smith (London: Rebel Press, 2006). This approach entered the mainstream through works like Michel de Certeau, *The Practice of Everyday Life*, trans. Steven Rendall (Berkeley: University of California Press, 1984), which draws its well-known distinction between tactics and strategies directly from Lefebvre's work, and more indirectly through approaches like that of Pierre Bourdieu and Michel Foucault, which have many obvious methodological points of convergence with the Marxist analysts of the everyday, the latter of whom often explicitly appears in Banner's work. The idea that sociology was the ideal academic location for politically engaged ethical thought was developed in one of the cult books of the 1968 movement, Pierre Bourdieu and Jean-Claude Passeron's 1964 book, now translated as *The Inheritors: French Students and Their Relation to Culture*, trans. Richard Nice (Chicago: University of Chicago Press, 1979). For this history, see Michael Sheringham, *Everyday Life: Theories and Practices from Surrealism to the Present* (Oxford: Oxford University Press, 2009); and Stanley Cohen and Laurie Taylor, *Escape Attempts: The Theory and Practice of Resistance to Everyday Life*, 2nd ed. (London: Routledge, 1992). The latter was first published in 1976, and the new introduction in the 1992 revised version (1–29) is especially illuminating.

7. This shift in emphasis still determines the most influential Marxist ethical analyses, such as Michael Hardt and Antonio Negri's widely influential *Multitude* trilogy: *Empire* (Cambridge, MA: Harvard University Press, 2000); *War and Democracy in the Age of Empire* (New York: Penguin, 2004); and *Commonwealth* (Cambridge, MA: Harvard University Press, 2009).

8. Henri Lefebvre, *Critique of Everyday Life: Foundations for a Sociology of the Everyday*, trans. John Moore (London: Verso, 2002), 11.

9. Zygmut Bauman, *Hermeneutics and Social Science* (London: Hutchinson & Co., 1978), 58.

10. Michael Trebitch, "Presentation: Twenty Years After," preface to Henri Lefebvre, *The Critique of Everyday Life*, vol. 3, *From Modernity to Modernism (Towards a Metaphilosophy of Daily Life)*, trans. Gregory Elliot (London: Verso, 2005), 15.

11. Trebitch, 16–17.

12. Lefebvre, *Critique de la vie quotidienne III*, 65.

13. David Graeber, *The Utopia of Rules: On Technology, Stupidity, and the Secret Joys of Bureaucracy* (Brooklyn, NY: Melville House Publishing, 2015), 101.

14. This has not always been the case, however, as indicated by the title of his inaugural lecture at King's College London, "Turning the World Upside Down—and Some Other Tasks for Dogmatic Christian Ethics," published in Michael Banner, *Christian Ethics and Contemporary Moral Problems* (Cambridge: Cambridge University Press, 1999), 1–46. The phrase is a direct reference to Marx. See Jerrold Seigel, *Marx's Fate: The Shape of a Life* (Princeton, NJ: Princeton University Press, 1978), 169.

15. Such a misreading is understandable given Banner's proximity to the heart of the British political, ecclesial, and educational establishments. See Robert Neild, *Riches and Responsibility: The Financial History of Trinity College, Cambridge* (Cambridge: Trinity College, 2008).

16. See Banner, *Ethics of Everyday Life*, 155–62.

17. See Banner, 201–4.

18. Ludwig Wittgenstein, *Zettel*, ed. G. E. M. Anscombe and G. H. von Wright, trans. G. E. M. Anscombe (Berkeley: University of California Press, 1967), remark 456 on p. 82e.

19. In common with several other British theologians, Banner parallels contemporary work being done in Germany in a much more systematic manner. See Alex Stock, *Poetische Dogmatik* (Paderborn, Germany: Ferdinand Schöningh, 2004).

20. "'I believe' means, 'I *exist* in believing.'" Karl Barth, *The Holy Spirit in the Christian Life: The Theological Basis of Ethics*, trans. R. Birch Hoyle (Louisville, KY: Westminster John Knox Press, 1993), 33. In a note Barth makes it clear that this is a repristination of Luther, whom he quotes as writing (in his commentary on Galatians), "'Doing,' in theology, is always understood as 'doing in faith,' so that 'faithful doing is a different orbit, and as it were, a new realm compared with 'moral doing.'" "Faith, in theology, should continually be the divinity of the works, and so diffused through the works as divinity is through the humanity in Christ . . . therefore it is faith that is the *factotum* in the works." See Barth, *Holy Spirit*, 56n80.

21. Robert W. Jenson, "What if It Was True?," in *Theology as Revisionary Metaphysics: Essays on God and Creation*, ed. Stephen John Wright (Eugene, OR: Cascade, 2014), 23–37.

22. See James D. Faubion, *An Anthropology of Ethics* (Cambridge: Cambridge University Press, 2011). A cognate effort closer to Banner's approach is differently prosecuted in Tim Ingold's work, which is nevertheless positioned to produce texts that tell us what the world is like for "those people." See Tim Ingold, "Anthropology Is *Not* Ethnography," in *Being Alive: Essays on Movement, Knowledge and Description* (London: Routledge, 2011), 229–43.

23. Banner, *Ethics of Everyday Life*, 54–55.

24. Gerald P. McKenny, "Technologies of Desire: Theology, Ethics, and the Enhancement of Human Traits," *Theology Today* 59, no. 1 (April 2002): 90–103.

25. McKenny, 93.

26. McKenny, 99–100.

27. Stanley Hauerwas, *Naming the Silences: God, Medicine and the Problem of Suffering* (Grand Rapids, MI: Eerdmans, 1990), 34.

28. Hauerwas is even less troubled by anthropologists' worries about objectifying their subjects than Banner, and he takes ethnographic work to be "documenting" the moral life worlds of others (*Naming the Silences*, 129).

29. Hauerwas, 34.

30. Banner, *Ethics of Everyday Life*, 209.

# PART II

# PRACTICES OF EVERYDAY ETHICS

EXTENDING THE PROPOSAL

# 5

# FORMING HUMANITY

===

## PRACTICES OF EDUCATION CHRISTIANLY CONSIDERED

### JENNIFER A. HERDT

AMONG THE MANY THEMES that might be illuminated by Michael Banner's "everyday ethics," I propose to take up that of education. It is a welcome and urgent, if somewhat daunting, task. Wherever we turn, there is some educational crisis to which we might attend, whether it be the precarious state of traditional seminary-based theological education, the failures of the public school system to ensure that no child is left behind (even amid the success of ensuring that no child is left untested), or challenges now posed by the digital revolution, not just to the integrative ideal of a liberal arts education but to the modern research university. Banner invites us to reconceive Christian ethics as an "ethics of the life course," an "imagination of human life (dwelling on and drawing from the life of Christ)" in conversation with "other moral imaginaries of the human."[1]

Before turning to education, I want to take time, following Banner's own example, for a preliminary expectoration on the proposal itself, of everyday ethics as a reconception of the task of Christian ethics. I suggest that we might fruitfully conceive of this turn to everyday ethics as a turn to ethics as social criticism rather than specifically as social anthropology or ethnography. This leads us to attend to the formative character of social practices both within and beyond the churches. Among these will be social practices that explicitly conceive of themselves as formative in some way, that is, those of education. Here we must grapple with the fact that many educational practices salient in contemporary culture are no longer conceived of as participating in ethical formation, even as we must identify the ways in which they in fact do continue to form patterns of perception, response, and action. Our task is to make explicit the ways in which we are being formed (and de-formed) by these educational and other social practices. We take responsibility for this dialectical task, striving to discern how these practices may be shaped, ordered, and directed to living into our vocation to enter into the be-friending love that is the life of God revealed in Christ.

## Quandary Ethics and the Call for Thick Description

Christian ethics as everyday ethics promises to be an abundantly fruitful enterprise. Yet it is not as novel a proposal as we might think. It stands in a tradition of Christian reflection as social criticism that reaches back at least to Augustine's therapeutic critique of the moral imagination of pagan Rome. Banner's proposal, then, stands in very good company. But perhaps it is also helpful to place it within the more immediate context of calls for the transformation of Christian ethics that date back to the middle of the last century. And even construed more narrowly, as a recommendation that moral theology engage with social anthropology, it is representative of a current trend in the field rather than a signal departure from it.[2] I will agree emphatically with Banner's call for a Christian ethics that is richly informed by "morality in its social context" while arguing that an engagement with social anthropology is only one form that this might take, and indeed perhaps a somewhat problematic one.[3] My proposal is for an everyday Christian ethics that openly confesses itself (as social anthropology rarely has the courage to do) as a form of engaged social criticism.

Banner's proposal is rooted in a diagnosis of the current ills besetting Christian ethics. "What both student and layperson have absorbed," he tells us, "is the notion that Christian ethics is an ethics of hard cases—for this is how the subject is predominantly presented and received."[4] Faced with a subject like "the crisis of old age," for instance, "what she or he has learnt as belonging to the subject matter of ethics is a set of question [sic] about the acceptability or otherwise of managing one's exit from this stage of life, but nothing much about what it might be to live it well." Moral theology, he argues, has acted "as if the good is natural in such a way that it needs no well-developed or considered narrative context to explain its character and existence."[5] It is characterized by a "historic and continuing unwillingness to undertake . . . cultural engagement"; it "shows no sustained interest in the deep character and logic of different forms of life."[6] Because of this failure, it offers nothing effective by way of treatment or therapy, "serious work" that "would go behind the symptoms, and would seek to understand and address the deeper individual, social, and cultural drives of which any symptoms are an expression."[7] He tells us that we need to be able to fathom the desires and aspirations of others, not simply to judge them.[8] Hence the turn to social anthropology, which will, Banner suggests, teach us how to "attend to the psychological and sociocultural depth of the different forms of life which we encounter" in order then to be able to "address pastorally and therapeutically other ethical imaginaries and forms of life."[9] This pastoral and therapeutic address will issue from something we currently lack, "a coherent and perspicuous account of the practice of the Christian life, which would, in a space of cultural contestation, describe and sustain this form of life as a particular way of being human in the world."[10]

This critique dates back at least to Edmund Pincoffs's 1971 article "Quandary Ethics," which worried about moral philosophy's focus on thinly described moral problems. Real quandaries, he noted, arise within particular personal and social contexts, and ethical reflection is distorted when these are forgotten.[11] We should, Pincoffs urged, return to the task of ethics as classically conceived, asking how to live well, not solving remote trolley problems.[12] This struck a chord and was taken up into a chorus of critiques of the state of ethical reflection at the time: of its abstract and formal character, its individualism, its failure to attend to moral psychology, its focus on right action, and its inattention to questions of the good, excellence, and flourishing.[13] These critiques, particularly as developed by Alasdair MacIntyre and Stanley Hauerwas, have had a significant and ongoing impact on Christian ethical reflection.[14] While the retrieval of virtue ethics that unfolded within analytic moral philosophy remained focused on fairly abstract questions concerning the justification of ethical discourse and practice, the unity of the virtues, habituation, weakness of will, and conceptions of happiness, within strands of Christian ethics influenced by MacIntyre and Hauerwas there has been much more attention to social context, in particular to social roles and practices, communally authoritative narratives and the shaping of communal identity, and the communally formed pursuit of the good.[15]

Of course, a turn to virtue and character, even if attentive to the ways in which character is formed in the context of communities and their practices, does not necessarily translate into attention to concrete social contexts.[16] The retrieval of virtue fed a surge of historical work on Aquinas, Aristotle, Plato, Augustine, and others, much of it not engaging in any explicit way with present social conditions. Moreover, while a great deal of attention has been given to contemporary liturgical and paraliturgical practices as forming Christian character, such work has not always attended in a close way to the culture at large, even when it has been accompanied by an assumption that such formation will be countercultural.

But the retrieval of virtue ethics was closely affiliated with other theological developments that called for attention to concrete forms of life. Postliberal theologians, influenced by Wittgenstein's insistence on meaning as use, called for attention to the concrete social contexts within which theological and ethical concepts have their life and being. Theology, on this understanding, can only be a reflection on a particular community's religious practices. Hans Frei, in lectures given in 1983 and published posthumously in 1992 as *Types of Christian Theology*, argued explicitly that Christian theology be conceived as a form of anthropology.[17] That is, the theologian's task is to interpret the particular culture that is Christian community, rendering its implicit rules and norms explicit. George Lindbeck's cultural-linguistic approach to religion was similarly inspired by anthropology, particularly by Clifford Geertz's understanding of anthropology as the interpretation of culture.[18]

We find ourselves, then, amid a theological and ethical turn to culture. As Ted Smith writes in a recent survey of the many and varied forms this turn has taken, "It has become a commonplace that there is no 'view from nowhere,' and that the somewhere from which all views look is, in some important sense, 'cultural.'"[19] Within this broad and manifold turn to culture, an engagement with social anthropology, in particular with ethnography, has gained momentum over the past decade and a half. We might, for instance, note the roundtable on the subject of ethnography and normative ethics at the Society of Christian Ethics annual meeting in 2003, the talk by moral theologian Todd Whitmore at the society's 2007 annual meeting, and the "Fieldwork in Christian Ethics" interest group, formed within the Society of Christian Ethics in 2009.[20] It was against this backdrop that Christian Scharen and Aana Marie Vigen's edited volume, *Ethnography as Christian Theology and Ethics*, was published in 2011, as Michael Banner notes, while he was at work on his own lectures on the subject.[21]

## The Cultural Turn: Three Caveats

I want to register myself as emphatically on board with the cultural turn. The task of the theological ethicist is not simply to interpret, with Frei, the particular culture that is Christian community, rendering its implicit norms explicit. It also involves interpreting the world generally. We act in the world according to how we perceive and describe it, what we see as good, what we take to be amiss. Unless we are "finely aware and richly responsible," to borrow a phrase from Martha Nussbaum, we can hardly hope to execute well the tasks of Christian ethics.[22]

However, I also want to issue three caveats about this enterprise. First, there is no reason to privilege an engagement with social anthropology over other forms the cultural turn can take. Second, we should be cautious about characterizing Christianity as offering a singular moral imaginary that can engage therapeutically with other moral imaginaries. Third, given these first two observations, we might do well to think simply in terms of promoting the ethical task of engaging in social criticism rather than aligning the Christian ethical task too fully with the academic enterprise of social anthropology. Let me say a bit about each of these before turning at last to the question of education.

First, social anthropology ought to have no privileged role in the conversation, even if it should have a place at the table. The heart of what is being called for in the cultural turn is attention to lived social realities, to thick description and embodied human experience, perhaps especially to the experiential realities of those other than ourselves, those to whom we have never bothered to attend, those who have remained invisible to scholarly attention. But this turn can come in many different forms. We might, for instance, turn to history, gaining greater awareness of the specificity of our own cultural moment by contrast with those of the past. Or we might turn to literature as a mode of attentiveness to concrete social existence. Social anthropology is only one mode of thick social description.

We might even need to exercise particular caution in engaging with social anthropology. Historically, this discipline, like other aspiring social "sciences," has had an uneasy relationship with the normative. To identify one's enterprise as openly normative is to lose the cultural authority attributed to the purely descriptive and hence properly scientific. Of course, social anthropology has always been normative, but the most problematic descriptions are those that fail to confess their normative character. This would include even social anthropologies *of* morality, insofar as these take morality simply as an object for study. Recent social anthropologies of morality are a very welcome development insofar as they help us to see the ubiquity and ordinariness of ethics rather than restricting ethics to explicitly articulated theories, norms, and principles. But the social anthropology of morality does not deliver a neutral description of everyday ethics, something to which a theological therapy might then be applied.[23] Rather, it offers a situated "take" on what it describes—a take that, in however inchoate or inarticulate a fashion, orients assessment and action.

Second, if an anthropological turn encourages us to think about Christian ethics and theology as imbricated in a particular communal way of life in all of its concrete, embodied character, it also encourages us to question whether one can speak of *a* Christian culture, community, or moral imaginary. As Kathryn Tanner has argued, "It is far from clear . . . that one can use 'way of life' in its full anthropological sense to talk about Christian churches apart from the wider cultural contexts in which they are set."[24] Christian practices are not self-contained, and Christians engage in a host of practices together with non-Christians. Christian practices are plural, and they are not static but rather are continually being formed and re-formed, something Tanner also points out.[25] Given these realities, everyday ethics cannot proceed by addressing itself to a particular moral imaginary served up by a particular social anthropologist and then offer up in response *the* Christian therapy, rooted in *the* Christian imaginary.[26] Rather, Christian ethicists are engaged as much in a normative, thick description of the manifold of Christian practices as of other cultural practices. Neither cultural practices at large nor Christian practices come to us predescribed, and our descriptions are always already evaluative, always already focused on what we think matters, what we think worthy of our attention.

Among those practices in which Christians and others are engaged are practices of interpretation, of making explicit the norms implicit in communal practices, of evaluating these norms and the practices in which they are embedded, of engaging in intentional acts of critique and revision.[27] What one might call a "social anthropological" or "ethnographic" moment is embedded within a more encompassing process of activity, reflection on this activity and its coherence with other activities, and reflective assessment of these activities. My third and final methodological suggestion, then, is that we characterize everyday ethics simply as social criticism and that theological ethicists encourage social anthropologists to concede that they too engage regularly in social criticism.

I have problematized talk of a singular Christian imagination of the human and argued that Christian communities, practices, and imaginaries are multiple. Of course, in another sense I agree that Christian imaginations of the human are always attempts to imagine the truly and fully human through the lens of Christ. When a Christian ethicist describes a particular social practice as "truly Christian," this is not simply to say that the people engaged in it call it, or themselves, Christian, or to see the practice as rooted historically in Christian communities. It is to pass judgment on that practice, to affirm it as properly responsive to the fully divine and fully human as revealed in Christ.

Christian practices are not self-contained or cut off from the culture at large, but we may, from an openly normative standpoint, affirm *truly* Christian practices as united in proper responsiveness to Christ. To return to Tanner once more, "What Christians have in common, what unites them, is nothing internal to the practices themselves. What unites them is concern for true discipleship, proper reflection in human words and deeds of an object of worship that always exceeds by its greatness human efforts to do so."[28]

We might note that this effort to articulate what all "truly Christian" practices have in common necessarily steps away from their concrete particularity. Any such attempt will do so. It is, of course, a *contestable* account of what makes some practices truly Christian. Contestation over its claims, and over the claim on the part of any particular practice to the title "truly Christian," will involve dialectical movement from the particular to the general and back again; this reflective moment is itself an aspect of ordinary practices as they unfold in time. Norms and commitments implicit in practices *claiming* to be truly Christian are made explicit and held up for examination. Such reflection naturally steps away from the ordinary flow of activity, if only momentarily, before plunging in again. The enterprise of articulating explicit norms and principles is thereby chastened and grounded, but also affirmed. It is in this way that Christian ethical reflection can aspire, in Banner's words, "to imagine, recount, and thereby hopefully sustain the practice and enactment of human being after the measure of Christ's human being."[29]

## Three Rival Versions of Education?

I now want to juxtapose two models of education that are quite at odds with one another—that of the modern research university (particularly in its American incarnation) and that of Tennessee's Highlander Folk School—in order to offer up a bit of everyday Christian ethics, that is, Christian social criticism. The one model enshrines highly specialized disciplinary education, the other the power of bringing ordinary people together to identify the problems they face and to develop their own solutions.[30] It might seem that Christians, seeking to be properly responsive to the fully divine and fully human as revealed in Christ, have reason to be suspicious of both of these and favor quite a different kind of education: the formation of faithful disciples. I will argue that this is not the case. Faithful disciples are found both in the research university and in settings like the Highlander School. Discipleship is not at odds with either disciplinary specialization or education for critical thinking. Crucially, we must recognize that all education is formation; it is never neutral. Making explicit the ways in which we are forming and being formed through educational practices is a first step toward taking responsibility for inhabiting and shaping these particular everyday practices in ways that are oriented to our final end, toward living out the be-friending love of God in relation to our neighbors.

We are all quite familiar with the research university; it is an educational setting most of us have at one time or another inhabited. As Chad Wellmon relates in a recent book on the invention of the modern research university, this social institution is rooted in an educational ideal that was formed in early nineteenth-century Germany in response to the Enlightenment-era explosion of print media.[31] Students no longer needed to attend a university in order to take verbatim notes as a professor read a book aloud from the podium; they could buy and read these books on their own. Why, then, attend university? The answer that emerged out of the reflections of such figures as Schelling, Kant, Fichte, and Humboldt, and that was so influentially implemented by Humboldt in the Prussian educational system, was to make the university primarily a place for the disciplined generation of new knowledge. Crucial to this vision of scientific education was the notion of peer review—experts in a particular domain, not state officials, should assess the value of scholarship.[32] Professors should lecture only within their domain of specialization, not beyond.[33] These innovations drove the processes of academic specialization familiar to us today. While the cultural impact of these changes is often bemoaned, without them it is hard to imagine many of the technological innovations on which our lives are now so dependent, from medical science to computer science and engineering.

What of the Highlander Folk School, probably less familiar to many? It was founded in 1932 by Myles Horton, a student of Reinhold Niebuhr. Horton was inspired by the Danish Folk School movement, with its vision of peer learning outside the reach of governmental regulation.[34] Highlander became a center first for union leaders, as the South underwent industrialization, and then, in the 1950s, for civil rights leaders. It was what has sometimes been called a "movement halfway house," a training ground for social activists.[35] Rosa Parks attended workshops there, and from her base at Highlander, Septima Clark established "citizenship schools" across the South to teach literacy and successfully prepare Black adults for voter registration requirements.[36] Horton was convinced that the poor and oppressed had the knowledge to create lasting social change, given the right conditions: "If they only knew how to analyze what their experiences were, what they know and generalize them . . . they would begin to draw on their own resources."[37] Education was about empowering people to think for themselves, to deliberate together, and to develop their own solutions. The Highlander philosophy was suspicious both of charismatic leaders and of experts. They did tolerate visits by the likes of Martin Luther King Jr., but only, in Horton's words, to give them "a chance to say they'd been at Highlander and write it up in their newspapers," not in order to pretend that they could be directly involved in the educational mission of the school.[38] Experts, like charismatic leaders, were dangerous because they typically disempowered people by telling them what to do, even "while having the semblance of empowering people."[39]

In one sense, the research university and Highlander enshrine diametrically opposed models of education—the one devoted to building up expert knowledge, the other to dismantling it; the one about constructing an elaborate institutional apparatus, the other about working around and outside of institutions. We might think that Christians should be suspicious of both, for both seem quite distant from an understanding of education as fundamentally a matter of being formed as a disciple, being formed within a tradition of faith and practice. Something like this stance seems to be reflected in Stanley Hauerwas's writings on education. He argues that "Christian schooling" ought to make students dysfunctional within the educational system as it exists in modern Western societies today. Education is properly a process of lifelong training within an ongoing tradition.[40] Only this kind of training can provide the material conditions necessary for resisting the overspecialization and abstraction endemic to the research university.[41] Christians must also reject the notion that it is liberating and educative to resist formation. Christians should recognize in calls for critical thinking a fatal resistance to formation. "Nothing is more destructive, nothing makes us less free," he writes, "than to have to do what we want to do."[42] Christians, then, should resist the disciplinary specialization of the research university while also resisting the relativistic goal of cultivating critical thinking, a cornerstone of Highlander's philosophy.

I want, however, to trouble this picture, for both the research university and Highlander are also about education as formation of desire, habit, and character, not simply about the training of experts or the cultivation of critical thinking. Wellmon skillfully makes this point with respect to the research university: "Specialized science, Wissenschaft, was not simply an ideology imposed by the vague imperatives of a rationalizing modernity. It was a normative and ethical framework that outlined particular internal goods (production of research and an ability to perceive the relationship of various sciences and forms of knowledge) and inculcated particular virtues (rigor, collaboration, intellectual capaciousness, a commitment to method)."[43] The research university, far from shelving the question of how one should live, offered an answer—in devotion to the endless pursuit of knowledge. The character of the scientist, and its disciplined formation, was essential to the enterprise.

The Highlander School, meanwhile, was scarcely about the cultivation of critical thinking to the exclusion of the formation of character. Horton is explicit about this. He distinguishes between organizing and educating, in that organizing campaigns are focused on achieving specific goals and so tend to choose the most efficient means to that goal. "If the purpose is to solve the problem, there are a lot of ways to solve the problem that are so much simpler than going through all this educational process."[44] Education, in contrast, is not finally about organizing a union, integrating a school, or registering voters. It is about developing people, helping them grow. As Horton comments, "I'd say if you were working with an organization and there's a choice between the goal of that organization, or the particular program they're working on, and educating people, developing people, helping them grow, helping them become able to analyze—if there's a choice, we'd sacrifice the goal of the organization for helping the people grow, because we think in the long run it's a bigger contribution."[45] Horton identifies this as a difference between himself and Saul Alinsky, even though Horton collaborated closely with the founder of community organizing. In fact, though, Alinsky himself differentiated broad-based community organizing from labor organizing and issue-based organizing on precisely these grounds: broad-based organizing is fundamentally about developing people, particularly their leadership capabilities. "We learn, when we respect the dignity of the people," Alinsky writes, "that they cannot be denied the elementary right to participate fully in the solutions to their own problems. Self-respect arises only out of people who play an active role in solving their own crises and who are not helpless, passive, puppet-like recipients of private or public services."[46] Alinsky and Horton agree both in their affirmation of universal human dignity and in their recognition that persons must be formed to affirm their own dignity. Critical thinking is not a firehose to be aimed indiscriminately at everything. It is to be directed, first and foremost, to the practices and institutions that have formed the people to be helpless and passive, to doubt their capacities, to lower their aspirations and dim their dreams. It is not an antiformative but a counterformative practice, aimed at a substantive good, the affirmation and concrete social realization of human dignity. As practically oriented as Highlander seems, it is worth noting that this also means that the educational process is an end in itself and to that extent also includes what we might call a contemplative aspect. Those who participate in it are situated to grasp the truth, beauty, and goodness (however flawed and partial) of human persons in communion as well as the ways in which these refer beyond themselves to God.

Neither the modern research university nor the Highlander School resists formation. Nor does either condemn its participants to enslavement by their own desires, to *having* to do what they *want* to do, to echo Hauerwas. Moreover, both the cultivation of disciplined researchers and of critically reflective citizens involves lifelong training in the context of an ongoing tradition of practice and reflection. In this sense, both traditions share much in common with the Christian tradition.

But Christians are called to be faithful disciples, something quite other than disciplined scientists or self-respecting citizens. If a Christian ethics of everyday life is, as Banner tells us, about sustaining "the practice and enactment of human being after the measure of Christ's human being," perhaps it is time to turn to that Jewish rabbi who made his disciples fishers of men. Let us briefly consider Jesus's farewell discourse in the Gospel of John: "You call me Teacher and Lord—and you are right, for that is what I am. So if I, your Lord and Teacher, have washed your feet, you also ought to wash one another's feet" (John 13:12–14). A disciple (*mathétés*) in the Hellenistic world was a pupil, a learner, an adherent of a philosophical school or of a master.[47] Being a disciple involved imitating the life of the teacher, not just learning some content from the teacher. To be a disciple of Jesus, then, is to regard him as an authoritative example to be imitated. At the same time, learning to be faithful to Jesus, submitting to being schooled by him, is nothing like simply being a passive recipient of formation. The example that Jesus offers—here, in washing his disciples' feet—is subversive and unexpected. It does not reproduce given traditional practices or norms but rather involves the upending of norms and the introduction of new practices. It is, in fact, an example that elicits critical reflection by virtue of its subversive and unexpected character. Is one who does the outrageous, who violates norms in this way, to be regarded as teacher and authoritative example? Christian education, I submit, can never be simply about submitting to formation. It can never be simply passively accepted. It jolts the learner into reflection and response.

And there is more. The example of this Teacher is not simply shocking and subversive. It is shocking and subversive in a particular way, for it is an authoritative example of a Teacher, even of a Lord and Master, who performs acts of humble service for his pupils. The distinctive mark of this school will be love—it is an example of self-giving love, even of the laying down of one's life for one's friends, that the Teacher gives; it is by their love that his disciples will be known as such (John 15:13; 13:34).

Our choice is not between education that is formative and education that is not. All education, in and outside of schools and universities, is formative of desire, of habit, of character. It is not between education that commands us to act against our desires and education that leaves us to do what we happen to want to do. For insofar as education is formative of desire and character, it shapes us not just to act in certain ways but to *want* certain things.

We cannot do without academic specialization and disciplinary experts. Without them, we cannot make headway on AIDS research, or climate change, or many of the most significant challenges that face us and our world. We need scientists trained in a lab that focuses, say, on the way one particular protein folds, willing day after day, year after year, to run variations on the same experiment under tightly controlled conditions. The danger is not specialization as such. Rather, the danger is in bracketing one's specialized discipline off from a broader context. It is in treating one's discipline as autonomous, as not needing to answer to any broader questions concerning what it is good for, why it matters, how it might find a place in a life worth living.[48] It is in regarding one's discipline as neutral. As Myles Horton argues, neutrality is "a code word for the existing system. It has nothing to do with anything but agreeing to what is and will always be. . . . Neutrality is just being what the system asks us to be."[49] To see one's research as neutral is to fail to see one's own formation and the goods one has been formed to desire by participating in these practices and institutions. All education is formation, but not all formation is good. Because of this we must be as aware as possible of the ways in which we are being formed, making explicit what would otherwise remain implicit. We must assume responsibility for the broader ends and purposes to which the practices in which we are engaged are oriented. It is because all education is formation that one aspect of education (although only one) should be education for critical thinking. Critical thinking is no more the real danger than is disciplinary specialization. Rather, what we should reject are both disciplinary specialization and critical thinking simply for their own sake, as ends in themselves, rather than as means to, and ways to participate in, greater love and service.[50]

The original ideal behind the Humboldtian research university was that of *Bildung*, the active self-development of humanity. In some respects, the eighteenth-century humanistic conception of *Bildung* associated with Herder, Humboldt, and Goethe represents a rejection of Pietistic conceptions of *Bildung*. Pietists sought to be passive vessels of divine agency, seeking to be conformed to Christ's suffering and remade in his image and therefore in the image of God that had been destroyed by original sin. Pietists, we might say, rejected any place for critical thinking in Christian schooling. The humanistic conception, in contrast, was one of active self-formation. Humboldt was insistent, however, that through *Bildung* the individual participates in something that transcends herself and her desires. She is no longer simply fulfilling her subjective desires, whether this be a desire to fit in, to be cherished, or to be exceptional or independent. Neither is the individual simply accepting objective burdens placed on her by the natural world or objective demands made on her by the social world. Rather, the individual discerns an ideal, not yet realized, toward the instantiation of which all of her energies can be directed—the ideal of humanity, of *Menschheit*.[51] This ideal does not coerce her either from within, like an overwhelming urge, nor from without, like the laws of the state. But neither is it an ideal that has no point of contact with the individual's agency. Rather, she encounters it as an ideal that *ought to be* realized, that makes a demand on her.[52] Encounters with others are key: when someone catches a glimpse in others of the ideal of perfection toward which she herself strives, she recognizes that the ideal of humanity transcends the realization of this ideal in her own person.[53] She also recognizes that her own instantiation of the ideal may require self-sacrifice, and that this sacrifice can be the realization rather than frustration of our pursuit.[54] Ironically, then, we find at the origins of the research university a commitment with which Horton and Alinsky would resonate, a commitment to education as forming people to recognize their own and one another's dignity.[55] It is even a commitment that Christians might well (re)appropriate from would-be secularizers like Humboldt: the pursuit of *Bildung* as inspired by the encounter with a Teacher who washed his students' feet and demanded that they do the same.

## Turning the Tide

Having begun with a preliminary expectoration, it seems only fitting to end with a concluding unscientific postscript (one far less disproportionate to the whole than Kierkegaard's *Concluding Unscientific Postcript* to his *Philosophical Fragments*!). Perhaps the original ideal of *Bildung* has not quite given up the ghost to the ills of creeping bureaucratization and overspecialization, despite announcements to the contrary from Max Weber to the present.[56] The Harvard Graduate School of Education recently released a set of recommendations for improving the US college admissions process, "Turning the Tide: Inspiring Concern for Others and the Common Good through College Admissions." Now, we might smile cynically at the thought that the college admissions process could do any such thing. But the study, to its credit, is rooted in the critical recognition of the non-neutrality of the process and its deeply formative character. "Too often," the study notes, "today's culture sends young people messages that emphasize personal success rather than concern for others and the common good."[57] Current admissions processes reward students who participate in more extracurricular activities rather than becoming deeply engaged in a few, who maximize the number of Advanced Placement courses they take rather than developing intellectual passions in key areas, and who accumulate as many community service hours as possible rather than building relationships with those they serve. Even more perniciously, current admissions processes penalize students who are unable to accumulate hours of community service because they are working to supplement family income or caring for younger siblings while parents work—in other words, penalizing students who have likely learned much more about concrete care and concern for others than their advantaged peers.

The study's recommendations, to be sure, take for granted that college education is a highly desirable good. It is because of this that the conditions for its successful pursuit are themselves so powerfully formative. In order to assess this proposal, one must ask *why* it is that colleges and universities should compete for students on the basis not solely of those students' intellectual capabilities and competitive achievements but also of their character and commitment to others and to the common good. At bottom, this is a recognition that college and university education is no more neutral than the admissions process. If students who have been formed to care only for individual prowess and achievement are rewarded with an elite education that opens up to them the most significant leadership positions in our society, the writing is on the wall for the character of the society they will lead. Admissions professionals can shift the structure of incentives presented to aspiring college students.

If this amounts merely to presenting students with a different game to play in order to achieve the goal of admission into a competitive college so that they may thereafter open the doors to positions of wealth and power, it is mere whitewashing. If it is instead a declaration that a true leader is one who serves the common good, not one who enhances his or her own power or wealth, it contains within itself two other remarkable confessions: first, that there is nothing neutral about education—that it is necessarily always about what is worth loving and pursuing, about what is true, good, and beautiful[58]—and, second, that colleges and universities have little hope of forming students for service to others or to the common good if they have *already* been formed for pursuit of personal achievement. For the pursuit of such external goods, once made into ends in themselves, subverts and undermines the pursuit of internal goods; the next cohort of college applicants could simply beg their parents for opportunities to babysit their siblings and hang out with Grandma, seeking to game the new system. Augustine's critique of the virtues of pagan Rome is apropos—the CVs of today's college applicants might continue to enumerate only vices, if splendid ones, just as Roman heroes sacrificed their lives for the sake of their city, but only because this was the path to honor and glory. But where are universities to find students already formed for love and service to others? Might some of them have learned to love the Teacher who washed his students' feet? Jacques Maritain believed that this was true even of Saul Alinsky, an atheist Jew. "The deep-rooted motive power and inspiration of this so-called trouble-maker," he wrote, "is pure and entire self-giving, and love for those poor images of God which are human beings, especially the oppressed ones."[59] Strange to think, in this post-Christian era, that elite institutions of higher education, those bastions of the secular vanguard, might yearn—as Michael Banner and I would both, I take it, suggest—for disciples of Jesus.

For here was One who could be trusted, to echo Augustine once more, to be left free to love and do as he pleased.[60] And it is in making it possible for this Truth to *appear*, to be *heard*, that everyday Christian ethics, Christian ethics as social criticism, can make a transformative contribution.

## Notes

1. Michael Banner, *The Ethics of Everyday Life: Moral Theology, Social Anthropology, and the Imagination of the Human* (Oxford: Oxford University Press, 2014), 3–4.

2. Banner cites two relevant books that were published as he was working on his lectures and book: Christian Scharen and Aana Marie Vigen, eds., *Ethnography and Christian Theology and Ethics* (London: Continuum, 2011); and Peter Ward, ed., *Perspectives on Ecclesiology and Ethnography* (Grand Rapids, MI: Eerdmans, 2012).

3. Banner, *Ethics of Everyday Life*, 4.

4. Banner, 9.

5. Banner, 12.

6. Banner, 12.

7. Banner, 13.

8. Banner, 16.

9. Banner, 23.

10. Banner, 28.

11. Edmund Pincoffs, "Quandary Ethics," *Mind* 80, no. 320 (1971): 552–71, at 570.

12. Pincoffs, 558.

13. See, e.g., G. E. M. Anscombe, "Modern Moral Philosophy," *Philosophy* 33 (1958): 1–19; Alasdair MacIntyre, *After Virtue* (Notre Dame, IN: University of Notre Dame Press, 1981); Bernard Williams, *Ethics and the Limits of Philosophy* (Hammondsworth, UK: Penguin Books, 1985); and discussed briefly in Jennifer A. Herdt, "Varieties of Contemporary Christian Virtue Ethics," in *The Routledge Companion to Virtue Ethics*, ed. Lorraine Besser-Jones and Michael Slote (New York: Routledge, 2015), 223.

14. An important anthology mediating between philosophical and theological discussion of these issues was Stanley Hauerwas and Alasdair MacIntyre, eds., *Revisions: Changing Perspectives in Moral Philosophy* (Notre Dame, IN: University of Notre Dame Press, 1983). It included Pincoffs's essay, together with essays by Iris Murdoch, Annette Baier, Simone Weil, J. B. Schneewind, Peter Berger, and others. The coeditors begin by noting that "in those periods when a social order becomes uneasy and even alarmed about the weakening of its moral bonds and the poverty of its moral inheritance and turns for aid to the moral philosopher and theologian, it may not find those disciplines flourishing in such a way as to be able to make available the kind of moral reflection and theory which the culture actually needs" (vii).

15. Herdt, "Varieties," 227.

16. Alda Balthrop-Lewis made this point effectively in her talk, "Avoiding Solution Thinking in Environmental Ethics," Society of Christian Ethics Annual Meeting, Toronto, January 9, 2016.

17. Hans Frei, *Types of Christian Theology* (New Haven, CT: Yale University Press, 1992), 11–14.

18. George Lindbeck, *The Nature of Doctrine: Religion and Theology in a Postliberal Age* (Philadelphia, PA: Westminster Press, 1984), chap. 2. Both Frei and Lindbeck are discussed, in relation to a social practical theory of religion, by Stephen S. Bush, *Visions of Religion: Experience, Meaning, and Power* (Oxford: Oxford University Press, 2014), 217–18.

19. Ted A. Smith, *The New Measures: A Theological History of Democratic Practice* (Cambridge: Cambridge University Press, 2007), 16. See also his prior article, "Redeeming Critique: Resignations

to the Cultural Turn in Christian Theology and Ethics," *Journal of the Society of Christian Ethics* 24, no. 2 (2004): 89–113.

20. Todd Whitmore, "Crossing the Road: The Case for Ethnographic Fieldwork in Christian Ethics," *Journal of the Society of Christian Ethics* 27, no. 2 (2007): 273–94.

21. Christian Scharen and Aana Marie Vigen, eds., *Ethnography as Christian Theology and Ethics* (New York: Continuum, 2011).

22. Martha C. Nussbaum, "Finely Aware and Richly Responsible: Moral Attention and the Moral Task of Literature," *Journal of Philosophy* 82, no. 10 (October 1985): 516–29.

23. Banner seems to leave social anthropology's aspiration to pure description untroubled, for example in suggesting that the moral theology he is promoting "will attempt to do prescriptively what is done descriptively in Juliet du Boulay's book" (*Ethics of Everyday Life*, 203–4).

24. Kathryn Tanner, *Theories of Culture: A New Agenda for Theology* (Minneapolis, MN: Fortress Press, 1997), 67.

25. Tanner, 78.

26. See Molly Farneth, chapter 1 in this volume.

27. As Tanner says, "Academic theology is therefore about Christian social practices in the sense that it asks critical and evaluative questions of them. It is . . . governed by those practices in the sense that it employs a strategy of criticism and evaluation similar to that used in everyday Christian life. Academic theologians ask how well the practices at issue hang together with other things that Christians believe and value." See Tanner, *Theories of Culture*, 80.

28. Tanner, 152.

29. Banner, *Ethics of Everyday Life*, 209.

30. Myles Horton and Paulo Freire, *We Make This Road by Walking: Conversations on Education and Social Change*, ed. Brenda Bell, John Gaventa, and John Peters (Philadelphia, PA: Temple University Press, 1990), 119.

31. Chad Wellmon, *Organizing Enlightenment: Information Overload and the Invention of the Modern Research University* (Baltimore: Johns Hopkins University Press, 2015), 4.

32. Wellmon, 229.

33. Wellmon, 231.

34. Horton and Freire, *We Make the Road*, xxi. The book records conversations between the two; subsequent references indicate the specific individual who is the source of the quotation.

35. Charles M. Payne, *I've Got the Light of Freedom: The Organizing Tradition and the Mississippi Freedom Struggle* (Berkeley: University of California Press, 1995, 2007), 70.

36. Payne, 71–75.

37. Horton, quoted in Aldon Morris, *Origins of the Civil Rights Movement* (New York: Free Press, 1984), 142.

38. Horton, *We Make the Road*, 114.

39. Horton, 120.

40. Hauerwas, *Sanctify Them in the Truth: Holiness Exemplified* (Edinburgh: T&T Clark, 1998), 221.

41. Stanley Hauerwas, *The State of the University: Academic Knowledges and the Knowledge of God* (Oxford: Wiley-Blackwell, 2007), 105.

42. Hauerwas, *Sanctify Them in the Truth*, 220.

43. Wellmon, *Organizing Enlightenment*, 232.

44. Horton, *We Make the Road*, 119.

45. Horton, 116.

46. Saul D. Alinsky, *Rules for Radicals: A Practical Primer for Realistic Radicals* (New York: Vintage, 1989), 123. "This, then, is our real job," Alinsky writes elsewhere, "it is the breaking down of the feeling on the part of our people that they are social automatons with no stake in the future, rather than human beings in possession of all the responsibility, strength, and human dignity which constitute the heritage of free citizens of a democracy." See *Reveille for Radicals* (New York: Vintage, 1969), 50. In his reflections on dignity, Alinsky was indebted to Jacques Maritain and his vision of

Christian democracy. See Luke Bretherton, *Christianity and Contemporary Politics* (Oxford: Wiley-Blackwell, 2010), 91–94.

47. Michael J. Wilkins, "Disciples," in *Dictionary of Jesus and the Gospels*, ed. Joel B. Green, Scot McKnight, and I. Howard Marshall (Downers Grove, IL: InterVarsity Press, 1992).

48. Jürgen Habermas, worrying about the infiltration of the "lifeworld" by the "systems world," seems to assume that we should seek to insulate the two worlds from one another as much as possible. See "Social Action and Rationality," in *Jürgen Habermas on Society and Politics: A Reader*, ed. Steven Seidman (Boston: Beacon Press, 1989), 157. Our concern should instead be to dismantle the factors that tend toward insulation, to place instrumental reason at the service of practical reason.

49. Horton, *We Make the Road*, 102.

50. Alasdair MacIntyre argues that education in America "takes it for granted that there is no such thing as the human good, but that each individual must at some point choose for her or himself among a variety of different and rival conceptions of the good. A good education is then an education that prepares individuals for making such choices. And by that standard a Thomist education is a bad education." See Alasdair MacIntyre, "Aquinas's Critique of Education: Against His Own Age, against Ours," in *Philosophers on Education: Historical Perspectives*, ed. Amelie Rorty (London: Routledge, 1998), 95–108, at 107. Critical thinking, on the account I am sketching here, is directed toward better articulating the human good, not toward arbitrary individual choice.

51. I explore this Janus-faced tradition and the ways in which we further it by engaging in its immanent criticism in Jennifer Herdt, *Forming Humanity: Redeeming the German Bildung Tradition* (Chicago: University of Chicago Press, 2019).

52. Wilhelm von Humboldt, "Über Religion," in *Werke in fünf Bänden*, ed. Andreas Flitner and Klaus Giel (Darmstadt, Germany: Wissenschaftliche Buchgesellschaft, 1960), 1:13. "Er will nicht mehr bloss dem Menschen Kenntnisse oder Werkzeuge zum Gebrauch zubereiten, nicht mehr nur einen einzelnen Teil seiner Bildung befördern helfen; er kennt das Ziel, das ihm gesteckt ist." See Wilhelm von Humboldt, *Theorie der Bildung des Menschen* (1793), in *Werke*, 1:238–39.

53. "Er geht aus sich heraus, fliesst in den andren über, und gelangt endlich zu dem erhebendsten und beseligendsten aller Gefühle, zu dem Gefühle sich alles eigne Geniessen und Wirken dahinzugeben für fremdes Wohl." Humboldt, "Über Religion," 14.

54. As he puts it in a letter to Schiller, "Des Menschen Wesen aber ist es, sich erkennen in einem Andern; daraus entspringt sein Bedürfnis und seine Liebe." *Werke*, 5:197, quoted in Erhard Wicke, "Der Beitrag der Bildungstheorie Wilhelm von Humboldts zur Selbstaufklärung der Aufklärung," in *Menschheit und Individualität: Zur Bildungstheorie und Philosophie Wilhelm von Humboldts*, ed. Erhard Wicke, Wolfgang Neuser, Wolfdietrich Schmied-Kowarzik (Weinheim: Deutscher Studien Verlag, 1997), 22.

55. As Bretherton writes of Alinsky's approach, "It prioritizes social relationships and refuses to subordinate these relations to political or economic imperatives." See Luke Bretherton, *Resurrecting Democracy: Faith, Citizenship, and the Politics of a Common Life* (Cambridge: Cambridge University Press, 2015), 21.

56. Max Weber, "Science as a Vocation," reprinted in *From Max Weber: Essays in Sociology*, trans. H. H. Gerth and C. Wright Mills (Oxford: Oxford University Press, 1946), 129–57.

57. Richard Weissbourd, "Turning the Tide: Inspiring Concern for Others and the Common Good through College Admissions," Making Caring Common Project, http://mcc.gse.harvard.edu/files/gsemcc/files/20160120_mcc_ttt_report_interactive.pdf?m=1453303517, 1.

58. We might add—education is about what is worth contemplating and, in light of that, about what is worth seeking to realize or bring about.

59. Letter to the Ford Foundation (May 29, 1951), Box 12, file 179, Industrial Areas Foundation Archive, quoted by Bretherton, *Christianity and Contemporary Politics*, 93.

60. Augustine, *Homily 7 on the First Epistle of John (1 John 4:4–12)*, para. 8. English translation in *The Works of Saint Augustine: A Translation for the 21st Century*, 3.14, trans. Boniface Ramsey (Hyde Park, NY: New City Press, 2008), 90.

# 6

# CHARITY, JUSTICE, AND THE ETHICS OF HUMANITARIANISM

## Eric Gregory

We are born into unjust relationships with people near and far. We benefit from these relationships and, in reaping the benefits, become increasingly complicit in them. This complicity is held in place through willful ignorance, disordered loves, and neglect of relevant social facts. The complex causal networks of late modern societies intensify this complicity. Efforts to mitigate injustice and relieve suffering often serve only to deepen them. Sin begets tragedy, even in those relationships we inherit through no fault of our own or in our capacity as a group member. This is not a metaphysical claim of the sort that theologians rightly have tried to deconstruct in avoiding a primordial tragedy written into creation. It is simply a recognition that all human institutions and practices, even the relatively just, are tainted by what theologians call sin. It is a morally shameful condition to be met with lament and repentance.

Yet Christians believe that the good news of the Gospel demands such realities might also be told as part of the story of God's redeeming work in the world. There is no social context—even ones as mundane, fallen, and tragic as humanitarian aid—in which the reality of Jesus Christ is not present. The largely unexamined world of Christian humanitarian work is to be related to this *missio Dei*. As with previous missionary encounters, ghosts haunt this work founded on prior injustices that we wish to repress. How do we judge and understand these contemporary expressions of loving the neighbor? What do we make of this domain of everyday human activity "nourished by forces of destruction, production, and salvation"?[1] This is the topic by which I intend to test Michael Banner's generative proposal.

Banner marshals recent anthropological study of the moral adequacy of the politics of humanitarian reason in ways that compel us to think critically about love's fleshly work. With anthropologist Didier Fassin, Banner joins humanitarianism to the material and social history of Christian compassion. For Fassin, humanitarianism is a "form of political theology" in the democratic order that "makes the intolerableness of its injustices somewhat bearable."[2] Its appeal to human solidarity focuses on the "condition of suffering people above all else."[3] Banner rightly notes Fassin's ambivalence about humanitarianism and the hierarchies of value and power that it sustains, especially to the extent that it obscures structural problems of inequality and domination. Fueled by appeals to critical theory and continental philosophy, others are more direct in their suspicion. Titles abound like *The Dark Sides of Virtue*, *Imposing Aid*, *Refugee Manipulation*, *Famine Crimes*, and *Toxic Charity*.[4]

Such critics pose a strong challenge to Christian communities deeply invested in humanitarian work as the embodiment of their confession that charity is the very heart of God. Surveys in the United States, for example, consistently rank helping the poor among the highest markers of Christian faith, even above reading the Bible regularly, attending church, supporting fair trade, or working to protect the environment.[5] One recent history found that "it is impossible to study humanitarianism without being impressed by the importance of religion."[6] We may live in an age of humanitarian care for distant strangers, but we are noticeably uneasy about this cultural ideal.

Like inventions of childhood and discoveries of the suffering Jesus, humanitarianism has a dappled pedigree. Recent genealogies often link it with a Christian sacralization of life coupled with a valorization of suffering and its strenuous relief.[7] Social historians tell us that it was the preaching of Christian bishops like Augustine (that great ethnographer of late antiquity) who invented the category of the "poor" in their exegesis of Jesus's new mapping of the social world and the redemptive power of almsgiving.[8] Others emphasize the salience of the rise of capitalism for the production of humanitarian sentiment in the eighteenth century, and still others highlight how technologies of science and medicine rendered visible the details of bodily suffering.[9] Recent debates about Christianity's relation to the vast legal and institutional framework of human rights is yet another sign of historicizing humanitarianism.[10] No doubt, different accounts of cosmopolitan compassion and sympathy—not to mention their cultivation—play an important role in various philosophical histories. Christian theology did not require a Nietzsche to interrogate the semblances of charity. But they only recently have been employed (or shall I say, embodied) in terms of a distinctive humanitarian discourse and practice that in many ways continue Enlightenment transformations of Christian charity, epitomized by John D. Rockefeller's "scientific benevolence."[11] As Luke Bretherton has put it, our age of humanitarianism "is part of the transmutation and re-description of theological categories such as sin and charity into more immanent and moralized ones such as vice and altruism."[12]

In *The Ethics of Everyday Life*, Banner seeks to "review and reconfigure" the relationship of moral theology with moral philosophy and social anthropology.[13] I read his book less as a methodological manifesto (of which there are now many in theology) and more as a salutary corrective and encouragement to his fellow moral theologians. He seeks "an ethics not of hard cases, but of the life course."[14] The path forward for a more incarnational moral theology is less analytic philosophy and more interpretive anthropology. While no grand theory, this qualitative engagement allows us to better track the "paradigmatically human moments in Christ's life" that take us to "sites of contention and controversy, where what it is to be human is discovered, constructed, and contested."[15]

Seeking both judgment and understanding is a familiar refrain among those dissatisfied with the social myopia and theological distortions wrought by those "hard cases" in "quandary ethics" that my undergraduates love in all their glorious abstraction and dilemmatic appeal. In fact, while they can pose an obstacle to practical reason, I confess that I still find them pedagogically useful as a hook for teaching Christian ethics at my secular university (even if it sometimes pains me to give yet another lecture on trolley problems to animate their moral intuitions). No doubt, the particularist turn to narrative and virtue also conceived itself as a revolt against the ahistorical and rule-driven simplicity of a "hard cases" approach, including its Pelagian temptations in shifting focus from the relational habitus of character and social practice to a calculus of right action and universal norms. Parallel developments in comparative religious ethics and Christian social ethics that tap into the field's origins in sociology have only added to the demise of an ethics of hard cases in favor of attending to dynamics of power and thick description of habits, practices, and dispositions (especially at the intersections of race, class, and gender).[16] Indeed, although I do not have empirical data to support the claim, my sense is that few American Christian ethics courses rely on hard cases and that few American Christian ethicists remain in dialogue with the current practices of analytic moral philosophy. Even fewer moral philosophers pay attention to the work of Christian ethics. Perhaps we need an ethnography of our own tribal practice to get a clearer picture of what constitutes the obsessions of Christian ethics today.

Of course, Banner knows other dissenters motivated by "the plausible narration of moral lives."[17] Readers of Alasdair MacIntyre and Charles Taylor (not to mention Max Weber or Pierre Bourdieu) know that such a narration entails more than an academic exercise. They serve as a proxy referendum on the politics of modern society, especially those aspects of everyday life celebrated in the wake of the Reformation and the rise of capitalism and democratic liberalism: for example, the "dominant individualist and bureaucratic modes of modern culture."[18] But Banner does more than add a twist to these familiar re-turns to ethical formation, ones that often maintain a close relationship with moral philosophy even when drawing on other disciplinary resources (albeit more Aristotle and Hegel than Kant and Mill). By calling us to engage more fully with social anthropology and its descriptions of ordinary life, Banner asks yet more of the moral theologian stretched between the doctrinal, the descriptive, and the practical.

Banner, for example, distinguishes the challenge that suffering poses to practical rather than theoretical reason. His interest in the "politics of compassion" turns to "our action in the world, not to our understanding."[19] It may be difficult to hold off questions of theodicy or familiar debates about agape and special relations. Funded by appeal to Luke 10 and Matthew 25, love's relation to justice was the central concern for much of twentieth-century Christian ethics. Despite efforts to question its abstractions, it continues without apparent resolution or exhaustion, especially for a Protestant tradition recovering from certain notions of disinterested agapism. Love of neighbor is perhaps the most discussed topic in modern Christian ethics, yielding a vast literature analyzing notions of human dignity, self-sacrifice, mutuality, the relation of self-perfection and other-regard, and the scope of moral responsibility rooted in a conception of a common humanity bound by moral obligation. My own recent work, admittedly more in dialogue with philosophy than anthropology, has examined how these concepts, so indebted to a theological heritage, might change with the globalization of the neighborhood.[20] But loving the neighbor assumes a different perspective for moral theology in dialogue with anthropology.

According to Banner, an everyday Christian ethics that is both therapeutic and evangelical must engage "other imaginations of human being" "on the ground" and in "a wider and richer context," attending "psychologically and socioculturally realistic" narratives.[21] That anthropologists have now made turns to morality and to Christianity only further highlights generative possibilities that ethicists have been prone to overlook in their skipping through the intellectual history of modernity on their selective way to casuistry. At its best, anthropologists and their ethnographic method will help direct us to "the routines, discourses, and practices of daily life" that we too often neglect in our pursuit of conceptual clarity and normative principles.[22] Many ethicists call for such description of forms of life necessarily interrelated with evaluation. Anthropology gives us another language for doing it.

I am sympathetic to the ambition for empirical sensitivity to the ordinary, not simply as an antidote to dominant strains of deontology and consequentialism but, equally important for our field, as a revealing challenge to those big narratives of modernity criticism that tell us we live "after virtue."[23] As Banner puts it, ethics often goes "without saying—and because it goes without saying, it will only be noticed and understood by the patient ethnographic enquirer."[24] Patient noticing of complex realities and multiple voices is a needed virtue for doing ethics today, consistent with current appeals to "lived religion" and the turn to practice. In fact, some advocate ethnographic fieldwork as itself an expression of loving the neighbor, a way beyond the "excarnation" of empty theorizing.[25] But if X is better than Y for moral theology, then we need more examples of where it fares better for a particular task.

I confess initial skepticism that social anthropology is the most promising empirical discipline for exposing the social constructions of our experience and our moral ecology. My skepticism is fueled by familiar questions now being addressed in the resurgent literature on ethnography and theological normativity.[26] Given its necessary contextualism, can it help us with needed comparative framing for normative inquiry? Does it privilege explanation of local embedded knowledge in ways that resist moral analysis and expertise? How do we get from ethnography to theology or do ethnography as theology? History, cognitive psychology, political theory, economics, literature, and sociology all seem as likely to be important conversation partners (and, in some cases, more important). Finally, one need not agree with everything John Milbank has said to wonder if this ethnographic turn risks even further marginalizing constructive theology within the neo-Kantian construction of university disciplines. That said, consider this chapter an experimental response both to Banner's act of fraternal correction and to what one prominent anthropologist helpfully terms "the lure of the concrete."[27]

## The Ethics of Humanitarianism

My focus emerges in chapter 4 of Banner's work: "Regarding Suffering: On the Discovery of the Pain of Christ, the Politics of Compassion, and the Contemporary Mediation of the Woes of the World." What might social anthropology teach moral theology about the ethics of humanitarianism and the "cultural representation of suffering" in light of our contemporary desires and postcolonial and post-Christendom circumstance?[28] In particular, how might anthropology—which has its own entanglements with empire, gift, and paternalism—inform Christian efforts to imagine (and practice) a humanitarian moral and political economy that escapes or at least responds to its many contemporary critics on the left and the right? Banner puts the question this way: What are the "resources to acknowledge and overcome the internal inconsistencies and external complaints that can be put to humanitarian reason"?[29] Or, as I might put it, how can we be humanitarians without humanitarianism?

The term *humanitarian* dates from early nineteenth-century theologies that emphasized the humanity of Christ and the value of everyday life, even to the point of seeking a more modest hope in humanity without divinity. It was quickly applied to various reform movements, including abolition and the promotion of international law.[30] Today it has multiple meanings that reflect religious and secular formations. It is "a structure of feeling, a cluster of moral principles, a basis for ethical claims and political strategies, and a call to action."[31] While development and human rights discourse are staples of Christian ethics, Banner's interest in humanitarianism—even a Christian humanitarianism—is anomalous.

This is especially surprising given the increasingly recognized role of religious actors and institutions in the aid industry, the globalization that fosters transnational interdependence among churches, and the dramatic rise of Christian humanitarian groups since the end of the Cold War, often compensating for state and market dysfunction as well as a vacated traditional denominational presence.[32] To the ends of the earth, it is not so much congregations but large-budget organizations such as the World Council of Churches, Habitat for Humanity, Salvation Army, Red Cross, Catholic Relief Services, World Vision International, Tearfund UK, Samaritan's Purse, Christian Solidarity International, Christian Aid, and Lutheran World Relief, as well as thousands of smaller NGOs funded by billions of dollars, seeking to address disaster relief, refugee resettlement, delivery of food and water, health care, and community development. They stand alongside the mega-philanthropy that now characterizes a Second Golden Age, with charitable giving by American individuals, foundations, and corporations exceeding $400 billion in 2017.[33] Public charities in the United States alone report more than $2.7 trillion in assets.[34] For example, at $50 billion the Gates Foundation is worth more than the GDP of many African countries, not to mention the billions circulating as remittances from migrants to their home countries. While difficult to gather data, it seems that economic development of the kind associated with the United Nations or official government transfers is now met with this older yet reconfigured form of care that assumes a cosmopolitan identity with technological capacities. Internationalization and institutionalization of humanitarian sentiment is one of the remarkable features of our age, especially since the end of the Cold War.

The neglected attention by moral theologians stands in sharp contrast to anthropology, in which humanitarianism and the suffering body occupy a central place. Despite their number and influence, attention to Christian humanitarian practices and organizations is not a hallmark of this burgeoning field of humanitarian studies, perhaps reflecting a continued secular bias and the ways Christians can seem a "disappointing subaltern" for the anthropological gaze (either not exotic enough given the long history, inherently suspect given this history, or mistakenly filtered only through the lens of American culture wars and neoliberal economics).[35] As one scholar notes, Christian NGOs are invisible, "counted on" but not "accounted for."[36] Those anthropologists who do focus on Christian humanitarianism often confess surprise at its "disturbing complexity" and the ways Christian workers challenge "dynamic binarism of good and evil."[37]

For anthropologists, humanitarianism once promised a "new, politically and ethically acceptable object of study . . . reflecting the growing presence of discourses and institutions that represented and protected a universal, 'global humanity.'"[38] Such study was not uncritical of the depoliticizing and dehistoricizing tendencies within humanitarianism. Work in the 1980s and 1990s, for example, focused on the perils of bureaucratic rivalries, Faustian bargains, the unintended consequences of humanitarian interventions, and the commodification of suffering bodies cast as victims through a "politics of pity."[39] The language of paradox appears more frequently in humanitarian studies than many a systematic theology.

In the 2000s, the anthropological literature became even more critical, leading to what one anthropologist termed a "cul-de-sac of critique," an apt description for much of contemporary Christian ethics as well.[40] It is pretty depressing reading that inspires little hope for resistance and the possibilities of human agency (and I say so as someone who has spent a fair amount of time reading Augustine). Much of this literature seeks to unmask the ways charity constructs victims as contemptible objects of vindictive pity and populations as objects of control in the liberal political imaginary, especially now with links to security interests and projects of nation building. In reinforcing social inequalities and hierarchies, it is the poisonous gift that keeps on taking.[41] Humanitarianism may be good for the giver but not for the vulnerable; or better yet, like the master-slave relationship, it corrupts both alike.[42] This relentless suspicion—littered with references to will to power, class control, and disciplining technologies—is at odds with the enthusiasm of my undergraduates and many churches for activities that go under the rubric of humanitarianism.

In fact, while a popular imagination—both secular and Christian—finds humanitarianism "morally untouchable," to read the work of most social anthropologists is an exercise in melancholia.[43] Shaped by their ethnographic experience (and the work of Michel Foucault, Pierre Bourdieu, and Giorgio Agamben), this literature seeks to expose the contradictions of a "charitable-industrial-complex" that misrecognizes its structures as disinterested.[44] In some cases, by my lights, ethnography serves primarily as an illustration of these philosophical critics. They are simultaneously the crushing regimes of modern formation and the leisure activity of the global bourgeoisie. The Foucauldian discourse of these anthropologists is less Banner's "technology of self" and more the hidden yet pervasive control exercised by "governmentality."[45] It seems, however, that this swing between warm embrace and total denunciation now has led to "more cautious, ethnographic examinations and descriptions of its complexities, limits, and boundaries."[46] This involves a shift "from an anthropological critique of the discursive power of development toward the ethnographic treatment of development as a category of practice."[47] What does this third wave of anthropology and its so-called aidnography tell us?

## What Empirically Sensitive Philosophy Teaches

Before turning to some examples, let me note briefly an analogy with Banner's discussion of bioethics. He shows us how much of bioethics is constrained by a focus on the licitness of certain practices and technologies. This narrow focus misses the broader cultural context and implicit moral imagination.[48]

In moral philosophy, one dominant empirical approach to humanitarian aid focuses on the private morality of charitable giving in light of metrics that determine which organizations spend most efficiently and make the greatest possible impact. Through organizations like GiveWell and Giving What We Can, "effective altruism" promises a clear, rational, and impartial decision procedure for individuals seeking to prevent or alleviate suffering due to global poverty. Recalling William Godwin and Bishop Fenelon, proponents offer calculations for helping to decide if it is better to cure the blind or improve the life of the AIDS patient.[49] While such a focus does not demand a utilitarian basis, one governs much of it in assessing the comparability of all goods through the lens of welfare economics. Effective altruists tend to focus on individual agents situated in a world whose only relevant features are units of suffering and pleasure plus disputed causal facts about which acts on the agent's part would raise or lower the overall balance of these units. Its critics issue familiar objections to utilitarianism that track theological reservations about impersonal ethics, rational choice theory, and the movement's antipathy to proximity as a morally salient feature of duties to aid.[50] I need not rehearse these reservations here, but I think they are consistent with Banner's criticisms of the type of work done in bioethics that wholly abstracts from the specificity and complexity of social structures of everyday life. This approach does not bring those relationships among multiple human beings into view. Indeed, it may reinforce fantasies of absolute power and condescension to the less powerful.

Effective altruists need not oppose collective and institutional reform, but I take their focus to be on what actions are required before a radical revolution in the global economic system.[51] Other philosophers, like Thomas Pogge, insist on a somewhat less demanding approach under the rubric of reparative justice rather than personal charity. He emphasizes responsibilities to institutions grounded in duties not to harm. For Pogge, our participation in unjust structures invites grief born of guilt: "We can compensate for our contribution to collective harm also by contributing to efforts toward institutional reform or toward protecting the victims of present institutional injustice."[52] Pogge's approach might dovetail with efforts in economics and public policy to expand our repertoire for measuring well-being in terms of capabilities rather than simply aggregation of economic utility.

While accountability and transparency are hallmarks of the "effective altruism" movement, questions of political morality are sometimes neglected by the attention to personal morality. Big philanthropy, often heralded with civic gratitude, represents an expression of power that deserves scrutiny in democratic societies, especially since these organizations benefit from an array of tax incentives and subsidies that complicate any strict division between state and civil society. This is not to deny the value of philanthropy or foundations, an ironic argument for a university professor to make. Philanthropic foundations serve a valuable and defensible function in democratic societies.[53] The point is simply to emphasize their political rather than merely moral nature.

At the same time, empirically sensitive philosophy raises important questions about how to engage empirical disciplines themselves. For example, in addition to measures of health and education, Angus Deaton's work celebrates the dramatic decrease in poverty (especially extreme poverty) on a broad historical scale, especially in China and India.[54] But, with others in development economics, Deaton poses a strong challenge to humanitarians for failing to achieve their goals. In fact, the literature on the "aid curse" or "aid illusion" argues that much of humanitarian aid displaces institutional innovation and existing public expenditures. Even with the best intentions, it can thwart long-term development of civic activities, induce state exit, create dependency, and contain popular discontent that might otherwise pressure political reform of corrupt governments through collective action. Deaton, for example, argues "citizens of the rich world . . . can best help the poor of the world by not giving them large-scale aid."[55] Some theologians who advocate ethnography have also found the contradictions of the so-called NGO effect: one informant reports, "When I want to gather the people in my parish, they all expect to be paid."[56] These are ironies of development and humanitarianism that any Niebuhrian or "effective altruist" should appreciate, even if they judge the benefits of aid outweigh its negatives (especially at a micro rather than macro level). These ongoing empirical debates about displacement and multidimensional poverty reduction, including more radical claims that development has passed its prime or advocacy of direct cash transfer, should matter for moral theology (not to mention churches and Christian NGOs).[57] Moral theology is about more than getting facts right, but it should not be about less.

## What Anthropology Teaches: Some Ethnographic Examples

But *these* empirical matters, driven by quantitative data, are different than those discovered by engaging more directly with social anthropology. While recognizing that to summarize ethnography is often to miss the point, let me simply report a few recent examples before concluding with some tentative implications for moral theology. In general, these examples show the value of attending not only to large-scale processes of international relations or economic systems but also to the lived realities of humanitarian work.

In his discussion of baptism and godparents, Banner argues that Christianity "scripted a practice which preferred kinship that is made over kinship that is given."[58] Reimagining kinship emerges throughout his book as a central descriptive task of social anthropology even as it becomes a normative task of moral theology working out the implications of early Christian transformations of ethnic and familial kinship. Banner describes this process not as "unkinning" but a "rekinning" of the community of disciples marked by a dramatically different sense of solidarity and obligation.[59] Godparenthood, for example, is a "highly structured and deeply socially embedded practice of spiritual kinship," which he tells us represents a "bold, profound, and influential attempt to express and realize the theo-logic of Christian kinship."[60] This theo-logic is one that fashions "kinship amongst strangers" as a mode of "organizing alterity."[61]

While there are relatively few ethnographic studies of faith-based humanitarianism, much of Christian humanitarianism can be seen as fashioning kinship among strangers. Despite the pressures of institutional isomorphism that shape these organizations, they also show the radical pluralism and shifting models of aid provision negotiating religious concepts and rhetoric with pragmatic demands of effective service.[62] I take that to be an epistemic strength of the ethnographic approach at odds with the homogenizing discourse of technocratic rationality. To put it crudely, social anthropologists focus on persons and relationships, while moral philosophers focus on concepts and rationalist decision procedures.[63]

In her ethnographic study *Disquieting Gifts: Humanitarianism in New Delhi*, anthropologist Erica Bornstein takes the reader into the lived intersections of global humanitarianism and what she calls the informal charity of "everyday life."[64] This intersection, she notes, is "riddled with ethical dilemmas."[65] Unlike many scholars, Bornstein does not separate realms of development, charity, and humanitarianism. However useful and morally salient those distinctions might be, Bornstein links them through the category of the gift and a "larger universe of giving marked by notions of global citizenship, relations of social obligation that entail rights and entitlements, and sacred conceptions of religious donation."[66] Inspired by debates surrounding Marcel Mauss's classic work on gift relations and Jacques Derrida's rejoinder, she hopes her readers will "pay attention to the impulses that inspire people to engage in humanitarian actions instead of solely paying attention to outcomes."[67] Her book focuses on the "tension between giving to strangers and giving to kin," connecting "how gifts to beggars and donations to organizations are infused with cultural codes that structure the expectations and experience of giving."[68] These codes, which differ dramatically in her account of religious traditions, provide the conditions for action that might be "discounted by those whose eyes focus solely on institutions."[69] Bornstein highlights the ways that the "rational mechanics of capitalism (accountability, governance, credibility, transparency)" are at odds with certain Hindu practices of spontaneous giving as an art of liberation. Bornstein is averse to normative evaluation. As an anthropologist, she claims to diagnose social facts. But she does argue that the liberal imagination to provoke empathy does not capture the desire for "relational empathy" that she found in her study of various groups in India. Similar to Banner, Bornstein concludes that "liberal empathy seeks to assist abstract others in need; relational empathy turns strangers into kin."[70] Liberal humanitarianism focuses on the needs of strangers who remain anonymous and distant. Relational humanitarianism imagines a kinship of humanitarianism that reduces social distance (i.e., a Canadian church group who saved their nylon stockings for bandaging despite its inefficiency, or a child sponsorship scheme of elderly British women who wrote letters about their everyday life that were unintelligible to their Indian recipients[71]). At the end of the day, she argues that both are necessary and valid. The rights-based critique of charity cannot account for donor-recipient dynamics that "resemble kin-based entitlements" and brings "small, often utopian, solutions to an unjust world."[72]

Consider another study of the International Health Mission, a Minneapolis-based Lutheran NGO that supplies medical technologies to Lutheran clinics in Madagascar, Tanzania, Cameroon, Papua New Guinea, Liberia, and Nicaragua. The ethnographer Britt Halvorson found that agencies like IHM "merge political discourses of humanitarianism with biblical motivations for their work."[73] In one of its best-supported projects, IHM collects a large number of painstakingly handmade bandages from a network of eighteen thousand US supporters (mostly elderly women) encouraged to see their gift as a devotional work that extends the healing ministry of Jesus. The primary scriptural appeal is not Matthew 25 or 28 but rather Luke 24: "accompanying" those who suffer through an imagined landscape of social connection. But through fieldwork, the author discovers that this practice stands in stark tension with the professionalized and bureaucratic model of aid that otherwise characterizes the agency's efforts to address health care inequities, especially through the institutional and industrial process of transferring the bandages overseas. The authors note how this process involves "the erasure of personal traces from produced goods."[74] At the warehouse where the bandages are collected, for example, the many handwritten notes attached to each bandage are removed. Following procurement directives from a cross-denominational network called the Technical Exchange for Christian Healthcare, many of the defective bandages are secretly discarded. The anthropologist concludes that this practice shows the "mismatch between relational caregiving and professionalized relief provision."[75]

This mismatch is starker in the case of an ethnographic study of a Ugandan charity home for orphans, children with disabilities, and the elderly run by the Franciscan Sisters of Africa. At Mercy House, the author finds "faith in providence encourages the sisters to focus on the eternal and intrinsic goods of action accomplished in the present moment" rather than "forms of rational planning and demands for lasting change that advocates of sustainable development call for."[76] The sisters' refusal to adopt practices of auditing disqualifies them from aid money from most foundations. Consistent with humanitarian critics like Davie Rieff, they see their Franciscan charism as meeting need directly and express skepticism that structural efforts will have much effect. Their activity was also an intentional form of "self-crafting, allowing them to perfect the virtue of charity and to foster their capacity to trust in divine providence."[77] The anthropologist asks the reader to "consider resistance to such forms of planning not as an obvious lack to be remedied through capacity-building exercises but, rather, as an alternative orientation to time and agency chosen for its own sake."[78]

In a final ethnographic study, "The Charismatic Gift," Simon Coleman identifies an even more dramatic effort to construct a social order of relational giving at odds with professional models of aid and Weberian ascetic religiosity. The community in focus is a Swedish-based Word of Life ministry, a conservative Protestant movement animated by the "Prosperity Gospel" that runs possibly the largest Bible school in Europe, associated with Oral Roberts University. Here the anthropologist's patience presents "sacrificial economics as something other than naïve submission to religious hucksterism."[79] According to Coleman, these Faith Christians offer a perspective that challenges "Western concepts of the bounded, autonomous social actor" by "suggesting the possibility of the mutual interpenetration of believing persons."[80] The spontaneous financial gifts and prospective rewards they encourage fund ministries central to charismatic identity. These gifts are not tied directly to aid as much as perpetuating the ministry, but the anthropologist here emphasizes that the circulation of gifts shows how these believers cultivate agency and intersubjectivity. Given the strong presence of other Pentecostal-charismatic traditions in many poor and highly indebted countries, it is important not to universalize this example.[81] In Tanzania, for example, the Tanzania Social and Economic Trust blends traditional development initiatives with a charismatic ministry that seems to tap into a long-standing Christian association of almsgiving with merit and atonement, of laying up treasure in heaven, one that other Protestants find mercenary and distasteful.

## Conclusion: Theological Tasks

Practices shape beliefs as much as they are shaped by them. Banner argues that forms of Christian practice that appropriate the suffering of Christ can help overcome "the implicit disregard for the Other which construes compassion as a grant and not a recognition."[82] Yet compassion is a form of the gift even if such recognition pushes us toward language of duty and righteousness. Banner is surely right that representations of Christ's suffering were "never bare representations" like flashes of suffering "in the manner of TV images with their ephemeral immediacy."[83] The technologies that shape Christian imagination and "practiced attention to Christ's suffering" can and should be distinguished from "mere spectatorship" complicit with a voyeuristic "iconography of suffering."[84] They stretch and fashion the agent in her attention "both in time and over time," troubling "estimations of the other which would proceed first of all and only from the perspective of pity."[85] Unlike much of the visual media sponsored by aid groups, Christian art and liturgy invite followers of Jesus to "occupy a range of subject positions: as witnesses to the sufferings, but also in various alternative modes of attention, as causes of the suffering and even as victim."[86] This may be good theology, but there is nothing in these technologies or liturgies themselves that guarantee these representations will have such a happy effect on sinners like us.[87]

Recent marketing trends by aid groups suggest an aesthetic shift toward "cool activism" in a digital age. It turns less to universal ethics backed by images of suffering and more to lifestyle authenticity for publics now skeptical of traditional humanitarianism.[88] Nevertheless, our ethnographic studies show that relational identities and desire for connection remain present amid the diversity of Christian humanitarian efforts. Banner lifts up the L'Arche communities as one example attentive to the dynamics of power in "one-sided acts of charity."[89] As Jean Vanier puts it, they do not "simply do good to the poor but discover God hidden in the poor"; they are sacraments of the hidden God.[90] Such discovery is not without its own sentimental temptations, but I take Banner to echo Luke Bretherton's emphasis on the ways in which the long history of Christian works of mercy require a formation on the "part of the giver so as to enable a deeper, intimate, and more meaningful relationship with those in need."[91] They both suggest that Christian practices of personal and material renunciation in a theocentric vision contrast with "the form of *noblesse oblige* and philanthropic donation, both of which emphasize rather than bridge the distance between giver and receiver and too often leave intact the structures of inequality."[92] For Bretherton, humanitarianism perpetuates "bureaucratic, colonial, collectivizing, and commodifying programs of rule" of privileged experts that legitimate "top down, technocratic schemes" in the name of development, modernization, and ending suffering.[93] According to Bretherton, we need a politics and an ethics oriented toward the formation of a people, the body of Christ and the body politic. Identifying "the paradox of care" as a "central dilemma in all means of welfare provision," he calls on the church to find ways to "take seriously the agency and wisdom of 'ordinary' people: that is, to put people before program."[94] Such charity directs us toward solidarity and communion, not the maximization of states of affairs.

People before program—for Stanley Hauerwas, this is what Christian worship makes possible, such that Christians "have time to be with the poor, to learn with the poor, to listen to the poor."[95] Christians "carry on with the small acts of kindness and mercy that are made possible by our conviction that God has redeemed the world" despite the apparent absence or impossibility of macropolitical change.[96] At the end of the *Church Dogmatics*, Karl Barth argued that diaconate ministry is a basic form of witness even as it is challenged by dramatic developments of state welfare provision. He recognizes that such ministries can "never be more than drops in the bucket."[97] But they are invested with the pathos of eternity and a freedom beyond obligation.

Christian humanitarians need not worry about humanitarian efficiency or the extent to which they might delay more radical forms of distributive justice; their charity is a parable of the kingdom.

Such charity is at odds with the transactional ethos of contemporary humanitarianism. Reflecting the power of professionalization and rationalization, one humanitarian worker reports, "Most of us avoid interacting on a one-to-one basis with the people. We don't have time. . . . We don't think that much can be gained that will help us do our job."[98] This report is no doubt fodder for Hauerwasian critique, not to mention fueling notions that humanitarian aid disregards not only friendship but also local perceptions and skill sets. Yet I remain wary of celebrating the *koinonia* of charity over against managerial philanthropy. The sources of my discontent are theological as well as political.

How does L'Arche help us think about the current scale of Christian NGOs? Are there limits to this community of mutual recognition? Is Christian charity—especially marked by personal, expressive, and even the whimsical spontaneity—simply not compatible with larger (let alone global) networks that trade in the language of quantities as well as qualities? I think charity is necessary but insufficient. Politically, I worry about a romantic imagination for non-bureaucratic forms of organization that insulate charity from the broader types of issues that give rise to Fassin's ambivalence (like domination and structural inequalities). Ironically, many ethnographers found a deep connection between an individualistic politics of volunteerism alongside a "romanticized ideal of Christian charity based on a belief in the possibility of creating profound interpersonal bonds that transcend social boundaries and status hierarchies."[99] Other anthropologists found that the effectiveness of aid matters more to recipients and promotes trust more than appeals to moral principles of solidarity.[100]

L'Arche certainly trains Christians in the virtue of patience and other fruits of the Spirit that bureaucrats may lack. It establishes a counterpolitics of friendship opposed to the transactional logic of market exchanges. But how does it help theologians understand the dynamics of public authority and the broader struggle for justice? This is not merely a question of scale, comparing the monastery to the administrative state. It is a normative question of political theology in a technological age.

It would be foolish and rather puritan to rise in defense of joyless bureaucracy, market fundamentalism, top-down aid, and Weberian rationalization against the witness of L'Arche. But perhaps some disorientation is needed given the power of stories that starkly contrast charity framed by transcendence to philanthropy framed by immanence. As Jennifer Herdt rightly asks in her compelling critique of Milbank's account of how social theory destroyed Christian charity, "Is there a single truly Christian vision of charity, or can Christian responses to poverty take on different incarnations given different social and economic circumstances?"[101] Organizational efficiency should not be an end in itself, nor one that dominates all other social goals. Efficiency for the sake of efficiency is no virtue, especially when wed to an implicit philosophy of human progress that turns the virtue of prudence into mere calculation of means and ends and leaves no room for divine action.[102]

But, like just war reasoning, does not humanitarian reasoning speak to a social practice that generations of our immediate Christian predecessors bequeathed to us as a possible good rather than merely an ill? Are they not also forms of human making and moral imagination that do more than cloak arbitrary power responsive to non-ideal arrangements? Indeed, might they be forms of the human spirit that participate in divine transcendence? While concern for effective giving has always been a part of Christian charity, debates about humanitarianism are "reiterations of a disagreement foundational to social science: the question if modernity is morally beneficial or not."[103] I propose a more charitable interpretation of both Christian charity and its recent expressions in the coordination of humanitarian work. Much like Oliver O'Donovan's argument regarding Christendom and liberalism, they stand as witnesses and traditions deserving our humble respect.[104] Humanitarianism might be narrated as both an achievement and a predicament, borrowing from Charles Taylor's general diagnosis of a secular age. When we demonize humanitarian reason, we risk enchanting it with divine power as much as when we bow down to its lordlike pretension.

In the 1930s, echoing Weber's contrast between instrumental rationality and value rationality, George Herbert Mead identified the ways philanthropy seeks to place the charitable impulse under "rational control."[105] One enthusiast for the rationalized turn in humanitarian aid argues that "the bureaucratic model allows parachurch organizations to produce more goods and services faster, more efficiently, and more predictably."[106] Of course, the question remains efficiency at what and for what. Some theological critics assume that regulation and institutionalization are at odds with acts of freedom, perhaps revealing a Protestant anxiety that charity should remain outside the space of reason, law, and justice. I worry that this can indulge the romance of powerlessness.

The founders of the Social Gospel were never quite sure how to mediate power and expertise in the face of the Gospel, especially after making peace with welfare state liberalism. Their dilemma remains, caught as we are between the Weberians and the Nietzscheans. To the extent that Christian humanitarian work is rationalized, it meets theological suspicion in the name of relationships. To the extent Christian humanitarian work resists professionalization, it meets empirical suspicion in the name of efficiency.

Theologically, the relational and the efficient risk both dualism and mystification. A strong version of the argument is that interpersonal charity is intrinsic to Christian faith, regardless of effectiveness. As one critic of philanthropy argues, Christian charity "was not a means, at least not primarily, of solving a social problem, redistributing wealth, or even growing the church. To practice charity was to make a statement about the world and the God who had created and redeemed it."[107] But one response might be that humanitarianism generates goods beyond efficiency, albeit fragile ones, especially for creatures like us who cannot always be counted on to mobilize willingness for right action.

Critique should not be total. The problems of humanitarianism are contingent ones that through constant trials of discovery can be at least mediated. They no doubt will change. Aid groups are not a natural kind embedded in a perennial ideology of the "rage for order." They represent experiments in living and social innovation; their metrics and technologies are tools for human flourishing. They not only optimize but can also institutionalize fairness, stabilize judgment, control willful individuals, and correct possible epistemic biases (i.e., the preference for homemade bandages or child sponsorship programs that skew family relations). As creatures of universities and churches, it is easy to criticize forms of social relations under capitalism as technocratic. But we need to do more than point out the power of soulless bureaucracy, especially as the pace of technology accelerates.

The "ism" in humanitarianism marks for its critics a technological understanding of practice and underwriting of certain aspects of the social order that we should resist.[108] But this is not to say that technologies and expertise are in themselves distorting and dehumanizing.[109] They are, no doubt, prone to manipulation and self-deception. But so too with charity in its distinctive way: without countervailing powers it can be chaotic and threatening. The goods internal to the practice of humanitarianism were at least thought to correct these dangers.

As many anthropologists now tell us, humanitarianism has become a form of faith, reoccupying a sacred canopy that "guards against a world in which interests and instruments trump values and ethics."[110] Perhaps not unlike Marx and Hegel, they reflect an aspiration for spiritually satisfying lives under the material conditions of modernity. Hannah Arendt credited Christianity with reversing the order of classical antiquity by substituting the immortal cosmos with the "most mortal thing, human life": what matters is not immortality but that life is the highest good.[111] For many Christians, humanitarianism simply is the modern rationalized expression of neighbor love in the face of desperate need occasioned by natural disasters, political corruption, and economic inequality.

In Bretherton's apt description, humanitarian faith is "simultaneously Christ-forgetting and Christ-haunted."[112] Like Banner's reading of Flemish art, humanitarian work reveals the sacred on the surface.[113] But it is a surface that coincides with depth. That requires a double vision: institutional structures that push toward justice yet without forsaking the transformation of a people toward a fellowship in virtue that such structures serve. Much of recent Christian ethics has sought to make democracy more humane, largely through debates about the role of religion in public life. We seem to be on the cusp of an era in which our economic practices once again merit the theological inquiry that a focus on liberalism has obscured. Humanitarian aid should be a part of this turn, as with any anthropological one: not simply as a moral argument or problem to be solved but as a Christian social movement that raises missiological and soteriological issues often neglected by moral theologians.[114]

Henry Dunant, founder of the Red Cross, thought that "while Christianity was supposed to save the world, humanitarianism would help to save Christianity."[115] Many Christians continue to agree. That is the social reality, the institutional context, and the moral ethos we inhabit. But most of our ethnographic evidence seems only to deepen recognition of tensions and ambivalence. As a good Augustinian, I will simply conclude by saying that sinful romance tempts us on all sides, both in the desire for relationships and the desire for effective giving. All of our incarnate loves are compromised and wounded in their cultural mediation, just as our moral theology will always be incomplete and premature. But love covers a multitude of sins. Any turn to the ordinary must not lose sight of the extraordinary grace that casts this light.

## Notes

1. Michael Barnett and Thomas G. Weiss, "Humanitarianism: A Brief History of the Present," in *Humanitarianism in Question: Politics, Power, Ethics*, ed. Michael Barnett and Thomas G. Weiss (Ithaca, NY: Cornell University Press, 2008), 15.

2. Didier Fassin, *Humanitarian Reason: A Moral History of the Present* (Berkeley: University of California Press, 2012), 251 and xii.

3. Erica Bornstein and Peter Redfield, "An Introduction to the Anthropology of Humanitarianism," in *Forces of Compassion: Humanitarianism between Ethics and Politics*, ed. Erica Bornstein and Peter Redfield (New York: School for Advanced Research, 2010), 6.

4. David Kennedy, *The Dark Sides of Virtue: Reassessing International Humanitarianism* (Princeton, NJ: Princeton University Press, 2005); B. E. Harrell-Bond, *Imposing Aid: Emergency Assistance to Refugees* (Oxford: Oxford University Press, 1986); Stephen John Stedman and Fred Tanner, eds., *Refugee Manipulation: War, Politics, and the Abuse of Human Suffering* (Washington, DC: Brookings Institution, 2003); Alex de Waal, *Famine Crimes: Politics & the Disaster Relief Industry in Africa* (Bloomington, IN: James Currey / Indiana University Press, 1997); Robert D. Lupton, *Toxic Charity: How Churches and Charities Hurt Those They Help* (New York: HarperCollins, 2011).

5. Pew Research Center, "Religion in Everyday Life," April 12, 2016, http://www.pewforum .org/2016/04/12/religion-in-everyday-life/.

6. Michael Barnett, *Empire of Humanity: A History of Humanitarianism* (Ithaca, NY: Cornell University Press, 2011), 17.

7. See Fassin, *Humanitarian Reason*, 248–51.

8. See, for example, Peter Brown, *Through the Eye of a Needle: Wealth, the Fall of Rome, and the Making of Christianity in the West, 350–550 AD* (Princeton, NJ: Princeton University Press, 2012).

9. See Thomas Haskell, "Capitalism and the Origins of the Humanitarian Sensibility, Part 1," *American Historical Review* 90, no. 2 (April 1985): 339–36; Thomas Haskell, "Capitalism and the

Origins of the Humanitarian Sensibility, Part 2," *American Historical Review* 90, no. 3 (June 1985): 547–66; and Thomas Laqueur, "Bodies, Details and the Humanitarian Narrative," in *The New Cultural History*, ed. Lynn Hunt (Berkeley: University of California Press, 1987), 176–204.

10. Samuel Moyn, *Christian Human Rights* (Philadelphia: University of Pennsylvania Press, 2015).

11. See, for example, Barbara Howe, "The Emergence of Scientific Philanthropy, 1900–1920," in *Philanthropy and Cultural Imperialism: The Foundations at Home and Abroad*, ed. Robert F. Arnove (Bloomington: University of Indiana Press, 1982), 25–54; and Robert Gross, *Giving in America: From Charity to Philanthropy* (Cambridge: Cambridge University Press, 2003).

12. Luke Bretherton, "Poverty, Politics, and Faithful Witness in the Age of Humanitarianism," *Interpretation* 94, no. 4 (2015): 447–59, at 449.

13. Michael Banner, *The Ethics of Everyday Life: Moral Theology, Social Anthropology, and the Imagination of the Human* (Oxford: Oxford University Press, 2014), 3.

14. Banner, 4.

15. Banner, 35.

16. See, for example, Richard Miller, "On Making a Cultural Turn in Religious Ethics," *Journal of Religious Ethics* 33, no. 3 (September 2005): 409–43; and Christian Scharen and Aana Marie Vigen, *Ethnography as Christian Theology and Ethics* (New York: Continuum, 2011).

17. Banner, *Ethics of Everyday Life*, 7.

18. Alasdair MacIntyre, *After Virtue: A Study in Moral Theory* (Notre Dame, IN: University of Notre Dame Press, 1981), 227.

19. Banner, *Ethics of Everyday Life*, 82.

20. See, for example, Eric Gregory, "The Gospel within the Commandment: Barth on the Parable of the Good Samaritan," in *Reading the Gospels with Karl Barth*, ed. Daniel L. Migliore (Grand Rapids, MI: Eerdmans, 2017), 34–55.

21. Banner, *Ethics of Everyday Life*, 6, 7, 11, 12, 24.

22. Banner, 128.

23. Of course, MacIntyre need not be committed to the idea that those who live after the Enlightenment do not lead lives of virtue. Rather, as Stanley Hauerwas argues, "the 'after' does not mean that some virtues are not still present, but that we no longer have the philosophical means to articulate their importance." *Performing the Faith* (Grand Rapids, MI: Brazos Press, 2004), 235n40.

24. Banner, *Ethics of Everyday Life*, 202.

25. Todd Whitmore, "Crossing the Road: The Case for Ethnographic Fieldwork in Christian Ethics," *Journal of the Society of Christian Ethics* 27, no. 2 (2007): 273–94.

26. See, for example, Peter Ward, ed., *Perspectives on Ecclesiology and Ethnography* (Grand Rapids, MI: Eerdmans, 2012).

27. Veena Das, "Action, Expression, and Everyday Life: Recounting Household Events," in *The Ground Between: Anthropologists Engage Philosophy*, ed. Veena Das et al. (Durham, NC: Duke University Press, 2014), 304.

28. Banner, *Ethics of Everyday Life*, 83.

29. Banner, 105.

30. See Craig Calhoun, "The Imperative to Reduce Suffering: Charity, Progress, and Emergencies in the Field of Humanitarian Action," in Barnett and Weiss, *Humanitarianism in Question*, 77.

31. Bornstein and Redfield, *Forces of Compassion*, 17.

32. See, for example, Robert Wuthnow, *Boundless Faith: The Global Outreach of American Churches* (Berkeley: University of California Press, 2009); Elizabeth Ferris, "Faith and Humanitarianism: It's Complicated," *Journal of Refugee Studies* 24, no. 3 (2011): 606–25; and Heather Curtis, *Holy Humanitarians: American Evangelicals and Global Aid* (Cambridge, MA: Harvard University Press, 2018).

33. *Giving USA 2018: The Annual Report on Philanthropy for the Year 2017* (Indianapolis, IN: Giving Institute, 2018). On religious participation and charitable giving, see Christian Smith and Hilary Davidson, *The Paradox of Generosity* (Oxford: Oxford University Press, 2014).

34. Michael Mascarenhas, *New Humanitarianism and the Crisis of Charity: Good Intentions on the Road to Help* (Bloomington: Indiana University Press, 2017).

35. Banner, *Ethics of Everyday Life*, 27. According to Barnett and Stein, evangelical agencies account for "almost 80 percent of all faith-based agencies and the bulk of the new population of faith-based agencies over the last three decades." Michael Barnett and Janice Gross Stein, eds., *Sacred Aid: Faith and Humanitarianism* (Oxford: Oxford University Press, 2012), 5. Mary Douglas reports that she once asked "Fredrik Barth, the Norwegian anthropologist and Islamicist, whether the day would come when Catholicism would be accorded by ethnographers the same benevolence as given to Judaism, Hinduism, and Islam, or to African religions. He replied, 'I doubt it, there is too much history.'" Mary Douglas, "A Feeling for Hierarchy," in *Believing Scholars*, ed. James L. Heft (Fordham, NY: Fordham University Press, 2005), 7.

36. Jonathan C. Agensky, "Dr Livingstone, I Presume? Evangelicals, Africa and Faith-Based Humanitarianism," *Global Society* 27, no. 4 (2013): 454–74. Elizabeth Ferris points out that "most of what is known about these organizations comes from the organizations themselves, from journalists, or from general observers of the humanitarian world who have not explored the particular orientations of faith-based organizations" (Ferris, "Faith and Humanitarianism," 16).

37. Erica Bornstein, *The Spirit of Development: Protestant NGOs, Morality, and Economics in Zimbabwe* (Stanford, CA: Stanford University Press, 2005), 169.

38. Miriam Ticktin, "Transnational Humanitarianism," *Annual Review of Anthropology* 43 (2014): 273–89, at 276.

39. See, for example, Luc Boltanski, *Distant Suffering: Morality, Media, and Politics* (Cambridge: Cambridge University Press, 1999).

40. Ticktin, "Transnational Humanitarianism," 283. Others have called anthropologists to "strive to do more than simply mobilize real-world messiness to expose predatory practices and complicate ordered philosophy and statistic-centered and cost-effectiveness-minded policy approaches . . . to advance people-centered analytics." João Biehl and Ramah McKay, "Ethnography as Political Critique," *Anthropology Quarterly* 85, no. 4 (Fall 2012): 1209–27, at 1223.

41. I borrow this formulation from Jeffrey Stout, "Christianity and the Class Struggle," in *The Kuyper Center Review: Calvinism and Democracy*, ed. John Bowlin (Grand Rapids, MI: Eerdmans, 2014), 40–53.

42. Cf. Georg Simmel: "When Jesus told the wealthy young man, 'Give your riches to the poor,' what apparently mattered to him were not the poor, but rather the soul of the wealthy man for whose salvation this sacrifice was merely a means or a symbol." *Georg Simmel: On Individuality and Social Forms*, ed. Donald N. Levine (Chicago: University of Chicago Press, 1971), 153.

43. Fassin, *Humanitarian Reason*, 244.

44. Peter Buffett, "The Charitable-Industrial Complex," *New York Times*, A19, July 27, 2013.

45. See Michel Foucault, "Governmentality," in *The Foucault Effect: Studies in Governmentality*, ed. Graham Burchell, Colin Gordon, and Peter Miller (Chicago: University of Chicago Press, 1991), 87–104. This critique extends not only to humanitarianism but to the welfare state that reconstitutes subjects in service to the state.

46. Ticktin, "Transnational Humanitarianism," 283. See also João Biehl and Ramah McKay, "Ethnography as Political Critique," *Anthropological Quarterly* 85, no. 4 (Fall 2012): 1209–27.

47. David Mosse, "The Anthropology of International Development," *Annual Review of Anthropology* 42 (2013): 227–46. In a section titled "Beyond Critique," Mosse reviews how critique ironically denies agency.

48. See Brian Brock, chapter 4 in this volume.

49. William MacAskill, *Doing Good Better: How Effective Altruism Can Help You Make A Difference* (New York: Gotham Books, 2015).

50. See Eric Gregory, "'Remember the Poor': Duties, Dilemmas and Vocation," in *God, the Good, and Utilitarianism*, ed. John Perry (Cambridge: Cambridge University Press, 2014), 192–208.

51. See Jeff McMahan, "Philosophical Critiques of Effective Altruism," *The Philosopher's Magazine* 73 (2016): 92–99.

52. See, for example, Thomas Pogge, *World Poverty and Human Rights* (Cambridge: Polity Press, 2002).

53. See Rob Reich, Chiara Cordelli, and Lucy Bernholz, eds., *Philanthropy in Democratic Societies: History, Institutions, Values* (Chicago: University of Chicago Press, 2016).

54. See also Steven Radelet, "Prosperity Rising," *Foreign Affairs* (January/February 2016): "Since the early 1990s, daily life in poor countries has been changing profoundly for the better."

55. Angus Deaton, *The Great Escape: Health, Wealth, and the Origins of Inequality* (Princeton, NJ: Princeton University Press, 2013), 318. Deaton argues that "giving more aid than we currently give—at least as it is given now—would make things worse, not better" (272). For response to Deaton's argument in development economics, see Martin Ravallion, "On the Role of Aid in the Great Escape," *The Review of Income and Wealth* 60, no. 4 (December 2014): 967–84. More generally, see Abhijit Banerjee and Esther Duflo, *Poor Economics* (New York: Public Affairs, 2011); and Abhijit Banerjee, *Making Aid Work* (Cambridge, MA: MIT Press, 2007). On the failures of aid, see also Fiona Terry, *Condemned to Repeat? The Paradox of Humanitarian Action* (Ithaca, NY: Cornell University Press, 2002).

56. Todd Whitmore, "Whiteness Made Visible: A Theo-Critical Ethnography of Acoliland," in Scharen and Vigen, *Ethnography as Christian Theology and Ethics*, 184–206, at 200.

57. See, for example, Majid Rahnema and Victoria Bawtree, *The Post-Development Reader* (London: Zed Books, 1997); and Joseph Hanlon, Armando Barrientos, and David Hulme, eds., *Just Give Money to the Poor: The Development Revolution from the Global South* (Sterling, VA: Kumarian Press, 2010).

58. Banner, *Ethics of Everyday Life*, 38.

59. Banner, 43.

60. Banner, 46.

61. Banner, 59.

62. See N. J. Demerath, Peter Dobkin Hall, Terry Schmitt, and Rhys H. Williams, eds., *Sacred Companies: Organisational Aspects of Religion and Religious Aspects of Organisations* (Oxford: Oxford University Press, 1998).

63. Cf. Didier Fassin: "Philosophy is interested in concepts, whereas anthropology is concerned with the world" (*Ground Between*, 52).

64. Erica Bornstein, *Disquieting Gifts: Humanitarianism in New Delhi* (Stanford, CA: Stanford University Press, 2012), 6.

65. Bornstein, 56.

66. Bornstein, 12.

67. Bornstein, 16.

68. Bornstein, 8, 14.

69. Bornstein, 18.

70. Bornstein, 22, 170.

71. Bornstein, 167–68.

72. Bornstein, 173, 174.

73. Britt Halvorson, "Woven Worlds: Material Things, Bureaucratization, and Dilemmas of Caregiving in Lutheran Humanitarianism," *American Ethnologist* 39, no. 1 (2012): 122–37, at 122.

74. Halvorson, 124.

75. Halvorson, 133.

76. China Scherz, "Let Us Make God Our Banker: Ethics, Temporality, and Agency in a Ugandan Charity Home," *American Ethnologist* 40, no. 4 (2013): 624–36, at 625.

77. Scherz, 627.

78. Scherz, 625.

79. Simon Coleman, "The Charismatic Gift," *The Journal of the Royal Anthropological Institute* 10, no. 2 (June 2004): 421–42, at 424.

80. Coleman, 424.

81. See, for example, Dana Freeman, ed., *Pentecostalism and Development: Churches, NGOs and Social Change in Africa* (New York: Palgrave, 2012).

82. Banner, *Ethics of Everyday Life*, 98.

83. Banner, 99.

84. Banner, 101. Susan Sontag, *Regarding the Pain of Others* (New York: Picador, 2003), 40; see also Susan Moeller, *Compassion Fatigue: How the Media Sells Disease, Famine, War and Death* (New York: Routledge, 1999).

85. Banner, *Ethics of Everyday Life*, 101, 102.

86. Banner, 102. Psychological studies suggest that donors respond more to stories of natural disasters than statistics and structural inequalities. See Richard Ashby Wilson and Richard D. Brown, eds., *Humanitarianism and Suffering: The Mobilization of Empathy* (Cambridge: Cambridge University Press, 2009).

87. A similar point is developed by Molly Farneth in chapter 1 in this volume. See also Stephen S. Bush, *Visions of Religion: Experience, Meaning and Power* (Oxford: Oxford University Press, 2014).

88. Lilie Chouliaraki, *The Ironic Spectator: Solidarity in the Age of Post-Humanitarianism* (Cambridge: Polity Press, 2013).

89. Banner, *Ethics of Everyday Life*, 103.

90. Jean Vanier as cited in Hans S. Reinders, "Being with the Disabled: Jean Vanier's Theological Realism," in *Disability in the Christian Tradition: A Reader*, edited by Brian Brock and John Swinton (Grand Rapids, MI: Eerdmans, 2012), 474, quoted by Banner, 103.

91. Bretherton, "Poverty, Politics, and Faithful Witness," 451.

92. Bretherton.

93. Bretherton, 455.

94. Bretherton, 448.

95. Stanley Hauerwas, "The End of Charity: How Christians Are (Not) to 'Remember the Poor,'" *ABC Religion and Ethics*, http://www.abc.net.au/religion/articles/2014/02/10/3941760.htm.

96. Stanley Hauerwas, *Performing the Faith: Bonhoeffer and the Practice of Nonviolence* (Grand Rapids, MI: Brazos Press, 2004), 235–36.

97. Karl Barth, *Church Dogmatics*, trans. G. W. Bromiley and T. F. Torrance (Edinburgh: T&T Clark, 1936–1975), IV/3 (891).

98. Michael Barnett, "Faith in the Machine? Humanitarianism in an Age of Bureaucratization," in Barnett and Stein, *Sacred Aid*, 202. See also Tony Waters, *Bureaucratizing the Good Samaritan: The Limitations of Humanitarian Relief* (Boulder, CO: Westview Press, 2001).

99. Omri Elisha, "Moral Ambitions of Grace: The Paradox of Compassion and Accountability in Evangelical Faith-Based Activism," *Cultural Anthropology* 23, no. 1 (2008): 154–89.

100. Dennis Dijkzeul and Claude Iguma Wakenge, "Doing Good, but Looking Bad? Local Perceptions of Two Humanitarian Organisations in Eastern Democratic Republic of Congo," *Disasters* 34, no. 4 (2010): 1139–70.

101. Jennifer Herdt, "The Endless Construction of Charity: On Milbank's Critique of Political Economy," *Journal of Religious Ethics* 32, no. 2 (Summer 2004): 301–24, at 310.

102. See Brian Brock, *Christian Ethics in a Technological Age* (Grand Rapids, MI: Eerdmans, 2010).

103. Peter Stamatov, *The Origins of Global Humanitarianism: Religion, Empires, and Advocacy* (Cambridge: Cambridge University Press, 2013), 189. According to Stamatov, "the precarious historical contingency of the genesis of our institutionalized model of long-distance advocacy is perhaps the strongest argument for us to do our best and preserve this important yet inherently fragile legacy of our history" (189).

104. Oliver O'Donovan, *The Desire of the Nations: Rediscovering the Roots of Political Theology* (Cambridge: Cambridge University Press, 1999).

105. George Herbert Mead, "Philanthropy from the Point of View of Ethics," in *Intelligent Philanthropy*, ed. Ellsworth Faris, Ferris Laune, and Arthur J. Todd (Chicago: University of Chicago Press, 1930), 133–48.

106. Christopher P. Scheitle, *Beyond the Congregation: The World of Christian Nonprofits* (Oxford: Oxford University Press, 2010), 35.

107. Jeremy Beer, *The Philanthropic Revolution: An Alternative History of American Charity* (Philadelphia: University of Pennsylvania Press, 2015), 26.

108. On technological understanding of practice, see Craig Dykstra, "Reconceiving Practice," in *Shifting Boundaries: Contextual Approaches to the Structure of Theological Education*, ed. Barbara G. Wheeler and Edward Farley (Louisville, KY: Westminster John Knox, 1991), 39.

109. See Paul du Gay, *In Praise of Bureaucracy* (London: Sage, 2000).

110. Barnett and Stein, *Humanitarianism in Question*, 8. On humanitarianism and sacralization, see also Gilbert Rist, *The History of Development: From Western Origins to Global Faith* (London: Zed Books, 2002); Stephen Hopgood, "Moral Authority, Modernity, and the Politics of the Sacred," *European Journal of International Relations* 15, no. 2 (2009): 229–55; and Peter Redfield, "Secular Humanitarianism and the Value of Life," in *What Matters? Ethnographies of Value in a Not So Secular Age*, ed. Courtney Bender and Ann Taves (New York: Columbia University Press, 2012).

111. Hannah Arendt, *The Human Condition* (Chicago: University of Chicago Press, 1958), 314.

112. Bretherton, "Poverty, Politics, and Faithful Witness," 451.

113. Banner, *Ethics of Everyday Life*, 33.

114. It is telling that the journal of the American Society of Missiology was originally titled *Practical Anthropology*, primarily aimed at anthropologically minded missionaries.

115. Barnett, *Empire of Humanity*, 228.

# 7

# THE ELIMINATION OF THE HUMAN WITHIN THE TECHNOLOGICAL SOCIETY

CRAIG M. GAY

W E SHOULD BE DEEPLY GRATEFUL for modern technology. None of us would enjoy our current everyday quality of life were it not for a series of technological revolutions that began in the eighteenth century and have continued with increasing frequency into the present. These include revolutions in science and medicine, production, transportation, communications, the organization of firms and governments, and so forth. Devising tools, techniques, and systems to get things done in the world is just something that we human beings do, something that we develop more or less "naturally," as it were, perhaps the product of the tension we experience between what our minds can envision and what our bodies can accomplish.[1]

Nonetheless, a large and growing body of evidence suggests that modern technology and, in particular, automatic machine technology is taking a toll on everyday embodied being. Michael Banner's project is in part to allow the creedal moments of Christ's life to disclose the Christian "imagining of the human."[2] He asks pointedly, "How does the Christian representation of human being relate to other representations of the human?"[3] In this chapter I propose to ask this question of modern technology—and in particular of automatic machine technology—in order to query whether, how, and why machine technology is diminishing everyday embodied human being. I will do this by means of a four-part argument. In the first part, I catalog a number of observations indicating that modern automatic machine technology is not necessarily—and perhaps not at all—conducive to ordinary, embodied human thriving. In the second part, I suggest why modern technological development seems to be trending away from ordinary, embodied human existence. In part three, I query why we are not more concerned about the elimination of the human from the technological society. Finally, in part four, I contend that Christians in particular cannot continue to acquiesce in the face of modern technology's diminution of ordinary embodied human being, for the Gospel of Jesus Christ confers staggering—and en-during—value on ordinary, embodied human existence. By questioning technology, the chapter responds to Banner's call that moral theology develop its own "everyday ethics." Few things are more "everyday" today than our use of modern technology.

## The Litany

It has, of course, long been lamented that the modern factory system is dehuman-izing. Yet as sociologists Peter and Brigitte Berger and Hansfried Kellner observed a number of years ago, it is not just workers on the assembly line who are encouraged to mimic the machinery they work with.[4] The modern workplace in general encour-ages us to envision ourselves as important yet nevertheless replaceable components within the work process.[5] The modern work environment tends to foster a cognitive style that is innovative and flexible, characterized in terms of "problem-solving in-ventiveness" and an "engineering mentality," yet it also tends to discourage personal formation and social relations and to foster a kind of "self-anonymization."[6]

The use of automated machinery has also been observed to have a "de-skilling" impact on its human users.[7] One rigorous examination of the effects of automation in a number of industries found that, although skill levels did increase slightly as power hand tools were introduced into the workplace, they dropped off quickly and sharply with the introduction of automated, self-regulating machinery.[8] Technology critic Nicholas Carr recounts how automated systems ironically contributed to sev-eral recent airline disasters; the human pilots, having become so used to computer control, had basically forgotten how to fly their aircraft.[9] A similar diminution of proficiency appears to extend to anyone who uses any kind of automated device for any purpose. While the design, development, and maintenance of sophisticated modern machinery continues to require the creativity and skill of highly trained professionals, philosopher Albert Borgmann notes that this skilled work "inevitably leaves in its wake a wasteland of divided and stultifying labor. Wherever there is a traditional area of skillful work, it is disassembled, reconstructed, largely turned over to machines, and artisans are replaced by unskilled laborers. This process leads to a continuing contraction of expertise and a corresponding expansion of unskilled labor."[10] Along this line, it has been suggested that the real cost of machines that can "think" may well be people who no longer can,[11] or as Carr put it even more suc-cinctly, "Sharp tools, dull minds."[12]

As Borgmann's observations suggest, skillful human labor has also increasingly been outsourced to machinery, a process now poised to colonize white collar profes-sions just as it previously automated large swaths of blue collar labor. In this connec-tion, economists have long used the term *technological unemployment* to describe the tendency of new technologies to displace human labor.[13] Just as steam and electricity revolutionized industry in the nineteenth and twentieth centuries, so information and communications technologies are now primed to "disrupt" (to use the currently fashionable term) nearly every aspect of the modern post-industrial economy.[14] This disruption will likely leave some, perhaps even a great many, people behind. Will the new machines think as insightfully and creatively as people can? Most likely not, but—here is the rub—they will not have to. As Bryan Appleyard commented recently, "It does not matter whether the new machines never achieve full human-like consciousness, or even real intelligence, they can almost certainly achieve just enough to do your job—not as well as you perhaps, but much, much more cheaply. To modernize John Ruskin, 'There is hardly anything in the world that some robot cannot make a little worse and sell a little cheaper, and the people who consider price only are this robot's lawful prey.'"[15]

Given these sorts of developments, it is not surprising that modern technological societies have witnessed an epidemic of depression and other anxiety-related disorders. Even as the technological milieu places more and ever-greater demands on human beings to adapt to its machine rhythms and logic, it seems to leave us increasingly without recourse and largely powerless to protest.[16] Furthermore, given that the Internet is even now being expressly designed to distract us, it is hardly surprising that modern men and women are increasingly falling victim to a variety of psychological disorders commonly grouped under the headings of "attention" and/or "attachment."[17] Just as the public workplace has become increasingly anonymous, so the devices that we have increasingly turned to in our private lives—for consolation, as it were—are interfering with the face-to-face conversations that make for mental health by nurturing empathy and intimacy. Although we are apparently connected with each other within vast social networks, the truth may be, as the title of one recent book suggests, that we are really only "alone together."[18]

The incidence of more serious psychiatric disorders appears to be increasing in our technological milieu as well, particularly disorders that exhibit a psychotic break with ordinary reality.[19] While the loss of oneself into unreality has always been possible, never before have we been so surrounded by technologies—indeed by entire industries—that have been expressly designed to encourage this loss. Never before has it been technically feasible for the possibilities of "hyperreality" to so convincingly eclipse the necessities of ordinary reality.[20]

Of course, this litany could be lengthened. We could also discuss the dehumanizing impact of cyberbullying, cybercrime, and other illicit uses of networked digital technologies; our tendency online to interact only with those who share our own views;[21] the rapid proliferation of "fake news" and the implications of disinformation for democracy;[22] the possibilities of cyber warfare; the demise of humanities curricula in favor of STEM programs; and the like. The point is not to exaggerate all of this, and neither is it to dispose of the many and remarkable benefits of modern machine technologies and systems. Nevertheless, everywhere we look today in our technological milieu, ordinary embodied human existence in the world appears to be at risk.

Banner rightly reminds us that moral theology should encourage self-examination and the evaluation of our way of living "against notions of the good, or the right, or the fitting" in order to offer what he refers to as a "therapeutic" and "pastoral" engagement with modern life.[23] That people do not, in any number of respects, appear to be coping particularly well with new technologies may be evidence of the kind of "unconscious moral code" to which Banner refers.[24] Indeed, this may be just the kind of social malaise that moral theology could use social anthropology to address. Whereas social anthropology raises the concern and, in this case, narrates the disorder, moral theology could offer a therapeutic response aimed at recovering those aspects of embodied human being that modern technologies are undermining.

## What Interprets These Developments?

In his classic work, *Technics and Civilization* (1934), Lewis Mumford contended that one of the crucial characteristics of modern machine technology is what he termed *automatism*.[25] Modern machines are designed and developed to function *automatically* and self-sufficiently, which is to say, to operate in a manner unimpeded—as much as possible—by human frailties, inconsistencies, and irrationalities. Marx was among the first to comment on this development in the early decades of the nineteenth century.[26] The world-historical importance of modern industry, Marx observed, was that it had succeeded in breaking the productive process down into a series of separately analyzable steps and had thereby freed itself from the capricious, unpredictable, and unreliable influence of human beings. While human beings continued to be involved in the industrial process—as owners, managers, and workers—the influence of individual human persons *as such* was minimized within what Marx called the factory system. Indeed, it was only as human influences had been thus marginalized that modern industry had been freed up to take full advantage of modern scientific findings.

The minimization of the human element within the modern factory system, as well as the characteristic automatism of modern technics, are, of course, aspects of what Max Weber termed rationalization, the master process that all but defines modern societies.[27] "Rational" conduct, Weber explained, entails deliberately choosing those means best suited to realizing a desired end or purpose. "Rationalization" refers to the submission of a particular practice—say, that of science, or medicine, or law, or accounting, or manufacturing, and so on—to rational methods that have been expressly designed to produce desired results, in effect enabling us to predictably control some aspect of reality. In contrast to their "traditional" counterparts, modern rationalized methods and procedures can be counted on—or at least so we have, in modern times, come to assume—to yield the fruit of practical mastery, and modern societies have come to be driven and characterized by the development and implementation of methods, procedures, systems, and techniques that stand the best chance of producing such things as health, prosperity, security, comfort, and convenience. This whole process, Weber contended, was—and continues to be—animated by the simple but powerful belief that we can, in principle, "master all things by calculation."[28]

The rationalization of modern life is also—and perhaps supremely—evident in the ubiquitous role that money plays in modern societies. Money is not simply an instrument useful for measuring rational effectiveness but is itself the end to which modern means are very often adjusted. Indeed, Mumford believed that "pecuniary pressure" is the essential clue to modern technological development. It is precisely the modern preoccupation with money, Mumford stressed, that interprets the seemingly automatic and uncontrollable dynamism of the whole modern technological system.[29]

Needless to say, the rationalization of modern life has been extraordinarily successful, providing us with a great deal of mastery over our practical and material circumstances and yielding the secular fruits of health, prosperity, comfort, security, and convenience. Yet the process has also been quite profoundly dehumanizing—and necessarily so, for a good deal of the volatility and unpredictability that must systematically be eliminated from the equations that link means to ends derive from human personality. As Jacques Ellul observed in his celebrated study of the technological society, this dehumanizing tendency must inexorably continue: "Every intervention of man, however educated or used to machinery he may be, is a source of error and unpredictability."[30] "The combination of man and technique," Ellul noted, "is a happy one only if man has no responsibility."[31]

Ironically, the process of rationalization appears to be the chief culprit behind the oft-lamented inversion of means and ends, for rational mastery requires life to be divided up into discrete problems for which rational and technical solutions can then be devised. Yet when life is divided up in this way, we lose sight of it as a whole—in effect, losing sight of the forest for the trees. As Ellul commented in *The Technological Bluff* (1990),

> And what is so reassuring as the rational? . . . All that we ask of people in this society must be rational. It is rational to consume more, to change immediately what is worn out, to acquire more information, to satisfy an increasing number of desires. Constant growth is rational for our economic system. We can take the ordinary actions of 99 percent of the population in a so-called advanced country and we shall find that the key to them is always rationality.[32]

That the rational actions of 99 percent of the populations of so-called advanced countries are even now contributing to global warming and exhausting the earth's natural resources, while simultaneously hastening that time when real people are no longer required within modern technological systems, suggests that the process of rationalization may not actually be very rational, or at least not from the standpoint of the purpose of human thriving.

Finally, we should note that the process of rationalization has been inevitably secularizing. Technical means and calculations now play the roles—and apparently play them much more predictably and reliably—that were once believed to be the prerogative of the gods. Shaped now by science, technology, and industrial capitalism, the modern world has quite literally become an artificial world, one that is much more obviously a human construction than the world of our ancestors. In the modern world, themes of human choice, responsibility, and control have become paramount. It is not difficult to see how all of this artificiality has created an intellectual climate within which traditional religious faith has become increasingly implausible.

Modern secularity has, in turn, made it difficult to question the relentless progression of rationalization on religious grounds, and, in the absence of substantive religious criticism, practical rationality has become, as Ellul's comments above suggest, something of an end in itself. As Robert K. Merton commented in the foreword to Ellul's seminal work *The Technological Society*, our modern technological civilization is characterized by the "quest for continually improved means to carelessly examined ends."[33]

## Why Not More Protest?

Modern machine technology appears to have arisen out of a novel understanding of the natural world and consequently—perhaps simultaneously—out of a new understanding of our place within, and our relationship to, nature. We seem to have become mechanical in our outlook roughly a century and a half before we began to develop the techniques and machinery adequate to early modern aspirations after the "mastery and possession" of nature.[34] Having once begun to develop new techniques, instruments, and eventually machines on the basis of this new scientific understanding, the mastery and possession of nature—including human nature—appeared increasingly justifiable in terms of the productivity and profitability that the new methods and machinery quickly made possible.

The powerful synthesis of scientific knowing with technological making is what sets modern technology apart from traditional tool making and technologizing, as ingenious and sophisticated as both very often were. Modern technology consists not simply of the application of scientific understanding to specific technical problems but also of the combination of scientific knowing and technological making such that it gives rise to a new and distinctively modern understanding of what the world is as well as of who we are within the world. As the Canadian political philosopher George Grant has observed in this connection, modern machine technology "is not simply an extension of human making through the power of a perfected science, but it is a new account of what it is to know and make in which both activities are changed by their co-penetration."[35] The thrust of this new account of what it is to know and to make is neatly schematized in the fateful progression from the objectification of nature, through the dissection and mathematization of discrete natural processes, to the technological manipulation of these processes. This is captured in the term *enframing*, that peculiar way of seeing things that Heidegger believed to be the essence of modern technology.[36] As a result, our world often appears to us as a neutral field of objects that stand ready for whatever uses we might devise for them. Within this worldview, furthermore, we tend to take it for granted that we are largely, if not entirely, free to determine the uses to which we will put the resources, both natural and human, that we find standing ready for use.

Unfortunately, the technological worldview is one in which genuine self-knowledge—which would be necessary for the wise use of technology—has become deeply elusive. In part, this is because the modern ethos has long been plagued by perplexing dualisms between scientific knowers and what is actually known, between minds and bodies, between selves and others. These persistent dichotomies undermine the possibility of self-knowledge by obscuring the nature of the relationships we have to ourselves, to others, to the natural world, and to God.

Genuine self-knowledge has also become elusive within modern technological culture because we have ourselves been objectified within it. We seem to have become objects even to ourselves. Whatever the reasons, in the absence of genuine self-knowledge, automatic machine technology has, in effect, been set loose to develop according to its own intrinsic logic. Newly empowered by vast networks of powerful digital computers and driven along by the bloodless requirements of the money economy, modern machine technology is now trending away from ordinary embodied human existence at ever-increasing speed. The assumption implicit in modern scientific understanding that nature is largely indifferent to human interests and aspirations has contributed to the emergence of a technological environment that has become increasingly and explicitly unresponsive to the hopes and fears of ordinary human beings.

And so modern machine technology has left us in a quandary. On the one hand, we cannot apparently live without it, for we have come to depend on the material and social conditions that our technologies have made and continue to make possible. On the other hand, neither can we truly live with modern machine technology, for within the technological purview we are ourselves objects that stand ready for use within systems that have been devised for the most part by others. To frame the dilemma somewhat differently, we have come to believe that we possess a right to technologically facilitated well-being and that anything that threatens this well-being thereby threatens freedom and human progress. Yet this same "progress" has by now—perhaps irreparably—despoiled the natural environment and seems to permit less and less room for ordinary embodied human existence, as Banner's Alder Hey example amply demonstrates.[37]

That modern secular culture has not offered much in the way of resistance to the dehumanizing thrust of automatic machine development is unfortunate but understandable. Given the material fruits of technological development and its alluring promises of more, better, faster, and easier; given the powerful monetary interests that attach to creative/destructive innovation; and given that the modern mind remains—Romantic protests not withstanding—mechanical in its outlook, it is not surprising that modern secular thought has been largely acquiescent in the face of recent technological developments.

That the Christian churches have not offered more considered resistance to modern machine development is, however, a tragedy. For the endorsement of ordinary embodied human being is one of the core truths of the Christian religion. True, the Christian hopes for salvation from this world and for eternal life in a world to come, but this hope has never—at least within the broad tradition of Christian orthodoxy—been understood in such a way as to disparage ordinary embodied human existence. Neither has the church ever kept silent in the face of gnostic promises of things like "transhumanism," that notion that human consciousness must eventually migrate out of our bodies and into machinery. On the contrary, if the eternal Word of God "became flesh and dwelt among us," as the apostle John declares, this confers staggering value on ordinary fleshly existence.

That modern technological development appears now to be trending away from ordinary embodied human existence should have triggered alarms in our churches. That it has not is puzzling. What appears to account for the church's silence is forgetfulness. Our churches seem to have simply forgotten how central embodied human existence is within the Gospel of Jesus Christ. Here we seem to have succumbed, along with most other "traditional" religious communities, to that peculiar amnesia fostered by the process of modernization. As sociologist Danièle Hervieu-Leger observed, "The growth of secularization and the loss of total memory in societies without a history and without a past coincide completely; the dislocation of the structures of religion's plausibility in the modern world works in parallel with the advance of rationalization and successive stages in the crumbling of collective memory."[38] Contrary to received secular opinion, Hervieu-Leger contends that modern societies have neither outgrown nor found secular substitutes for religion, nor are they more rational than traditional societies. Rather, they have simply become "amnesiac," in some cases repudiating and in others simply failing to maintain the "chain of memory" that binds them to their traditions.[39] For modern Christian churches, this has meant forgetting, among other things, the shape and implications of basic Christian theology. Having forgotten this theology, it has become all but impossible for the church to speak prophetically or, in Banner's terms, therapeutically into modern society and culture about the dehumanizing trajectory of modern technological development.

Our response now to the dehumanizing arc of automatic machine technology must, in the first instance, be one of remembering. Christians must seek to remember why, from the point of view of our belief in an *embodied* Savior, this might be a problem. Even more crucially, Christians must try to remember why, from the standpoint of the Christian religion, both the mechanical world picture and the modern habit of enframing must be supplanted with an outlook and practices that celebrate God's good creation and our particular human vocation within it.

## What We Need to Do

So what can we do in view of the disembodying thrust of modern technological development? Well, in the first instance (and at the very least), we can determine to take modern technology's long-standing promise to "disburden" us from the toil and drudgery of the "traditional" past with several large grains of salt.[40] While this promise has been kept in a great many ways, automatic machine technology has also saddled us with the additional—and in certain respects far heavier—burdens that stem from disengagement from one another as well as disengagement from ordinary physical reality.

Of course, it is conceivable that these new burdens are due to the fact that our technologies are not yet good enough and that newer and better technologies will successfully reconnect us with each other and with reality. Yet this is doubtful, for, as Borgmann has noted, whatever newer and better technologies lie just around the corner will still be made available to us as commodities to be purchased and consumed and, as such, will probably not demand too much from us in the way of commitment, discipline, or skill.[41] New technologies may be more entertaining and diverting, but this will likely only lead to the further scattering of our attention and atrophy of our capacities.[42] Of course, new technologies might very well make our lives better in certain respects. Yet unless they somehow reconnect us to each other and to our world, they will only exacerbate the sorts of problems we have enumerated above.

In addition to looking askance at technology's promises, the single most important thing Christians must do in light of the divergence of modern technological development away from ordinary embodied existence is to remember and to announce the truth of Christ's incarnation and its astonishing endorsement of ordinary embodied human being. Indeed, the importance of the incarnation can hardly be overstated. It is the foundation of the "Christian imagination of the human" that Banner so frequently invokes.[43] That the eternal Word, the One who was with God in the beginning and who *is* God, the One through whom all things were made, that this One was—and remains—enfleshed in a human body confers shocking significance on embodied human existence. True, Christians believe that our mortal bodies will one day be clothed with immortality and that we will be raised in glory and power and in the Spirit (1 Cor. 15). Yet the eyewitness testimony that is the basis for Christian faith affirms that the risen Christ, "the firstborn from among the dead" (Col. 1:17), was a recognizably human being who walked with his disciples along the road to Emmaus, who conversed with them at length, and who ate fish and bread with them by the Sea of Galilee. The risen Christ was not *trans*human. Rather, Christians believe that he was (and is) the first *fully* human person, and he clearly moved within the confines of ordinary space and time. The apostolic testimony further attests that Christ was taken up bodily into heaven, where he is now seated at the right hand of the Father. It is an embodied Christ who will, finally, as the Apostles' Creed states, "come again in glory to judge both the living and the dead."

The implications of Christ's incarnation spread out in all directions. In the first instance, it affirms the primacy of the ordinary, embodied, face-to-face, unmediated relations that we have with each other. It is in these relations that human beings will be and become most fully themselves. And so we can ask, Are our technologies enhancing ordinary, embodied, face-to-face relations, perhaps by creating or protecting time and space for these relations? Are our devices making these relations more vivid, more meaningful, more empathic? Are our technologies enabling us to become *more* of ourselves? Are they enhancing our embodied experience of and relationship with others and the world? If they are, we ought to employ them with deep gratitude.

Of course, it may also be the case that our technologies are in other respects undermining our relations. Our technologies may be interposing themselves between us, making our interaction and communication less meaningful. Our technological systems and devices may, in other words, be doing things for us but all the while leaving us either unchanged or even diminished. If this is the case, we should seek either to reform the systems in question or refrain from using them. Will we disagree on such things? We almost certainly will, and we must make room for disagreement. Still, keeping the incarnation consciously in view should help to guard us against some of the more gnostic tendencies within our technological milieu.

In addition, Christ's incarnation affirms the value and standing not only of embodied human being but of created reality as a whole, ordered as it is by space, time, and what we commonly call place. The gnostic longing after some presumably more spiritual or otherwise better reality might once, prior to the incarnation, have been plausible, but it is so no longer.[44] On the contrary, the Christian religion has always asserted this reality is redeemed in Christ, that salvation is not from this world but rather *of* this world. This, to use Banner's terms, is the "counter logic" it narrates. And so we must ask again, Do our technologies enhance ordinary reality? Do they give us time to think? to experience? to reflect? to listen? time for each other? Do our technologies ground or root us in place? Do they enable us to dwell richly in those places where we are most at home? If so, again, we should use them enthusiastically and gratefully.

Yet if we find that our technologies are compressing time such that it is becoming unlivable, and if we find that our technologies are somehow flattening what were once places for us into mere spaces, then we should either reform them or refrain from using them. The evaluations we make along these lines need not be vexed or complicated, and the decisions we make in respect to various technologies may well vary from one of us to the next. Yet in the current climate of technological enthusiasm in which we are encouraged to eagerly anticipate—and save up for—whatever is coming "next," basic questions about the impact of our technologies on ordinary lived experience are rarely asked at all. Christians, of all people, should be asking these questions. Just raising them is to be "salt and light" in the current environment.

One Christian thinker who has encouraged his readers to ask basic questions in respect to modern technology is Albert Borgmann, who has argued that our use of technological devices—despite their promises to make an expanded range of things and possibilities conveniently available to us—has frequently only resulted in the loss of skills, habits, and shared practices that once graced and oriented our lives.[45] Under the headings of focal things and focal practices, Borgmann has sought to encourage his readers to consider whether their use of technological devices has actually enabled them to develop the disciplines, habits, and skills that make for an enriched engagement with reality.[46] If so, he reasons, then by all means continue to use them. But if our devices are somehow undermining our engagement with reality, then he suggests that we reconsider their use. In doing so, we might apply what we could call the "Borgmann test." We know that we have arrived at a focal practice when we can answer no to the following three questions: Is there anywhere else I would rather be? Is there anything else I would rather be doing? Is there anyone else I would rather be with? If we can honestly answer no to all three questions, it is likely that we have landed on what, for us, is a focal practice, a practice that somehow enhances our engagement with and experience of reality. An additional clue for identifying such a practice is when we find ourselves thinking "This is something I will remember." We need to pay attention to these practices and not let the use of technology undermine them.

We must also remember that while humanly developed technologies may well be therapeutically beneficial in temporarily restoring our bodies to health, the Christian religion teaches that technologies become particularly problematic whenever they promise to do more than this. Human ingenuity, as remarkable as it is, cannot overcome the consequences of human sin, and we must be deeply suspicious of technologies that promise, even if only implicitly, to resolve the root difficulties that attend the human condition. As clever and sophisticated as it may well be, modern machine technology remains a human work and is therefore subject to the "thorns and thistles" of unintended consequences, frustration, and futility. Indeed, given its scale and scope as well as the hubris with which it is often deployed, it is not surprising that modern technologies regularly produce unintentionally negative consequences that dwarf the problems they were originally developed to solve.

Finally, from the point of view of the Christian religion, the hoped-for consummation of all things will not necessarily entail a return to the original garden, nor a reversal or unmaking of all that we have made by technical ingenuity. On the contrary, the Christian hope for the resurrection of the body—following on from the resurrection of Jesus Christ, the "first born from among the dead"—means that much of the work that has been (and is even now being) done "in the body" will, in the power of the Holy Spirit, find its place in the coming kingdom of God. In this connection, we might suspect that the work that will last is work that restores and enriches ordinary embodied human existence, work that quickens and awakens us to created reality and, in so doing, better enables us to admire and love created things as we were originally intended to love them. Putting this in Banner's terms, a therapeutic moral theology that is engaged with the embodied practices of everyday life can help us to remember who we are, where we find ourselves, and the kind of work we have been called to do within God's good creation, all of which would go some distance toward enabling us to properly evaluate modern technological development. This will require us to repent of enframing as well as of autonomous self-construction, but it will also begin to make possible a new way of seeing and being. And although the creation eagerly awaits the future revelation of the sons and daughters of God (Rom. 8:19), we can surely begin—and on the basis of what we *already* know—to, as the poet Wendell Berry so vividly puts it, "practice resurrection."[47]

## Notes

The material from this chapter is taken from Craig M. Gay, *Modern Technology and the Human Future*. Copyright (c) 2018 by Craig M. Gay. Used by permission of InterVarsity Press, P.O. Box 1400, Downers Grove, IL 60515, USA. www.ivpress.com.

1. Nicholas Carr, *The Glass Cage: Automation and Us* (New York: W. W. Norton, 2014), 215.

2. Michael Banner, *The Ethics of Everyday Life: Moral Theology, Social Anthropology, and the Imagination of the Human* (Oxford: Oxford University Press, 2014), 3.

3. Banner, 3.

4. Peter L. Berger, Brigitte Berger, and Hansfried Kellner, *The Homeless Mind: Modernization and Consciousness* (New York: Vintage, 1974).

5. Berger, Berger, and Kellner, 26.

6. Berger, Berger, and Kellner, 33.

7. See, for example, Carr, *Glass Cage*.

8. Carr 110–11 cites a Harvard Business School study conducted by James Bright in the 1950s.

9. Carr, 43.

10. Albert Borgmann, *Technology and the Character of Contemporary Life: A Philosophical Inquiry* (Chicago: University of Chicago Press, 1984), 118.

11. George Dyson, cited in Carr, *Glass Cage*, 113.

12. Carr, 78.

13. A term originally coined by John Maynard Keynes in "Economic Possibilities for Our Grandchildren," in *Essays in Persuasion* (New York: W. W. Norton, 1963), 358–73.

14. See Nicholas Carr, *The Big Switch: Rewiring the World from Edison to Google* (New York: W. W. Norton, 2013).

15. Bryan Appleyard, "The New Luddites: Why Former Digital Prophets Are Turning against Tech," *New Statesman*, August 29, 2014, http://www.newstatesman.com/sci-tech/2014/08/new-luddites-why-former-digital-prophets-are-turning-against-tech.

16. Jacques Ellul, *Perspectives on Our Age: Jacques Ellul Speaks on His Life and Work*, ed. William H. Vanderburg (Concord, ON: Anansi, 1981), 89.

17. See Susan Philips, *The Cultivated Life: From Ceaseless Striving to Receiving Joy* (Downers Grove, IL: IVP Books, 2015).

18. See Sherry Turkle, *Alone Together: Why We Expect More from Technology and Less from Each Other* (New York: Basic Books, 2011).

19. See Ian McGilchrist, *The Master and His Emissary: The Divided Brain and the Making of the Western World* (New Haven, CT: Yale University Press, 2009), 407.

20. See Albert Borgmann, "Matter and Science in an Age of Science and Technology," *Crux* 47, no. 4 (2011): 36–44.

21. See Emerson T. Brooking and P. W. Singer, "War Goes Viral: How Social Media Is Being Weaponized," *The Atlantic*, November 2016, 70–83. "For all the hope that comes from connecting with new people and new ideas," Brooking and Singer write, "researchers have found that online behavior is dominated by 'homophily': a tendency to listen to and associate with people like yourself, and to exclude outsiders" (74).

22. See, for example, Niall Ferguson, *The Square and the Tower: Networks and Power from the Freemasons to Facebook* (New York: Penguin, 2018).

23. Banner, *Ethics of Everyday Life*, 13, 23.

24. Banner, 201, quoting Lesley Sharp.

25. Lewis Mumford, *Technics and Civilization* (London: Routledge & Sons, 1934), 10.

26. See Nathan Rosenberg's discussion of Marx in *Inside the Black Box: Technology and Economics* (Cambridge: Cambridge University Press, 1982), 34.

27. See, for example, Stephen Kalberg's helpful overview of Weber's understanding of "rationalization" in "Max Weber's Types of Rationality: Cornerstones for the Analysis of Rationalization Processes in History," *American Journal of Sociology* 85, no. 5 (1980): 1145–79.

28. Max Weber, "Science as a Vocation," in *From Max Weber*, ed. Hans Heinrich Gerth and Mills C. Wright (New York: Oxford University Press, 1946), 139. In his chapter on pregnancy and birth, "Being Born and Being Born Again," Banner cites Robbie Davis-Floyd's observation that "technology has become 'technocratic'" because it is deployed by technical experts "who deploy the technology technocratically" in order to manage society (Banner, *Ethics of Everyday Life*, 66).

29. Lewis Mumford, *The Myth of the Machine: Pentagon of Power* (New York: Harcourt, Brace & Jovanovich, 1964), 169.

30. Jacques Ellul, *The Technological Society* (New York: Vintage, 1964), 136.

31. Ellul, 136.

32. Jacques Ellul, *The Technological Bluff* (Grand Rapids, MI: Eerdmans, 1990), 161.

33. Robert K. Merton, foreword to Ellul, *Technological Society*, vi.

34. Mumford's discussion of this is particularly helpful; see "Cultural Preparations," in *Technics*, 9.

35. George Grant, *Technology and Justice* (Concord, ON: Anansi, 1986), 13.

36. See Martin Heidegger, "The Question concerning Technology," in *The Question concerning Technology and Other Essays*, ed. William Lovitt (New York: Harper & Row, 1977), 3–35.

37. See Banner, *Ethics of Everyday Life*, 22, 155–62.

38. Danièle Hervieu-Leger, *Religion as a Chain of Memory* (New Brunswick, NJ: Rutgers University Press, 2000), 127.

39. Hervieu-Leger, *Religion as a Chain*, from abstract on back cover.

40. See Borgmann, *Technology and the Character*, 35.

41. Borgmann, 151.

42. Borgmann.

43. See Banner, *Ethics of Everyday Life*, 204.

44. See Oliver O'Donovan, *Resurrection of Moral Order: An Outline for Evangelical Ethics* (Grand Rapids, MI: Eerdmans, 1986), 14; see also Oliver O'Donovan, "The Loss of a Sense of Place," in *Bonds of Imperfection: Christian Politics Past and Present*, ed. Oliver O'Donovan and Joan Lockwood O'Donovan (Grand Rapids, MI: Eerdmans, 2004), 296–320.

45. Borgmann, *Technology and the Character*, 157.

46. Borgmann, 182.

47. Wendell Berry, "Manifesto: The Mad Farmer Liberation Front," in *The Country of Marriage* (New York: Harcourt Brace Jovanovich, 1973).

# 8

## ON NEW NEW THINGS

---

### WORK AND CHRISTIAN THOUGHT IN FLEXIBLE CAPITALISM

### PHILIP LORISH

W<small>E ARE NEARLY NINETY YEARS</small> on from the publication of John Maynard Keynes's short but important essay "Economic Possibilities for Our Grand-children."[1] Published in 1930, it begins by dismissing what Keynes calls a "bad attack of economic pessimism." This pessimism comes in two opposing forms: the "pessimism of the revolutionaries who think that things are so bad that nothing can save us but violent change, and the pessimism of the reactionaries who consider the balance of our economic and social life so precarious that we must risk no experiments." Against this, Keynes decides to "disembarrass" himself "of short views and take wings into the future," and what he sees in that future is a world wherein the "economic problem" has been solved."[2]

For Keynes, the interesting question was not about economic development but what he described as our permanent problem: what will we do with the leisure of our abundance? Once the economic problem is solved (or within reach), "must we not expect a general 'nervous breakdown'" roughly similar to the kind he sees within the non-working spouses of "well-to-do classes" in England and the United States? When they are "deprived of the spur of economic necessity," they suffer insofar as they cannot find any aspect of the life of leisure sufficiently *amusing*. They do not fully appreciate or somehow cannot see "the art of life itself," as Keynes puts it, and therefore live a kind of numbed, impoverished existence.[3]

There are provisos to Keynes's prediction, of course. He was hopeful but not naive. Global conflict could get in the way of economic progress. So too could an inability to control our population or an imbalance in the rate of accumulation. Given this, "the time for all this is not yet." Rather, "avarice and usury and precaution must be our gods for a little longer still," for "only they can lead us out of the tunnel of economic necessity into daylight."[4] And that daylight is marked by something looking a lot like the abolition of work—that is, the conclusion of the long, arduous struggle for self-sufficiency through labor.

This chapter addresses the question of what moral theologians can and should say about work in our current social order. My view is that any morally serious assessment of work in our time should attend to both the effects of a macroeconomic shift toward what Benjamin Snyder and others have called "flexible capitalism" and the moral norms emanating from Silicon Valley. When these two features of our current moment come into proper focus, moral theologians will find themselves within a historical period not too dissimilar from the flurry of work produced by the church at the end of the twentieth century. Whether it be the emergence of Catholic social thought or the relief and reform movements spawned by the Protestant Social Gospel, at this point in time the churches found a way to make use of their conceptual and pastoral resources to lead a broad-based social effort to curb the most inhumane features of an incredibly powerful economic order for the common good. And they offered their counsel to the world by paying sustained attention to the lived experiences of citizens of that economic order, articulating just how that order had come into being and providing some basic account of what could and should be done. It is time, in other words, for an account of the new new things.

## Sweat without Security: The Shift to Flexible Capitalism

In recent years, labor historians, sociologists, and political theorists have been grasping for common language to describe one large and unavoidable shift in the nature of work.[5] Seemingly, the grand bargain between capital and labor in the "managerial capitalism" of the mid–twentieth century has been called off. In the so-called Fordist economy, workers exchanged their fidelity for security, their daily labor for the tacit promise of stability. Assuming a baseline level of competence, once a worker was credentialed and brought into a company at an entry-level position, there were discernible and obvious paths for growth and, crucially, the presumption of continued employment. The entailments of this bargain were many, not least of which is the fact that *obtaining*—not *retaining*—a good job was the central objective of maturation, the central feature of growing up. For this reason, all the credentialing agents and experiences of youth and emerging adulthood culminated in establishing a career. There was sweat, to be sure, but for blue collar and white collar workers alike, sweat was exchanged for security.[6]

But this deal is either in the process of being called off or, more likely, has already been called off altogether. In its place is the rise of the contingent worker and the moral order it represents.

In March, 2016, economists Lawrence Katz and Alan Krueger published a short paper titled "The Rise and Nature of Alternative Work Arrangements in the United

States, 1995–2015."[7] What prompted the paper was the fact that although economists, journalists, and pundits have given the impression that a higher percentage of American workers are, in fact, in alternative or "nonstandard" work relationships, the last major survey by the US Bureau of Labor Statistics took place in 2005, prior to the market crash and "Great Recession" of 2008 and the emergence of the newfound "gig economy."[8] Their conclusion is straightforward and revealing: "The percentage of workers engaged in alternative work arrangements—defined as temporary help agency workers, on-call workers, contract company workers, and independent contractors or freelancers—rose from 10.1 percent in February 2005 to 15.8 percent in late 2015."[9]

While this statistic alone should establish the fact that a substantial shift in the nature of work has taken place, two further data points support the observation. First, while the increase in contingent work between 2005 and 2015 is itself quite dramatic, it is even more so when we realize that the Bureau of Labor Statistics reported a near-negligible rise in contingent work arrangements for the ten years prior. So the rise of contingent work relations is fairly recent. But the importance of this rise comes into prominence when Katz and Krueger place the rise of contingent work against the backdrop of stagnant growth in the so-called standard labor market.[10] When viewed in the context of stagnant growth in traditional forms of employment, Katz and Krueger come to the "striking implication" that "all of the net employment growth in the US economy from 2005 to 2015 appears to have occurred in alternative work arrangements."[11]

Some commentators are prone to place this entire shift toward alternative work at the feet of the emerging app-based "platform economy." Because the platform economy has such strong cheerleaders and seems to be on an upward trend, it deserves sustained attention when we consider the future of work.[12] But according to Katz and Krueger's analysis, from a macroeconomic standpoint, the growth in the platform economy between 2005 and 2015 accounts for a very small percentage of contingent work. The major shift was not primarily from legacy institutions to new, disruptive, emergent platforms; rather, it was primarily *within* legacy institutions themselves. It was, in effect, the difference between a local school employing a custodian to keep the school clean and a local school contracting with a cleaning service that hires contingent workers on temporary contracts to clean the school. In either case, the school is cleaned and jobs are filled, but when this experience is repeated and extended across a variety of sectors, the bargain of sweat for security is broken decisively. And, according to Katz and Krueger, that rupture largely *preceded* the emergence of the kind of "gig economy" in which custodians become Uber drivers on nights and weekends.[13]

Following Benjamin Snyder, I think the macroeconomic shift is best characterized as a move from managerial capitalism to "flexible capitalism." For Snyder, flexibility is the preferred term because it capably "summons images of movement, change, and unsettledness."[14] In the first chapter of *The Disrupted Workplace: Time and the Moral Order of Flexible Capitalism*, Snyder identifies three essential features of this emergent moral order, each of which expresses itself as a preference over and against the moral norms that established the bargain between capital and labor in the postwar economy. First is a preference for improvisation over planning; second, for fluidity over fixity; and third, for abstraction over concreteness. Given their importance, a word on each is in order.[15]

The preference for improvisation over planning expresses itself most directly in the establishment of "core" and "periphery" employees. Because companies are increasingly distancing themselves from the kinds of mass production that responded to much more uniformity in consumer demand in mid-century societies, "flexible capitalism favors arrangements that can respond to rapid and unpredictable change."[16] In terms of labor, gone are "bloated" workforces, which are replaced by "agile" and "nimble" teams.

The result is the displacing of the forty-hour workweek, which Snyder describes as the preference for fluidity over fixity. Crucially, this displacement affects both sides of the core/periphery employee divide. As Snyder makes plain, "*core* employees, made up of mostly skilled professionals, receive a lot of investment from their employers, including a great deal of decision-making power, so that they will align themselves with the goals of the company and work passionately."[17] As a result, these employees are frequently granted all the benefits of "flexible workplaces"—most of which amount to the expectation that they will always be working. On the other side of the core/periphery divide sits lower-skilled workers with lower pay. Flexibility exists for these workers as well, albeit in a quite different form. As multiple recent studies have shown, the insecurity low-wage workers now feel can be attributed just as much to the irregularity of their working schedules as to their relative lack of work. Low-wage workers are "finding it difficult to get enough hours with high enough wages to make ends meet, but they are also finding it difficult to get *regular* and *predictable* hours."[18] While many of us are grateful to have the freedom to end work at four o'clock in order to coach a child's soccer team, knowing full well that we will return to our inboxes after the kids are asleep and perhaps again before they wake up, there is a shadow side to flexibility, and it disproportionately affects the working poor.

The third and final feature of flexible capitalism is what Snyder describes as the preference of abstraction over concreteness. By this he means the emergence of the "knowledge economy" and its displacing effect on other areas of work. "Flexible capitalism goes beyond an emphasis on the flexibility of schedules and contracts," he writes. "It also involves flexibility in the actual stuff of work." In his analysis, the "objects of work" across multiple sectors of the economy are now functionally the same—emails, spreadsheets, codes, reports, and so on.[19]

While Snyder is happy to theorize this shift and leans heavily on a variety of social theorists, the main task of his ethnographic study of three kinds of contemporary workers—truck drivers, finance professionals, and the unemployed—is to display just how these elements of flexible capitalism show themselves time and again, most often on the backs of contemporary workers. With exquisite detail, Snyder highlights how, in our moment, workers, work itself, and what he calls "work-time" have become flexibilized.[20] To a substantial degree, this is because Silicon Valley wanted it that way.[21]

## Working in the Valley of Dreams

The setting is important. I had come to Silicon Valley to visit James, a friend who had become a source. My intuition was that if I wanted to understand the massive shifts in the labor markets and the changes in the lived experience of everyday work, I should pay sustained attention to the moral norms, work culture, and rhetorical innovations emanating from Silicon Valley. And so, across the street from the coffee shop where James launched the app that would later be acquired for an unfathomable sum of money, we sit over a delicious lamb vindaloo for an unrestrained discussion of Silicon Valley and the future of work.

From the start, James tells me that the world of Silicon Valley is not too dissimilar from an undergraduate philosophy seminar—the current hot topic being the nature of distributive justice and various proposals for a universal basic income. Major differences exist, of course, the most glaring being that the "students" were now multimillionaires and there were no teachers, no grades, and not even close to sufficient attention span to read whole books. But *ideas* are the currency of the place, he tells me, before saying that the real difference between "guys like him" and the "next level" is whether you rent your private plane or own it outright.

Our first topic of extended discussion was just that: inequality. More specifically, we were discussing Harry Frankfurt's "doctrine of sufficiency." As Frankfurt sees it, if we care about using language precisely and locate the moral harm of extreme inequality in the right place, we should not be worried that two people's incomes are unequal; we should be concerned that each person "has enough."[22] Morally speaking, inequality is not really the problem in Western societies; *poverty* is. James was familiar with the argument and shared Frankfurt's view.

The issue, he thought, was that the main way that most Americans ensure they have "enough" is through employment, and, as I learned during our discussion, steady, meaningful, well-compensated work is not necessarily at the center of Silicon Valley's vision of a well-lived life. Technological development is, and where technological development and "full employment" clash, technological development wins.

James explained the implications of technologies for mass employment through his current work as the project lead for one of the largest divisions of a company that generates roughly $75 million per day.

"We're on track to reach a billion users in 2016," he told me. "With a staff of 100. That's scale; and that's what technology can do."

"You ever read a short piece called 'Economic Possibilities for Our Grandchildren?'" I responded.

"Nope," he said, "but give me the argument and I'll tell you what I think." When I concluded my synopsis with a brief editorial comment on how Keynes prefigured a strand of economic utopianism that was obviously inadequate and likely wrong, he responded with a question.

"Keynes wrote that in 1930, you said?"

"Yep. Between the wars and just after the crash."

"Right. And did he say much about technological developments?"

"Not that I can remember, though he was concerned about population control and the massively destructive effects of war."

"Right. And the number was one hundred years you said?"

"Yep."

"Seems about right to me. Fourteen years to go. The iPhone is not even ten years old yet and think of what it has done. You're gonna be amazed by what is coming next. Trust me."

## Collaboration, Disruption, Optimization

James, like the "Fairchildren" of mid-century Silicon Valley lore, was born and raised in the middle part of the country and educated in an elite university on the East Coast. After making the move to the West Coast, he can no longer envision living anywhere else. Whether he fully appreciates it or not, his story trades on well-established narratives that present life in Silicon Valley as a fundamental alternative to life "back East."

The three terms that best capture the development and ethos of Silicon Valley are *collaboration*, *disruption*, and *optimization*. While there is little uniformity in their use, these terms have become a kind of currency within Silicon Valley, in large part because so few dissenters exist.[23] They also represent three distinct epochs within Silicon Valley marked by the main products that emerged in those periods: *collaboration* representing the essential premise behind the development of semiconductors in the late 1950s and 1960s; *disruption* being the catch-all term within the world of personal computing and the first wave of Internet-based technologies; and, finally, *optimization* being the word for the app-based economy centered on the smartphone.

AnnaLee Saxenian is the first and most prominent scholar to highlight the role of collaboration in Silicon Valley. In her comparative account of the cultures of Silicon Valley and its chief rival, the Route 128 corridor outside of Boston, she attributes the successes of Silicon Valley almost exclusively to different approaches to collaboration in entrepreneurial endeavors.[24] Back East, fidelity to one company required employees and managers to treat all other companies as threats. This was codified into employment law such that it was very difficult, specifically in Massachusetts, to move quickly from company to company or take one's work from one organization to another.

Not so in California, and Saxenian provides two basic reasons why. The first is cultural. As Saxenian has it, the basic difference between the two cultures was as fundamental as the distinction between feudal and democratic societies. According to a 1983 essay by Tom Wolfe, which Saxenian quotes approvingly, "Corporations in the East adopted a feudal approach to organization. . . . There were kings and lords, and there were vassals, soldiers, yeomen, and serfs, with layers of protocol and prerequisites." By contrast for the first generation of tech entrepreneurs who had migrated west, "it wasn't enough to start up a company; you had to start up a community, a community in which there were no social distinctions, and it was first come, first served in the parking lot, and everyone was supposed to internalize the common goals."[25]

The mentioning of parking lots and the built environment highlights the second reason: whereas Route 128 was populated with large, vertically integrated firms with clear delineations of responsibilities and "chains of command," Silicon Valley was made up of highly specialized firms with flat organizational charts clustered in close proximity to one another. Living in consistent fear of "the big one" has even produced zoning regulations that prohibit builders from building tall buildings, which facilitates a kind of collaborative spirit. Collaboration rather than competition, in other words, seems to be built into the architecture of the valley itself. In fact, as early as the 1950s, the joke was that Silicon Valley was the place where you could change companies without changing parking lots, and what made this joke funny was the fact that workers in East Coast companies found such a scenario absurd. According to Saxenian's account, the unique features of the office spaces within the valley and, crucially, the paucity of drinking holes in Palo Alto, Sunnyvale, and Menlo Park, fostered a uniquely collaborative working ecology. The emphasis on the network and the unusually high level of job-hopping in the valley is the result not only of differences in management style or philosophy but also of the built environment.[26]

This means that the language of collaboration is so worn into the grooves of Silicon Valley that it is, at times, difficult to pick out. Not so with disruption. It has become notable in large part because of its capacity to migrate from one industry to another. Although it was appropriated by tech firms before the publication of

Clayton Christensen's widely successful *The Innovator's Dilemma*, since then the rhetoric of disruptive innovation has become ubiquitous. So ubiquitous, in fact, that in his book *The Disruption Dilemma*, Joshua Gans dismisses disruption as "an overused term rendered almost useless as a conveyor of meaning."[27] The only reason it is not entirely useless, Gans explains, is that he is capable of reinvigorating the term with its original meaning, which refers to "what a firm faces when the choices that once drove a firm's success now becomes those that destroy its future."[28] The classic example of this is the demise of Blockbuster, which, tragically for them, perceived that prior success justified their refusal to adapt their basic business model to accommodate shifting technological norms regarding how people watched movies. Netflix's disruption became Blockbuster's demise.

While much could be said about the logic of disruption and its ubiquity in the modern world, the term is now employed within Silicon Valley as a conclusive argument against so-called status quo bias.[29] When considering whether we should change a given aspect of our lives, the question is which gets pride of place: our current experience and history or our best sense of what the future could hold? Generally speaking, tech entrepreneurs reverse the burden of proof. It is our current experience that must be justified, not an underdetermined future. Within business, this has led organizational leaders to live in a kind of constant state of innovation. Disruption is what happens to firms who rest on their laurels, falsely assuming that what has worked in the past will continue in perpetuity.

Our third and final term is *optimization*. Although this term is more recent and less theorized, it is the term de rigueur within Silicon Valley, perhaps because it is first and foremost a coding term. But it also justifies the turn to the so-called platform economy that depends so heavily on the ubiquity of powerful smartphones. To optimize code is not just to remove any bugs that might render that code unreadable; it is to remove any and all inefficiencies, understood as unnecessary parts. The reason to optimize a program, therefore, is to pursue a kind of frictionless experience—what developers frequently refer to as a "seamless" interaction. As a cultural ideal rather than merely as coding script, however, optimization refers to the whole of one's life.[30]

Optimization is now big business. The investigative journalist Sarah Kessler writes that from roughly 2007 to 2012 when the "sharing economy" was really catching fire, entrepreneurs and cheerleaders alike were searching for the appropriate metaphors to describe this new economic reality.[31] In time, the preferred image became the ubiquitous "power drill" from Rachel Botsman's 2010 TEDx event in Sydney.[32] In that event, Botsman asked the audience a simple question—How many of you own a power drill?—to which the majority of the audience responded affirmatively. The follow-up statement exposed the central premise of the emerging economic order: "That power drill will be used around twelve to thirteen minutes in its entire lifetime. It's kind of ridiculous, right? Because what you need is the hole, not the drill."[33] The essence of lifestyle optimization and the sharing economy based on it is unveiled in that very sentence: "What you need is the hole, not the drill." It is a kind of game of economic Mad Libs: swap out the nouns in that sentence with any number of possibilities and, presto, you have optimized your life![34]

The end of optimization is the emergence of artificial intelligence as a substantial feature of everyday life. In discussing this with a tech worker, the value of AI was described to me in precisely these terms: "If you want to understand the value added by AI," this subject said, "think of all the things in your life that need the power of a human brain." "But," he continued, "ask yourself how many of those tasks require *your* human brain to be completed to your satisfaction. What the AI guys are doing is outsourcing anything that requires the power of a human brain and allowing you to optimize your life accordingly." This is the next wave of flexible capitalism that is, in many ways, the culmination of Silicon Valley's long interest in disruption, collaboration, and optimization and the technologies those terms represent.

## Pursuing a Common Path

Because moral theologians are in the business of making judgments, I have come to see ethical thought—Christian or otherwise—as including three components: an assessment of contemporary conditions (what business types call a problem statement), a retrospective glance to see how such conditions came to be, and, finally, a prospective glance at what can and should be done.

So what can be said about Michael Banner's proposal for the future of moral theology? And what sorts of judgments can we make about the nature of work in flexible capitalism? From my vantage point, Banner's work and the turn to description more broadly comes at a time of great strength for Christian ethics as a whole. Confronted with profound questions about the shape of their lives, students (and others) are willing to grapple with the claims moral theologians make about what it would mean and take to be a faithful Christian, Jew, or Muslim in our contemporary context. And those claims and that context are anything but clear. So, to put it crassly, there is substantial market demand for the work as well as intelligent and faithful people capable of producing work from the contemporary, retrospective, and prospective angles of vision.

For that reason alone, the turn to description in Christian moral theology is a welcome rebuke to the tendency toward abstraction in Christian ethical thought. Taking up new conversation partners that push theologians to consider alternative ways of working is fantastic, and Banner is certainly right to point out that allowing analytic moral philosophy to set the agenda for moral theology has not, all things considered, been a boon for Christian moral thinking. In fact, it has likely had more deleterious effects on Christian moral thinking than Banner admits—not the least being that even Christian analytic philosophers find very little of what moral theologians say interesting.[35] New conversation partners shed new light on the problems and provide us with new "final vocabularies" to contend with (to borrow Richard Rorty's phrase), and this is all to the good.[36] The more, the merrier.

I confess, however, that I am not convinced Christian ethics should simply swap out moral philosophy with social anthropology. Nor am I convinced that Banner wants to have a straight swap. This is for two reasons. First, for all its obvious weaknesses, the strength of continuing a conversation with moral philosophers lies in its capacity to enliven our sense of agency. Of course, it is quite odd that a course in Christian ethics all too often reaches for absurd examples to illustrate, say, the differences in ethical theories. And Banner is quite right to insist that our moral judgments should be tied to the quotidian features of our everyday lives rather than hypothetical scenarios that we will likely never find ourselves in. But the absurdity of some examples does not in and of itself dismiss the unique pedagogical value of examples that bring our most basic and unexamined moral intuitions into conflict with one another.[37] It could be that we just need better examples.

The more fundamental reason to resist a straight swap is that social anthropology, as I understand it, has a difficult time encompassing all three components of moral thought described above: the contemporary, retrospective, and prospective. And that is as it should be. Disciplines exist to recognize differing inclinations and skill sets, and the ethnographic work I have read on the work culture of Silicon Valley has been immensely helpful, particularly in highlighting the physical effects of "techwork" on a variety of tech workers.[38] Frequently, however, to the degree that those studies interact with other disciplines or forms of thought, they most often look to social theorists who provide them with tools of an explanatory nature. Some, like Ben Snyder's ethnographic study, do more to situate contemporary norms in their historical precedents, but all too often there is less attention to the historical development of cultural norms than is needed, and rarely, if ever, do cultural anthropologists grant themselves license to pay direct and perhaps speculative attention to the proximate future—that is, what is likely to happen if current trends hold. For the most part, they stick to tasks in which they excel: attending to current phenomena and providing useful categories or concepts to elucidate interesting features of social life.

Pointing out these features of social anthropology in no way diminishes the real contributions it can make to moral thinking. As Banner says, tending to the so-called ubiquity of the ethical can be a "healthy corrective to the concerns of moral theology (and more so of bioethics), where the interest in difficult questions is an interest especially in what is novel, contentious, and changing." This "reminds moral theology" of "where its work might, at the very least, begin."[39]

But if moral theologians are to be sufficiently pastoral, the very real presence of moral hazard in the world should provoke them to run the risk of being proven wrong. Moral theologians, in other words, must be willing to offer counsel.[40] In addition to owning up to their own status as individual moral agents among others, they must be willing to make a reasoned judgment not only about the current state of affairs but also what a prospective future may hold, what forms of harm could be avoided, or what sorts of goods could be protected. So how could we do that in relation to work? What kinds of judgments does the preceding analysis enable or disable?

I identify four. When put together, these provisional judgments form a kind of prospectus for moralists interested in taking up the question of work within flexible capitalism. They pertain to likely disruptive effects of technology in three basic areas of life that have corresponding areas of study in Christian thought: the nature of human persons, the requirements of neighbor love, and the appropriate place of the state in a common life.

The first claim is that the continued rise of the contingent worker and the expansion of "self-assembled careers" will mean that economic precariousness and economic optimism will travel together for the proximate future.[41] And they will do so across a variety of sectors of the economy. This came home to me in a conversation with James about his own financial security. "I got 10 percent richer this week," he told me, after a better than expected quarterly report boosted his company's stock price. "But," he continued, "let me tell you about my back-up plan." As I came to find out, this back-up plan is in fact a 1991 Volkswagen Bus and an untouchable emergency fund of $12,000. The specificity with which James describes this plan suggests he has really thought it through. He can live on a thousand dollars a month, he tells me, and the great value of the 1991 VW Bus is that it is the last model before changing auto safety standards made it impossible to place a full-sized bed in the back. Yes, he tells me, if the bubble bursts and it all falls down, his backup plan is to live on a thousand dollars a month in the back of a twenty-five-year-old bus.

The second prospective judgment is that the emerging platform economy stands to reconfigure neighborly relations far more fundamentally than we have yet thought. It will do so in two ways that call for specific Christian responses. In the first place, an increasing number of us will partake in this economy—both as clients and providers. This means that if current trends continue, we will all have a growing network of technologically mediated labor arrangements aimed at mutual benefit. These may well include almost every feature of our daily life throughout our lifespan. The logic of optimization is one of efficiency, value maximization, and the possibility of a frictionless existence, and although I do not myself hold that efficiency is a virtue in and of itself, I see very few institutions resisting this logic. This means that for all the access we will have to one another (technologically mediated though it may be), a true gift economy will be harder and harder to preserve.

But we should preserve it, and Christian witness should require us to retain commercial-free neighborly relations. Imagine, just to take one example, that you are an avid cyclist who knows a thing or two about fixing bikes. Furthermore, a new, slightly out-of-shape neighbor moves in and, after a few months, you see an aged Raleigh ten-speed emerge from his back garden. Both neighbor and bicycle look in need of renovation and, as it happens, you have the skills and tools to perform a minor repair on your neighbor's bike. In a TaskRabbit-saturated world, this encounter presents itself as a perfect market opportunity. While the neighbor may be more likely to go to his iPhone than your front door for help, it is not a foregone conclusion that he will, and one of the basic responsibilities of Christian ethicists is to characterize the neighbor and neighbor love in such a way that Christians can resist the logic of the market when it threatens to infect every aspect of social life.

The second and perhaps less obvious opportunity for Christian witness in this domain is a rearticulated and reimagined defense of the goods inherent in structures of management. One of the most interesting features of Uber's ongoing legal troubles is the extreme lengths they are willing to travel to define themselves as a platform rather than an employer. This is painfully obvious in a speech given by David Plouffe, former architect of President Obama's presidential campaign and current communications guru for Uber. In an address called "Uber and the American Worker," Plouffe goes to extreme lengths to avoid characterizing Uber as a conventional employer who may have substantial management responsibilities. While he is happy to tout the positive social and economic effects Uber has in a world of wage stagnation and contingent labor—more than 400,000 active drivers in the United States! And, look, traffic is down! Underserved neighborhoods have more transportation options! Drunk driving is going down!—his main point is to characterize Uber in a way that avoids all responsibility for management. "To be clear, Uber was not started with the idea it could become a powerful economic engine. It was started by two guys who had trouble finding taxis and wanted to help their friends get around San Francisco a little bit more easily."[42]

Fair enough, but the logic of optimization is one that denies the fact that, in many cases, for labor to be humane, it should be overseen by other human beings who take responsibility for the whole. Have you ever tried to reach customer service at Facebook? Petitioned Twitter to minimize well-documented online abuse, particularly of women and minorities? We can and should resist management-by-platform and find ever-new ways to humanize work by ensuring it is overseen by humans.

Finally, the rise of flexible capitalism gives Christian moral theologians occasion to reconsider the proper relation of the market and the state. My time in Silicon Valley leads me to conclude that you do not have to be a techno-utopian to see that technological developments will require a much more robust social safety net than our current age of austerity will allow for—and perhaps in very short order. This means that there should be an urgency to moral claims on the state to address particularly vulnerable populations of workers (through retraining programs, a more robust social safety net, and perhaps both), particularly because the benefits of technological development will have a disproportionately positive effect on the knowledge classes and a disproportionately negative effect on all the disrupted peoples who suddenly find themselves made redundant. According to the developers of driverless cars, to take one example, mass unemployment of drivers of all kinds is frequently understood as an externality, a problem for the state to solve. This is why, for example, when Silicon Valley's most esteemed tech accelerator and source of venture capital, Y Combinator, began doing basic research in January of 2016, their first project was a five-year investigation of the effects of a universal basic income. Their justification for doing so echoed Keynes's "Economic Possibilities for Our Grandchildren," but it posited a new timeline for solving the economic problem of self-sufficiency.

However specific the churches can get regarding the merits of particular proposals by their governments and civic organizations to address the needs of redundancies, retraining programs, and social welfare, Christian ethicists can be buoyed in this task by the fact that we have a history of addressing new things before they become old. In this, the basic shape, if not the substance, of Leo XIII's insights in *Rerum Novarum* can and should be reproduced and repurposed to pursue faithfulness in this time and no other.

## Notes

1. John Maynard Keynes, "Economic Possibilities for Our Grandchildren," in *Essays in Persuasion* (London: Macmillan, 1931).

2. Keynes, 193–97. This seems to be an instance of what Robert Skidelsky has called Keynes's willingness to "address the world as a priest." Whether it was due to his "colossal self-confidence" or the fact that, according to Skidelsky, Keynes was of the last generation "which claimed to direct human affairs in the name of culture rather than expertise," Keynes, like all priests, I'd think, was well aware of the pastoral *utility* and *danger* of an over-realized eschatology. In times of crisis and social unrest, in times where a society seems to be coming apart at the seams, what we, as citizens, are prone to want is someone who can lift our eyes beyond our current malaise to the breaking of a new dawn, to show us that our future is secure and our current task is to live in light of that future. For more on this, see Robert Skidelsky, *John Maynard Keynes: 1883–1946: Economist, Philosopher, Statesman* (New York: Penguin, 2003), 455–72.

3. See Keynes, "Economic Possibilities," 197–98.

4. Keynes, 201.

5. Some theorists, like Luc Boltanski and Eve Chiapello, have sought to establish continuity with former versions of capitalism by discussing the "new spirit" of capitalism. See, in particular, part 2 of Luc Boltanski and Eve Chiapello, *The New Spirit of Capitalism* (London: Verso, 2005). In *The Precariat: The New Dangerous Class* (London: Bloomsbury, 2011), Guy Standing argues that the neoliberal state is tied to a neo-Darwinian social order he describes as a "politics of inferno" wherein collective forms of self-governance are set aside in favor of "The Precariat." These more theoretical accounts are complemented by recent popular accounts of the shift in modern work with dramatic titles like Rick Wartzman, *The End of Loyalty: The Rise and Fall of Good Jobs in America* (New York: Public Affairs, 2017); David Graeber, *Bullshit Jobs: A Theory* (New York: Simon and Schuster, 2018); David Weil, *The Fissured Workplace: Why Work Became So Bad for So Many and What Can Be Done to Improve It* (Cambridge, MA: Harvard University Press, 2014); and Sarah Kessler, *Gigged: The End of the Job and the Future of Work* (New York: St. Martin's Press, 2018). Whatever their differences, each

is grasping for language to describe the essential period of transformation that took place in the globalized economy beginning in the 1970s.

6. Notice, for example, the place of stability in the list of the constitutive features of "good jobs" and "bad jobs" in Arne Kalleberg, *Good Jobs, Bad Jobs: The Rise of Polarized and Precarious Employment Systems in the United States, 1970s to 2000s* (New York: Russell Sage Foundation, 2011), 7–10.

7. Lawrence F. Katz and Alan B. Krueger, "The Rise and Nature of Alternative Work Arrangements in the United States, 1995–2015," Working Paper 22667, National Bureau of Economic Research, September 2016.

8. The "gig economy" has entered our common vocabulary as a way of signaling a shift away from standard work arrangements like the forty-hour workweek, the presumption of continuous employment, and so on. Rather than stable, long-term employment arrangements, workers of all kinds now take on "gigs"—that is, short-term projects frequently consisting of multiple freelance workers who come together around a common project. For an interesting take on the gig economy in the world of arts and entertainment, see Adam Davidson, "What Hollywood Can Teach Us about the Future of Work," *New York Times*, May 5, 2015.

9. Katz and Krueger, "Rise and Nature," 2.

10. As Katz and Krueger's data show, the percentage of those jobs in the American economy actually declined by .3 percent between 2005 and 2015. See Katz and Krueger, "Rise and Nature," 2.

11. Katz and Krueger, 7.

12. See Geoffrey G. Parker, Sangeet Paul Choudary, and Marshall W. Van Alstyne, *Platform Revolution: How Networked Markets Are Transforming the Economy—And How to Make Them Work for You* (New York: W. W. Norton & Company, 2016).

13. See Katz and Krueger, "Rise and Nature," 17–18.

14. Benjamin Snyder's work on the relation of work to time has been invaluable for me in understanding the shifting moral norms that mark work in our contemporary moment. His ethnographic study of truck drivers, financial executives, and the unemployed is *The Disrupted Workplace: Time and Moral Order of Flexible Capitalism* (Oxford: Oxford University Press, 2016). Much of this section draws from the opening chapter of that work.

15. Snyder, chap. 1.

16. Snyder, 5.

17. Snyder, 5–6.

18. Snyder, 5–6, emphasis original.

19. Snyder, 7.

20. Snyder, 7. Although Snyder does not attend to the work habits of Silicon Valley tech workers, this is precisely the purpose of J. A. English-Lueck's important and prescient ethnographic work, *Being and Well-Being: Health and the Working Bodies of Silicon Valley* (Stanford, CA: Stanford University Press, 2010), which follows a group of tech workers to map their daily bodily rhythms.

21. See, for one example, Reid Hoffman, Ben Casnocha, and Chris Yeh, "Tours of Duty: The New Employer-Employee Contract," *Harvard Business Review* 91, no. 6 (June 2013).

22. Harry Frankfurt, *On Inequality* (Princeton, NJ: Princeton University Press, 2015).

23. Tech workers and entrepreneurs frequently debate whether it is appropriate to describe a given product as "disruptive," to take one example, and in so doing slightly different definitions of the term may emerge. I witnessed a debate just like this when I visited the Hacker Dojo, a wild and wonderful place that carries forward the spirit of the early Homebrew Computer Club while fusing it with a kind of quasi-anarchic distrust of centralized power. But such debates, however vigorous, about the precise meaning of the term only support the basic point: the essential features of terms like *disruption, collaboration,* and *optimization* are debated precisely because there is so much consensus within this community that they form the basic grammar of the industry.

24. AnnaLee Saxenian, *Regional Advantage: Culture and Competition in Silicon Valley and Route 128* (Cambridge, MA: Harvard University Press, 1996).

25. Tom Wolfe, "The Tinkerings of Robert Noyce: How the Sun Rose on the Silicon Valley," *Esquire*, December 1983, 346–74.

26. The legacy of collaboration for product development has now carried over into the platform economy and "collaborative consumption" more generally. On this, see Rachel Botsman and Roo Rogers, *What's Mine Is Y(ours): The Rise of Collaborative Consumption* (London: HarperCollins, 2011); and Parker, Choudary, and Van Alstyne, *Platform Revolution*.

27. Joshua Gans, *The Disruption Dilemma* (Cambridge, MA: MIT Press, 2016), 13.

28. Gans, 13.

29. The main source here is Nick Bostrom and Tony Ord, "The Reversal Test: Eliminating the Status Quo Bias in Applied Ethics," *Ethics* 116 (July 2006): 656–79. As they put it, regarding cognitive enhancement, there is an "inappropriate favoring of the status quo." For Bostrom and Anders Sandberg, taking what they call the "Evolutionary Optimality Challenge" means that when evaluating a proposed enhancement of human nature, the question of why such an enhancement is yet to take place should be asked. Their evolutionary heuristic is, interestingly, very similar to the way the language of optimization is utilized throughout Silicon Valley. For that argument, see Nick Bostrom and Anders Sandberg, "The Wisdom of Nature," in *Human Enhancement*, ed. Julian Savulescu and Nick Bostrom (Oxford: Oxford University Press, 2009).

30. And this is precisely what passes itself off as the platform-based "on demand" economy. As I mentioned briefly earlier, one of the dominant features in the rise of the contingent worker is the replacement of management with the platform, and it is precisely the language of optimization that funds this shift. Consider, for example, the basic features to the gig economy that NYU's Arun Sundararajan has established in the introductory chapter to *The Sharing Economy: The End of Employment and the Rise of Crowd-Based Capitalism* (Cambridge, MA: MIT Press, 2016). The gig economy (1) is platform based, that is, it relies on some sort of digitally enabled marketplace for exchanging goods and services; (2) downplays the place of professionals, favoring instead "peer to peer" relations for exchanging goods and services; (3) sidesteps the role of centralized institutions in favor of linked networks of consumers; and (4) is almost always a form of supplemental income rather than full-time employment.

31. As demonstrated in her 2015 piece for *Fast Company*, Kessler was one of the earliest critics of the developments within the gig economy. See Sarah Kessler, "The 'Sharing Economy' Is Dead, and We Killed It," *Fast Company*, September 14, 2015, https://www.fastcompany.com/3050775 /the-sharing-economy-is-dead-and-we-killed-it. In 2018, Kessler developed the argument further in *Gigged: The End of the Job and the Future of Work* (New York: St. Martins, 2018).

32. Rachel Botsman, "The Case for Collaborative Consumption," TEDxSydney, May 2010, https://www.ted.com/talks/rachel_botsman_the_case_for_collaborative_consumption? language=en.

33. Botsman.

34. Here's how the major players in the sharing economy work: "What you need is a ride, not a car" (Uber); "What you need is a bed, not a hotel" (Airbnb), and so on. But what about some of the more exotic peer-to-peer networks in the new economy? For a nominal fee, Washio and Rinse will come to your home, pick up your laundry, wash and fold it, and return it to your apartment. With Shyp, instead of taking a trip to the post office, you can simply take a picture of the care package you'd like to send to a friend and, before long, someone will come to your house with the appropriate box, pack up your care package, and take it to the post office. Or, in addition to all the food delivery services, consider what I take to be one of the weirder platforms: Leftover Swap. The purpose of this app is to connect "leftover takers" with "leftover givers." That's right: Order a bit too much vindaloo? No problem. With Leftover Swap, someone will be right over to pick up your leftovers and take them over to a neighbor who has the munchies.

35. Although I see Banner's work in the light of other efforts to resist the tyranny of hard cases, and, as such, am prone to draw direct lines between Banner's project and the turn to ethnography within religious studies departments in the United States, the ease with which I draw those lines is likely less principled in nature than I'd like to think. Rather, it is most likely due to the fact that most of my graduate studies occurred in places where what we called the "Marvin Gaye question" of "What's going on?" was always present. But, crucially, most of my colleagues and teachers in

those institutions where interested not just in the Marvin Gaye question but also Lenin's question of "What is to be done?" That is to say, for description of a given practice to be adequate, it must be a thoroughly moral description, and in order to be a thoroughly *moral* description, it cannot shrink back from the basic task of moral judgment.

36. Richard Rorty discusses a "final vocabulary" in *Contingency, Irony, and Solidarity* (Cambridge: Cambridge University Press, 1989), 73.

37. Eric Gregory also mentions the pedagogical value of hard cases in chapter 6 of this volume. This conflict between two deeply held impulses is what Michael Sandel calls the "impulse to philosophy" in *Justice: What's the Right Thing to Do?* (London: Penguin, 2010).

38. English-Lueck, *Being and Well-Being*, and Snyder, *The Disrupted Workplace*, are paramount here.

39. Michael Banner, *The Ethics of Everyday Life: Moral Theology, Social Anthropology, and the Imagination of the Human* (Oxford: Oxford University Press, 2014), 26–27.

40. Theology as counsel is the way Charles T. Mathewes and I describe the unique approach of contemporary Anglican moral theologians Nigel Biggar and Oliver O'Donovan. See Philip Lorish and Charles Mathewes, "Theology as Counsel: The Work of Oliver O'Donovan and Nigel Biggar," *Anglican Theological Review* 94, no. 4 (2012): 717–36.

41. See Carrie Lane, "Self-Assembled Career," *The Hedgehog Review* 18, no. 1 (Spring 2016).

42. David Plouffe, "Uber and the American Worker," *Uber Newsroom*, November 3, 2015, https://newsroom.uber.com/1776/.

# 9

# THE EVERYDAY ETHICS OF BORROWING AND SPENDING

EVALUATING ECONOMIC RISK AND REWARD

## Justin Welby

I AM NEITHER A PROFESSIONAL THEOLOGIAN (or even a very good amateur) nor a professional economist, but I am a jobbing practitioner in both. For that reason, the reflections in this chapter have many questions and relatively few prescriptions. At their heart is the thesis that, at least at a popular level, there is a lack of engagement between moral theology, social anthropology, and economics that is very dangerous for all three in the development of a foundation for understanding our economic activities at all levels.

The Great Recession avoided being another Great Depression by no more than a whisker, and it is quite possible that economists of the next generation may look back and say it was. Certainly, if you live in Greece, the difference is entirely academic. Even in the UK, the economy did not recover its 2007 peak until 2013, and the gap between where the economy would have been without the recession and where it is remains around 15 percent.[1]

There have been many attempts to explain the causes of the prolonged crisis in which we are still enmeshed. They tend to break into the technical analyses of the intricacies—especially of the US housing market in subprime loans—and macro analysis. Few venture too far into ethics.

One of the best analyses I have read is Adair Turner's *Between Debt and the Devil*, in which he exposes how the great period of the "Goldilocks Economy," which ran in Europe and the United States from 1992 until 2008, was largely built on debt.[2] Even worse, the levels of debt rose faster than the levels of GDP, and thus the economies slowly became increasingly leveraged. The crash was a debt crisis, not a casino bankers' crisis. Very few banks went under because they were gambling in the derivatives market. Most failed because they held debts or debt instruments that could not be serviced, which tied in with their use of derivatives to manage risk that were not effective at their task and, ultimately, were mispriced.

It is tempting for those who are practitioners in the financial markets, or who deal in commodities, to feel that the market is a random, impersonal force. The market is treated by most people in the same way as continental drift and tectonic plates; it is a mysterious and little-understood force that just happens, occasionally causing earthquakes. But it is neither random nor impersonal—it is made up of the billions of personal decisions of billions of everyday people that cumulatively establish the course and progress, or regress, of the global economy. I remember the bafflement of a colleague in the oil industry who said, "When you look at the economics, the price of oil should be double what it is today." The answer was simple: it is not. The market sets the price. It may make no sense, but it is so because that is all that people will pay.

This relates to what Michael Banner discusses in *The Ethics of Everyday Life*. In diagnosing the dangers of focusing only on "hard cases," "conundrums," and "dilemmas," Banner highlights the need for moral theology to turn in pastoral and therapeutic ways to the "regular practice of the everyday," those forms of human living that shape our decisions, actions, and being in ways that are quite ordinary but occasionally hidden.[3] The same applies to economic ethics, which tends to focus on the abstract morality of the market and various hard cases related to major economic policy decisions without considering the more mundane ways in which our economic activities and assumptions condition daily life. This more abstract approach has informed how we often assess the "hard case" of the economic crash, which was preceded and propelled by billions of everyday ethical choices. In turn, each of these decisions was determined by human nature, that is, by our fallen selves. If we are ever to create a financial system that promotes flourishing for all, that serves us rather than enslaves us, and that offers not just the superficial appearance of ethics but a deep change of culture, then we must understand the nature of the billions of everyday human beings who shape our global economy.

In this chapter, I examine the everyday financial decisions (and the human brokenness that influenced them) that led to a culture in which the crash of 2007 could occur. Drawing on my experience working in the financial sector and serving as a leader in the Anglican Church, I go on to discuss why a better understanding of human nature, achieved through the insights of social anthropology, moral theology, and economics, is the only way we can reform our financial sector and global economy. In particular, I explore how regulation (like much moralizing in Christian ethics) fails to grapple with the complexities of human nature and does not treat the cause of our problems but merely attempts to manage the symptoms—and often perpetuates them. While this approach can never bring about lasting change, it is what we continue to accept. My chapter is a call for us to find a better way.

## Risk and Reward

Risk is a factor of life. Even the most mundane economic decision is based on a risk/reward paradigm. We make a shopping list with the expectation that the supermarket will stock the items we want. But there is always a risk that other factors—for example, issues in the supply chain—will get in the way of our aims. We may not notice the consequences of risk in our personal economic lives (we simply reach for a different brand or quantity), but risk is always there. Other factors often obscure the risk/reward paradigm. Consumer choice means that only rarely do we fail entirely to buy the product we want, and often there is an (unexpected) reward—we find a lower cost for a different brand or we discover that we actually prefer the alternative.

With borrowing in everyday life, we know—or at least we indicate awareness—that certain products come with a risk, such as credit cards or mortgages. We must accept the terms of such products (the risk) to gain the benefits (the reward). But much of the time, we expect the reward to outweigh the risk. The immediate purchasing power that a credit card gives us, or the means a mortgage gives to purchase one's own home, is alluring. Without an ethics that recognizes the risk/reward paradigm as a fundamental feature of all financial actions and sets boundaries for that paradigm, we are liable to encounter problems. These are not abstract risks but rather the lived reality for those who find themselves in debt or unable to keep up with mortgage repayments.

We delude ourselves when we think that personal financial decisions do not have genuine risk attached to them. At a systemic level, the level of risk is acknowledged based on the size of the transaction. A loan of £250 million is a "risk" for a bank, not because we have an ethics that acknowledges risk as a factor of everyday life but because £250 million is a large sum of money. The absence of such an ethics was brought home to me during a hearing of the Parliamentary Commission on Banking Standards (PCBS), of which I was a member. We were looking into the payment protection insurance (PPI) scandal, a product that was often embedded in the cost of personal loans and that made the banks a great deal of money but gave no realistic protection to those to whom it applied. One witness, who had been in a leading position in a bank involved, denied vigorously the idea that the bonuses paid to those who sold PPI could have been an inducement to do something wrong like sell products that were of no use and, in some cases, demonstrably negative for the client. He argued that because the sellers earned very little; a 10 percent bonus was worth only £2,000. He could not grasp that, for someone earning £20,000, a bonus of that size made all the difference. It had infinitely greater value to those employees than the bonuses earned by those at the top. The individual reward on offer was, understandably, of far greater significance than the risk of the product, which was often not communicated to the sellers.

Early on in the oil business, I learned the rule that if something looks too good to be true, it almost always is. Risk and reward are joined at the hip. A low-risk product producing a high reward almost certainly has unidentified risks. So when commercial banks in the period before the crash were producing returns on equity over 20 percent, it looked fishy. Of course, they argued that this time it was all different. Since the crash in the Far East markets in the 1990s, the sophistication of risk-management instruments had grown extensively. By clever use of the right instruments, in which the numbers and risk profile and correlations were plugged into some clever person's computer, the senior management could be sure, without understanding anything, that nothing would go wrong. I exaggerate for effect. But few had the sense of my old boss, who once sent away a banker peddling one of these things, saying, "If you can't explain it so that I can understand it, then *you* don't understand it."

Risk management was an art or science (personally, I went for art) that moved corporate treasurers to become corporate risk managers between the late 1980s and the turn of the century. It was an attractive move, implying greater skill and erudition across a range of disciplines. But it was an illusion.

Risk is a factor of life, and in financial markets or in business, it can seldom be eliminated; it is merely transferred. To buy insurance is to transfer the risk of a catastrophe one cannot afford to someone who can. The risk remains, although it can be mitigated. It is mitigated on an exploration rig, for example, by intense discipline over health and safety and the use of sophisticated blow-out preventers, down-hole management, and fire detection and suppression. In the financial markets, risk is mitigated and passed round. A bank underwrites a debt issue for a company for £250 million. Immediately they sell it to investors, who buy and sell the bond through its life at prices reflecting interest rates in the economy and the likelihood of the borrower servicing the debt. They have numerous risks: inflation, an economic downturn that affects the borrower, or foreign exchange rate movements affecting them all. These risks may be reallocated by hedging, but they still float around the market, and someone somewhere is taking them. The more sophisticated the risk management, the more risk there is of someone somewhere defaulting on the obligations. The control of the risk turns out to be an illusion; it has simply been reallocated.

Economists analyze risk, and regulators make rules about it. Yet two disciplines are often missing, at least at the level of everyday ethics. We have not yet properly understood the everyday ethical impact of the risk/reward paradigm, so we cannot expect social anthropologists to have a broad-based impact on the understanding of why markets move, or moral theologians to comment extensively on the ethics of trading or risk allocation.

One rarefied aspect of market movement is based around the study of charts. My first boss, a Norwegian with otherwise impeccable English, used to say, "These bankers, they are just sheeps." Markets move in herds, and the herd movement is seen in the price. When a currency or commodity rises or falls, it tends to hesitate in its trend at key points, such as the highest or lowest point it has been at recently. These are called resistance levels. If it breaks through, it may well accelerate to the next resistance level. It has momentum or runs out of it. Herds of people trading are good subjects for anthropologists, as they are for moral theologians, but only if anthropologists and theologians work together to understand the habits as well as the mathematics of markets.

Everyday ethics must recognize the realities of risk and must develop an understanding of the underlying conditions that enable risk to be justifiable. A life without risk, the ignoring of contingency, is an illusion, but one often peddled. A life with too much risk becomes unbearable and irresponsible. Whether at the individual or market level, a positive approach to risk accounts for the movements of crowds in economics and also enables growth and development. Risk and reward must be joined ethically and not asymmetrically. This has been slowly recognized by regulators, but it remains something little absorbed at other levels.

## Hoarding

A *Punch* cartoon that has long stuck in my mind was drawn shortly after the publication of John Maynard Keynes's *General Theory* in the mid-1930s. A crucial part of his analysis of the Great Depression, and therefore the economic cycle, was the danger of "hoarding," of excessive saving in times of insecurity. Hoarding diminishes demand and lowers the volatility of the circulation of money, and both factors accentuate downturns. In the cartoon a wealthy couple is in a shop that sells fur coats. The wife is eagerly trying on everlasting coats in front of her pained husband, saying, "But darling, we must spend lavishly; Mr. Keynes says so."

Modern economies depend on adequate demand *and* adequate supply, but on a more global level. Excessive saving and inadequate demand for investment lie behind the "popular" notion that this will be a generation of secular stagnation, with slow-growing economies and rapid increases in inequality. Inequality is seen not only as unjust but also as a marker of potential instability in societies at a national, regional, or global level.

Catholic social teaching speaks of the universal destination of goods,[4] solidarity,[5] and the common good.[6] What God has created is for humanity and is to be shared, and the aim must be not just a general rise in the economic tide (the general interest) but a rising tide that lifts all boats (the common good). Yet the way the economy is currently working drives people toward debt to "float their own boat" because wealth and equity are too intentionally concentrated to spread out. Should moral theology say to the rich "spend, spend, spend"? Is there merit in the adage that wealth runs out in three generations—one to make it, one to fail adequately to preserve it, and one to squander it?

An ethic of spending that charges us to hold lightly that which we have, to have a self-awareness of our mortality and our small role in a wider story, offers a counter to the hoarding nature that at its heart says, "What we have, we hold." Yet mere spending is not an appropriate answer. Pope Benedict XVI developed the idea of gratuity in his encyclical *Caritas in Veritate.*[7] The issue of hoarding involves both non-investment and thus inadequate demand and a lack of velocity of circulation. Money becomes static and nonproductive. The couple in *Punch* was wrong. Gratuity is the release of surplus accumulation when it goes beyond what is necessary. It may be through philanthropy (although that can have its own problems of manipulation) or through not seeking the maximum profit in a transaction. I worked for an oil company during an oil price crash in the 1980s that chose not to push the cost of renting offshore drilling rigs to the lowest possible level because that would have bankrupted the suppliers. By not squeezing the last penny (gratuity), community was improved, businesses kept going, and human beings flourished in a time of crisis. Gratuity is an expression of everyday ethics.

## Power

The anthropological and economic examination of the sources and expression of power in society are necessary if we are to have an everyday ethics of borrowing and spending that enables us to have a sense of the boundaries and limits of their use and abuse.

Money and power are closely related. It is almost impossible to see the impact of one without understanding the desire for the other. An ethic of borrowing and spending that recognizes the relationship between power and money is therefore vital. Power flows to a large degree from money, and money is easier to acquire when one has power. One of the characteristics of poverty is that you are the object of other people's power rather than the subject who decides what to do with your own power.

Money gives power. A dictum widely attributed to Jean Paul Getty, who was in his day the richest man in the world, points out, "The meek may inherit the earth, but not its mineral rights." Humility is widely seen as the antithesis of power, indeed as a very good way of surrendering power to others. The interaction between money and power is complex and deceptive. In the first place, money buys certain capacities. It is obvious to most neutral observers that, for good or ill, the world's economic system is dominated by the wealthy, who through their wealth have the power to set the terms of engagement in international trade and commerce as well as in the exercise of political power.

Without an ethics that sets the terms of the relationship between money and power, we run into trouble. In the everyday setting, this manifests itself in the assumption that money has the power to dictate what is and is not possible for human beings. Success—in our personal life and choices—is seen through the prism of money. In the financial sector, the power of finance to govern the well-being of our economy has led to a system of "too big to fail." Here we might reflect that there has been little success in attempts by moral theology to overcome the fallacy that money is the protagonist in the human story. Our ethics around money, borrowing, and spending is governed by a philosophy that places money at the center of all things.

In order to truly change the nature of the economy, to develop an everyday ethics of borrowing and spending, we must endeavor to understand the social, emotional, and spiritual factors that cause people to make the decisions they do. This is the only way to see sincere and lasting cultural change.

## Inhibitors to Everyday Ethics in the Global Economy

The second part of this chapter examines two factors that inhibit the development of an everyday ethics of borrowing and spending: moralizing (i.e., regulation without a social anthropology) and technology. I examine both of these in the context of household finances and personal credit and apply them at a wider macro level to demonstrate how the lack of an everyday ethics leads to market failure.

A surprising amount of time in my first years as archbishop has been taken up with the issue of consumer credit, particularly high-cost short-term loans and credit unions. The sector has been in enormous flux over the last ten years. There was rapid growth in payday lenders, linked to firms who lent money for household goods at exceptionally high interest rates. The former ranged up to 5,000 percent annually, the latter not usually above 1,500 percent.

In the United Kingdom, this development was seen at the tail end of the great expansion of debt of which I have spoken, and it is similar to equally serious developments in finance for housing, such as 100 percent mortgages. As good credits reached saturation, the markets forced lenders into the subprime area to lend to people with short-term needs or inadequate capital. They are a larger proportion of society who, historically, either scraped by with great hardship or simply did not borrow, perhaps remaining in the social housing sector or forced into the hands of illegal loan sharks who were usually linked to wider criminal activity including drugs, protection, and trafficking.

For various historical reasons, including a regulatory system that constrained growth and prevented adequate returns on loans sufficient to maintain capital, the community credit sector remained underdeveloped in Britain compared to elsewhere in Europe. Reforms to regulation following the crash and severe restrictions on payday lenders are beginning to take effect. Credit unions have grown significantly in reach and in depth since 2008, up by over a third in activity. A number of payday lenders have closed. But a gap has reemerged as a result, with the credit union movement unable either to grow fast enough to replace the loss of high-cost lending or to become flexible enough to meet demand. As a result, there is a grave danger, and possibly already a reality, of loan sharks filling the vacuum.

The everyday ethics of household finance is dominated by meaningless moral imperatives. Polonius bleats in our ears that we should neither borrow nor lend, thankfully ignored because the alternative is cash under the mattress and no bed to put it on.

The reality for many people is that when the washing machine breaks down, it needs replacing. The old Ford Focus in which someone earning minimum wage gets to work has to have a new tire to pass its inspections. The sole trader needs money to buy equipment to carry out the jobs he has secured as a painter decorator, after weeks of putting photocopied leaflets through people's letter boxes on the local estate.

As with the macro picture of global finance, the formulation of moral theology requires an interaction with other disciplines, especially social anthropology and economics. Questions should be raised around the pressures to adopt a particular lifestyle and what is seen as essential in the home. What are the signs of a home that merits respect?

The responsibility for providing goods and food varies between areas, especially in outer city estates, where provision often comes in diverse forms. One school I knew well in the UK's Midlands, attended by two of my children, had 70 percent single-parent or step-parent families, with a high turnover around the often stable and usually female head of the household. This nuclear grouping was combined with extended family networks across the estate with strong support from siblings, grandparents (again, usually the women), and friends. While purely anecdotal, this illustrates that the basic power structures of many parts of society require further study in order to craft a moral theology that has some bearing on day-to-day experience, as in Michael Banner's discussions of infertility and the need for a child.[8]

A second example of moralizing is the repeated and regular restructuring of Greek debt. We are all familiar with the problem. Greece entered the Euro on essentially a false prospectus, with declared debt well below the reality and thus outside the criteria for Euro entry. There was a level of suspicion and collusion by all concerned, who wanted to include more countries. By taking on what is essentially a foreign currency, like a state of the United States, a country loses the ability to service its debt by printing money. It thus depends on trade balances and economic activity to generate income sufficient for all its needs, including debt service. Asymmetries in the European economies and a program of changes to the German labor market, along with demographic factors and changes in how power was exercised, led to Germany developing large surpluses on trade and commerce, much of them derived from sales to southern Europe, to which it lent the money to buy its goods. As a game of economic musical chairs, the potential flaws are obvious in retrospect, but as I have already said, there was a sense that "this time it is all different." Ethical questions about relative power, the nature and wisdom of debt, and corruption in the Greek state were suspended. Everyday ethics was absent without leave.

Throw in a global recession and, when the bill arrived, Greece could not pay. So far, so tragically normal. What is less normal is that, through previous mismanagement and even corruption by an elite, the poor of an entire nation have been put into a sort of involuntary bankruptcy. The weight has fallen on those least able to survive, and when their own suffering was aggravated by the desperate plight of hundreds of thousands of refugees, little help was given. "Debts must be paid, it is a moral obligation" is the litany of redemption of the creditors, and even the IMF has said it cannot happen since the debt is too large to be paid off.

So the global market system, and especially the EU, lends people money to buy things and then strangles their hopes and futures when they cannot repay. I have looked in vain for the outrage that this should cause or for excellent moral theology that recognizes the rulers' misrepresentation of the borrower and the deep hardness of heart that has created the biggest debtor's prison in Europe among the creditors.

The Parliamentary Commission on Banking Standards (PCBS) spent two years working on recommendations for the stabilization of the UK banking system, aiming to create a financial sector that worked for the good of all in society. I sat on the commission, an education of extraordinary interest, not least from witnesses such as Paul Volcker and fellow commissioners such as John McFall, Nigel Lawson, and the commission's chairman, Andrew Tyrie. Yet in one aspect, I remain unhappy about the outcomes. Discussion of ethics was discouraged as being too intangible, and, of course, the commission did not "do God." As a result, law, basically through regulation, became the default response to the appalling behavior we examined. Yet regulation has continually proved to be ineffective. It slams stable doors when all the horses have fled except those too dozy to notice that the door was open at all. The rate of innovation and the size of banking organizations by comparison with the number of regulators makes law an ineffective and incompetent tool.

Regulation has been the default response to human behavior since Moses and is relatively incapable of delivering the desired result. Telling foreign exchange dealers to be good is as likely to be successful as telling King David not to commit adultery. Some are good, and on the whole David did not frequently commit adultery, but in general it does not work. The habits and cultures of groups dictate behavior, constrained or liberated by a sense of personal morality and most profoundly by the work of the Holy Spirit in transforming the will and desires. When we try to control the symptoms of the illness through rules and punishment, we fail to treat the cause. It just does not work.

Both examples highlight that regulation without ethics, and therefore law without a recognition and understanding of human nature, are doomed to fail. More problematic than a failure to recognize human nature is perhaps the active disassociation of borrowing and spending from any sense of human interaction.

One of the most significant problems in the high-cost credit sector was the ease with which credit was available, particularly online. One simply had to find the right website, enter the amount of money one wished to borrow, and away one went. Many websites had very limited or no affordability checks and no requirement or means to understand individual circumstances. In numerous cases, this led to people incurring huge levels of debt by taking out multiple loans across various lenders. Worse, it led to situations in which people's personal well-being was badly affected by enslaving them to requirements for repayment. In a small number of cases, people were even driven to suicide because the terms of the loan and the amount of money owed became so completely impossible.

The impersonal nature of this system—through the development of certain technologies—inhibits the development of an everyday ethics of borrowing and spending. Where there is a focus only on laws and regulations and no human interaction between borrower and lender, we lack an adequate ethical framework. The ethics that underpins the ideal of the credit union movement stands in contrast to the algorithms that govern online lending. The ideal of the credit union and other forms of community and microfinance is to provide proper accountability and affordability checks for people. The face-to-face encounter (an increasing number taking place within churches) goes beyond the financial, seeing the individual not simply as an economic unit but as a person with value beyond their financial status. An everyday ethics of borrowing and spending needs to be fundamentally connected to the concepts of embodied personhood and human flourishing that Michael Banner emphasizes.

The absence of an everyday ethics is perhaps no more evident than in the practice of flash trading. Once upon a time, people like me in corporations needed to buy and sell foreign exchange as part of our daily business—for example, to transfer the dollars received from selling a cargo of North Sea oil into pounds to pay our staff and hire the exploration rigs. Two colleagues and I would ring one bank at the same time, greet our counterparts, and then ask politely, "Please could you give me the cable in 10?" Cable was the market slang for the dollar/pound exchange rate, first traded in the 1860s on the sub-sea cable across the Atlantic. Ten meant $10 million. Back would come the answer, "40/46," for example. The "big figure" was assumed, so what they meant was $1.3840–1.3846. The phone went on hold, we each called out the rate we had, and the best one was answered with "$10 yours at 46"—that is, a rate of $1.3846. We confirmed by letter or telex.

How it has changed! Through the PCBS, I visited a number of banks operating high-speed trading. The trades—in their case, on the stock exchange—are driven by algorithms through computers that trade thousands of times a second, gaining advantage by being thousandths of a second quicker than someone whose computer may be a few hundred meters further from the Stock Exchange server. On the whole, this trading is not for clients but for the bank's own account. Not surprisingly, it causes problems. In 2010 a computer error temporarily caused a near meltdown on the New York Stock Exchange that was so quick that several firms went bust before they recognized they had a problem.

The algorithms are fast and ruthless. They seize every opportunity for profit. They have neither ethics nor grace. Human error is nailed. There is no humanity left in a system that was once quite a strong community of traders, often merciful to mistakes. One major bank withdrew from flash trading because of its worries over ethics and control. Others continue. It is the rule of the robots, and one must question whether it can be ethical for a system to do such work or, if so, how and by whom the boundaries are established. With such technology, there is, in theological terms, an absence of incarnation.[9] There is no living human presence in relationship, no human activity that intermediates between buyer and seller or the thing bought and sold. It reduces the economy to a system that is autonomous and independent of human existence; it could presumably go on trading if everyone went on indefinite holiday.

What all this is doing is accepting the market's claim to power. Once the context of the entire system is the exercise of power, it follows that its ethics will be based on power. Challenging this notion requires an everyday ethics that puts human flourishing at the center of existence.

Flash trading eliminates the human and thus should be curtailed. Contingency provisions that enable and reward human participation might make more companies hesitate. Restrictions on usury recognize the imbalances of power in high-cost credit markets. An everyday ethics would treat imbalances of power with suspicion and look on them at a global as well as a local level. These imbalances need to be equalized.

Underlying many of the cultural and legal challenges of the market is the sense that it stands beyond ethics, itself demonstrating a failure of engagement by moral theology. The market exists. The question has become how we deal with it, as though we had taken an elephant as a pet and were only now wondering, as it reached maturity, how to house-train it or whether it could be house-trained.

These examples show that the imposition of rules and regulations, while necessary for restraining the worst abuses, does little to change our attitudes to borrowing and spending. The dehumanization of financial interactions is worse still. We must endeavor to understand the natures that drive these problems—our propensity to risk, hoard, and desire power—if we are ever to understand, and so redirect, the course of our global economy.

An everyday ethics of borrowing and spending would above all look more just, leave consequences closely attached to actions, and reduce asymmetries of power. Keynes created the post-war architecture of the world economic system; it is time we looked for another, based not on crisis but on our everyday interactions.

Underlying the sense of the inexorable force of the market and, with it, the concomitant disasters for the poor caught up in its gnashing teeth, is a failure of moral theology since the late twentieth century to engage effectively and in terms that make sense, using the language of other disciplines as well as its own, for the creation of an everyday ethics of borrowing and spending. Michael Banner's book is a wonderful remedy, and I am grateful to him for compelling me to think afresh in the areas in which I work.

## Notes

1. Brian Griffiths, "Faith, Leadership and the Global Marketplace," Max and Esther De Pree Presidential Lectureship, April 10, 2015, Fuller Theological Seminary, 12, http://theceme.org/faith-leadership-and-the-global-marketplace-april-2015/.

2. Adair Turner, *Between Debt and the Devil: Money, Credit, and Fixing the Global Finance* (Princeton, NJ: Princeton University Press, 2015).

3. Michael Banner, *The Ethics of Everyday Life: Moral Theology, Social Anthropology, and the Imagination of the Human* (Oxford: Oxford University Press, 2014), 3–4. In this chapter, I use "everyday ethics" in a broader way than Banner but one that resonates with his attention to the lived reality of human existence.

4. See *Catechism of the Catholic Church*, 2nd ed. (New York: Doubleday, 2003), 2402–6.

5. *Catechism of the Catholic Church*, 1939–1942; Pope John Paul II, *Encyclical Letter Sollicitudo Rei Socialis of the Supreme Pontiff, John Paul II, to the Bishops, Priests, Religious Families, Sons and Daughters of the Church and All People of Good Will for the Twentieth Anniversary of Populorum Progressio* (Washington, DC: Office of Publishing and Promotion Services, United States Catholic Conference, 1988), 40: "Solidarity is undoubtedly a Christian virtue. It seeks to go beyond itself to total gratuity, forgiveness, and reconciliation. It leads to a new vision of the unity of humankind, a reflection of God's triune intimate life."

6. *Catechism of the Catholic Church*, 1905–1912; Epistle of Barnabas 4:10: "Do not live entirely isolated, having retreated into yourselves, as if you were already [fully] justified, but gather instead

to seek together the common good," as cited in *Catechism of the Catholic Church*, 1905. See also Augustine, *The City of God against the Pagans*, ed. and trans. R. W. Dyson (Cambridge: Cambridge University Press, 1998), 19.5–17; Pope Leo XIII, *Rerum novarum*, 1891, http://w2.vatican.va/con tent/leo-xiii/en/encyclicals/documents/hf_l-xiii_enc_15051891_rerum-novarum.html, which addressed the conditions of workers; and *Compendium of the Social Doctrine of the Church* (Washington, DC: United States Conference of Catholic Bishops Publishing, 2005) chap. 4, part 2, which summarizes Catholic social teaching on the common good.

7. Benedict XVI, *Caritas in Veritate / Charity in Truth* (San Francisco, CA: Ignatius Press, 2009), 34–42.

8. See Banner, *Ethics of Everyday Life*, 35–81.

9. See Craig M. Gay, chapter 7 in this volume.

# 10

## SHARING TABLES

═══════════════

### THE EMBODIED ETHICS OF EATING AND JOINING

### RACHEL MUERS

IF SHARING FOOD HAS TO DO WITH how "our sociality is reaffirmed, negotiated, enhanced, and celebrated," there is ethical reasoning embodied in food sharing.[1] Following Michael Banner's suggestion in *The Ethics of Everyday Life*, in this chapter I use food and food sharing—or as Banner prefers to call it, "commensality"—as a starting point for exploring questions raised by the juxtaposition of theological ethics and social anthropology.[2]

My discussion also advances a broader proposal that I develop through the example of food sharing and in critical conversation with Banner. Theological ethics currently does not stand in need of renewed attention to practices per se—for, as Jennifer Herdt demonstrates in chapter 5, the "turn to practice" is already quite well established within both theology and ethics—but rather of ways of thinking about the value-laden interrelations, conflicts, shifts, and tensions *around* and *between* practices, about what happens where practices meet and interact. Food sharing, considered at the intersection of theology, ethics, and social anthropology, provides a valuable way into thinking about these questions. I use food, and specifically food sharing, as a metonym for embodied encounter across social and cultural difference.

It is not surprising that a chapter on food is included in a book on everyday ethics. Eating is at once a common or universal everyday phenomenon and one that varies enormously across cultures and contexts. Moreover, it is freighted with moral meaning—with obligations, prohibitions, and evaluations that are bound up both with the learned habits and tastes of individuals and with wider social, political, and ecological systems. From this obvious starting point, however, there are various directions in which theological everyday ethics could go—depending, inter alia, on whether we look at the coherence and continuity of food practices or at their edges, tensions, and transitions.

Consider, for example, how we look at practices of food sharing. The historical and anthropological literature gives numerous and diverse examples of contexts in which having food generates an obligation to share food, in particular ways and with particular people.[3] Sharing food in these contexts is not exactly an act of generosity, not what would ordinarily (in the contemporary study and teaching of ethics) be called an ethical decision. Rather, it is a recognition of how food *works*. You have to share it in order to keep the social body alive, which in turn is what keeps you alive. Material interdependence, and its enactment by sharing food, is not an optional extra; it is the way things are.

It would be easy for moderns tempted toward the romanticization of the premodern—and troubled by the loss of shared practices and narratives—to idealize such logics of food sharing and place them at the center of a discussion of food ethics. However, romanticization is not the only "ethical" way to look at systems of food sharing. In most contexts where the obligation to share food applies or has applied, food sharing mediates a set of power relations that are open to contestation. Just because there is an obligation to share food does not mean that there is an obligation to share food in the same way with everyone and anyone. In medieval Europe, for example, there was a very clear hierarchy of food sharing and the distribution of leftovers that mirrored the social hierarchy—starting with an enormous banquet set on the lord's table, with the copious leftovers of various grades distributed to people of various grades and eventually to the household animals. Later medieval challenges to that social hierarchy (for example, by the friars) were often formulated as challenges to the hierarchical pattern of food sharing.[4] To take a contemporary example, a study of food sharing in urban Burkina Faso demonstrates that the romanticized picture of a close-knit African household in which all food is shared and everyone is fed ignores how food sharing and distribution is a site of the exercise of and struggle for power and shows how this aspect of power is freely acknowledged and discussed by the members of the household.[5] The decision to eat alone in this context might not be a willful rejection of social solidarity or the social order but rather a protest against particular ways in which the social order is operating.

So where should we look for ethics in these pictures of food, in particular of food sharing? We could choose to look in detail at practices that maintain a group and a known social order—perhaps focused on the "shared and ordered occasion," in Banner's words—performing a stable pattern of differentiated interrelation that would "reaffirm" and "celebrate" (again in Banner's words) a distinctive embodied social ethos. If we were doing Christian theological ethics, we might at this point decide to look at recognizably *Christian* food practices—perhaps to contrast them favorably with the practices of secular modernity, with or without hints of nostalgia for premodern harmony. Alternatively, we might decide to look at the ethical questions that arise when somebody tries to do food sharing differently, or to bring together different food practices or different patterns of sharing. In this paper, I propose that theological ethics, however much it is tempted toward the former, needs to pay attention to the latter.

The reason for this, as I have already hinted, is about more than just the ethics of food and food sharing; it is about theological ethics' self-understanding as a discipline, particularly its recent history. It is not possible within the scope of this chapter to diagram the complex network of moves in late twentieth-century theology that comprise the "turn to practice," the "turn to virtues," and the "turn to culture" in theology and ethics. It is possible, however, to see that in some of their forms they tend to play on and reinforce a strong church-world boundary. Postliberal appropriations of Barth and Wittgenstein draw theology toward accounts based on internal coherence. Ethical attention to narrative and community pull toward an account of Christian ethics that focus on recognizably *Christian* practices (despite the warnings from Kathryn Tanner, and others broadly sympathetic to the project, that the boundary lines around both Christian culture and Christian practice prove difficult to draw).[6] The recent burgeoning interest in the specifically *ecclesiological* use of ethnography—while by no means assuming a particular ecclesiology—further draws the weight of academic theological attention toward recognizably Christian practices.[7] Banner's own project, while not primarily ecclesiological, finds its center of gravity in Christian traditions of liturgy and spiritual practice and seeks to highlight and recover their resources for modernity.

As Tanner and others have noted, a focus on Christian practice—contrasted, more or less explicitly, with secular practices or habits—poses theoretical problems of identification and delimitation. I suggest further, however, that this focus needs to be questioned on theological and ethical grounds. If theological ethics looks to the obviously Christian for its good examples of practices and patterns of life that lead toward human flourishing—particularly if the perceived point of contrast is modernity—it will tend to privilege the established, the predictable, and the institutionally authorized. It will tend to de-emphasize the perspective of the laity, whose Christian practice *just is* full participation in particular instances of the everyday life of families, neighborhoods, cities, workplaces, however "secular" those places may be.[8] It will also tend to de-emphasize the significance for theological ethics not only of the created goodness of the world but of the active and transformative presence of God in the world—the extent to which theological ethics might be "found" in the world and its history rather than being brought there by its ecclesial or academic practitioners.[9]

One obvious response to this possible problem is for theological ethicists to conduct or use studies of "non-church" situations or contexts—and not only as negative points of contrast or as imperfect approximations to a Christian vision. A further set of resources is found in theological-ethnographic studies of "crossing-points" in religious-and-secular contexts, sites in which the narratives and habitual responses of Christian communities interact with those of others.[10] In this chapter, rather than developing specific ethnographic studies in detail, I focus on another aspect of the task. I use the idea of food sharing as a basic feature of human sociality to present a theological and ethical exploration of the boundaries or joinings of practices. If it is the case that *everybody* works out their specific forms of embodied sociality by sharing food, what can we say, ethically, about the presence at a "common table" of many food practices, many ways of sharing food, many forms of embodied sociality? What happens when different food practices, different forms of embodied sociality, join together? How are these forms of embodied sociality maintained, challenged, repaired, or shifted through their encounters? I suggest that the study of Christian practices needs to look at their boundaries and joining points, and I propose theological and ethical starting points for this consideration.[11]

I argue, moreover, that attention to what happens around and between practices enables the theological ethicist herself, and the practice in which she is engaged, to enter the frame of ethical consideration and evaluation. In discussions of works such as *The Ethics of Everyday Life*, questions often emerge about the emergence of normative or evaluative judgments in "ethnography as theological ethics," about the relationship between the ethnographer's thick description of what *is* and the ethicist's constructive proposals about what *should* be the case. Questions also often emerge about the norms of Christian ethics—whether, for example, attention to the practices of "everyday life" is a sine qua non for the ethicist or simply an optional extra. In the discussion that follows, I draw these two sets of questions together. If we grant that theological ethics is itself a complex, located, and embodied practice, the question of how ethicists reach judgments about the everyday life they encounter is a question about the lived encounter between the ethicist and her practice, on the one hand, and some other people and practices—both in everyday life and in interdisciplinary research—on the other.[12] It is another question about the joining of practices.

The larger frame within which all this discussion is set is a theological concern about how embodiment is thought and represented. All Christian theology is obliged, in one way or another, to talk about bodies.[13] There are, however, ways of talking about bodies—and about one particular body, the body of Christ—that systematically denigrate ordinary embodiment. As successive generations of feminist theologians have argued, to think a body as securely bounded, without vulnerability, without attention to its production from and ongoing relation to other bodies, is not really to think a body at all.[14] Moreover, as Willie Jennings and others have demonstrated, a hierarchical way of thinking about embodiment, which excluded the possibility of "joining" social bodies across places and cultures, formed the basis for the racist colonial project; white supremacy relied on the idealization of certain bodies and the denial of their contingency, dependence, and relationships.[15]

In the main body of this chapter, rather than conducting an extensive survey of anthropological literature on food or food sharing, I draw out a few specific historical examples of attempts to do food ethics across difference and ask what can be learned for contemporary theological ethics. I suggest that a theological practice of everyday ethics needs to avoid idealizations of the Christian social body, constituted by Christian practices, that forget its relation to other bodies. We need to attend to the life and practice of the Christian body in ways that do not separate it from the material everyday contexts in which it is produced, encountered, joined, and struggled over. This takes us back again to the metonym of food sharing, for, as we shall see, from the earliest decades of Christianity, food sharing was a place where Christians experienced, and worked through theologically and ethically, the messiness of "joining" in or as a body in a social and historical context.

## Differences, Boundaries, and Joining Points: What Is Christian Food Sharing?

As I have noted, one possible approach to the theological ethics of food sharing (which seems to have some contemporary purchase) is that theological ethicists should examine Christian practices as examples of how food sharing is supposed to work. In this section, I consider why this might seem a good idea and a good use of theology's encounter with social anthropology—and why it might be problematic.

Two approaches to the appropriation of social anthropology for theology, in particular for theological ethics, can be traced in Banner's work and elsewhere in the literature. On the one hand, theologians use the "denaturalization of the natural," the examination of the unexamined, to call into question various contemporary assumptions about what is natural or inevitable in human behavior.[16] On the other hand, the conversation with social anthropology facilitates the naming of certain constants of human life (like food sharing) that we might go so far as to call natural, even while recognizing that this labeling is itself socially and culturally conditioned. These constants include not only biological needs but social, relational, and emotional features of what it is to be *Homo sapiens*. In practice, the theologian can argue with an eye to social anthropology that there are anthropological constraints on "denaturalization"; there are some limits, proper to human creatures, on *how* different we can be or become from one another or from what we are now.

What should theological ethicists make of this conjunction of the denaturalization of the natural and the recognition of the given? Food sharing is, rather obviously, a good place from which to think about this. Food practices are both constrained to a greater or lesser extent by given features of what it is to be human (humans have certain nutritional requirements) *and* an obvious area for the "denaturalization of the natural" given that food practices are both deeply ingrained habits and enormously varied across cultures and contexts. In *Theology on the Menu*, David Grumett and I draw attention to a forerunner for "theology learning from social anthropology,"

Jerome, as an example of both of these moves. Jerome's arguments for asceticism provide my first historical example of an attempt to do food ethics.

The argument that Jerome presents in *Against Jovinianus* for the Christian ascetic diet incorporates a rapid tour of the known world of his day. He shows off its dazzling—and we must assume, for his intended audience, frequently off-putting—diversity of everyday food practices and some of the associated diversity of evaluative judgments. Libyans eat locusts, Syrians eat land crocodiles, and some barbaric tribe in far-off Britain considers shepherds' buttocks a particular delicacy. In fact, says Jerome—denaturalizing the natural long before it was fashionable—"each race follows its own practices and peculiar usages, and takes that for the law of nature which is most familiar to it."[17] Jerome's world tour, and his suspicious conclusion about all that is called natural, clears the ground for radical ascetic practices that challenged his critics' assumptions about human nature, bodily flourishing, and embodied limits. The conclusion of the section lifts the "denaturalization of the natural" to another level, from the anthropological to the theological, from the multiplicity of human difference to the one key difference made by incorporation into the Christian body: "But suppose all nations [ate] alike . . . how does it concern us . . . who . . . are not bound to the circumstances of our birth, but of our new birth?"[18]

At this point Jerome, as was his wont (and as his historical opponents must have recognized), was playing with rhetorical and theological fire. A radical suspicion, concerning *both* the claims that people make about human nature *and* the social and cultural formations that embody these claims, risks slipping into a suspicion or denigration of embodiment per se. This is liable, in turn, to slip over into the denigration of people or groups who are read as failing adequately to overcome the limitations of their cultures, their bodies, or their food practices. If we think that we, uniquely, can float free of the "circumstances of our birth"—which notably, for Jerome, means not just biology but also social and cultural context—we are fooling ourselves, and we are liable to find it hard to deal with anything that reminds us of the "circumstances of our birth," for example, by challenging or interrupting our ingrained habits. If Christians or anyone else do not have the social and imaginative resources to acknowledge their own embodied contingency and its constraints, the affective body-response of disgust to unfamiliar food practices (reported or witnessed) is liable to be externalized into revulsion against the people (*or* the other animals) who eat *that* or who eat *like that*.[19]

On the face of it, the turn to practice in theological ethics appears to be a good way of developing the social and imaginative resources to acknowledge embodied contingency—and hence, perhaps, of developing the resources that might guard against this othering of the unfamiliar. In fact, Jerome's text already points in this direction. It is focused not on demonstrating that eating practices are all equally irrelevant to Christian life but rather on advocating a particular sort of ascetic practice.

This is the point of the reference, in the quotation given above, to "new birth." When Jerome relativizes all social and cultural differences—and indeed similarities—in the face of the difference that the "new birth" makes, what he is arguing for is a specifically *Christian* way of eating. This new way of eating, rhetorically at least, transcends the effects on food practices that the circumstances of birth create. Elsewhere in his work, he freely appeals to arguments about the health and flourishing of the human body per se in order to advocate a simple diet and, in particular, abstinence from animal flesh.[20] Following his line of argument in the most charitable direction, then, we might suggest that, far from simply denigrating the body in the name of Christianity, Jerome sees Christian food practices as the way to recover the body's flourishing by escaping the "circumstances of birth," understood as social and cultural *malforma*tions of eating.

If this reading of Jerome is correct, there is an analogy between what he claims about Christian diet and what Michael Banner implies in relation to Christian food sharing. As I have mentioned, Banner claims that food sharing is a basic site of human social formation. Shortly thereafter, at a key point in his discussion, he refers to how "Christians solemnly share bread and wine round a single table, in a meal that is open to all and from which no one is excluded."[21] Even if Banner's own account is not intended to imply a claim about how a specifically Christian way of "doing food" (namely, the Eucharist) calls humanity away from its various socially malformed "circumstances of birth" back to the true pattern given to human creatures for embodied and social flourishing, something like that claim *does* appear from time to time elsewhere in theological ethics based on the turn to practice.[22]

My concern about such a move, though, is its tendency to obscure the fact that specific Christian food practices—whether it be the Eucharist or Jerome's asceticism—always also have their circumstances of birth. They arise within, and relate to, everyday contexts. They challenge some existing relationships, including relationships of power and gender, and reinscribe others. And they join with a wide range of food cultures and food-sharing patterns. The idealization of the Eucharist as a radically inclusive, hierarchy-inverting shared meal, the answer to modernity's eating disorders, carries the risk of isolating Eucharistic eating and setting it up in contrast to, rather than in relation with, the everyday food practices in which its participants engage.

An alternative and productive approach—and this is the direction in which I think Banner's work points—is for the critical and self-reflexive attention to everyday embodied moral judgments, characteristic of the work of social anthropology, to be turned toward the food-sharing practices of the Eucharist. Among other things, such a study, rather than assuming that the Eucharist is the central point and the starting point of a distinctively Christian way of sharing food, might pay particular attention to the reciprocal relationships between the Eucharist and its social contexts, including its context of food practices. It might attend, for example, to how everyday meanings, relationships, and patterns of action associated with food enter the Eucharistic space and are repeated, shifted, or, in some cases, deliberately reversed. A rich example of this kind of reading of Eucharistic celebrations is Siobhán Garrigan's work on worship, sectarianism, and the peace process in Ireland. She provides, for example, an account of how "not drinking in church" (i.e., refusing the cup) for Irish Catholics interacts with the complex history of, among other things, the famine, the hunger strikes, the role of alcohol in stereotypical images of the Irish, and church-state relations north and south of the border.[23]

I want to suggest that this sort of attention to the thoroughly contextual character of Christian eating and the body formed by Christian food sharing—to the ways in which the "distinctively Christian" is formed and re-formed out of its wider social and material contexts—is not a second thought or an afterthought for theology and theological ethics. Just because food sharing is "everyday" and because food practices and habits (with their associated affective force) are carried from site to site, liturgical food sharing draws in, and draws on, the everyday food-sharing practices that surround it. Bread, the body of Christ, and social bodies are all assembled from bits of what is already there as well as being broken up and dispersed. Proper attention to embodiment entails attending not only to particularity and contingency but also, to use Jennings's terms again, to "joining"—to how the particular and contingent social body is formed in and through relation to others. In a later section, I shall consider how the theology and ethics of Christian eating in the New Testament are intimately bound up with the troubles and possibilities of joining.

My wider interest in this chapter, as indicated earlier, is in how theological ethics' turn to practice engages with the encounters and joinings between different practices, communities, and bodily formations. The key suggestion at this stage is simply that theological ethicists need not worry about whether and how the practices they discuss are special, irreducibly distinct, or set apart, and they should not assume that failure to assert "specialness" in this way means a loss of theologically significant identity or location. In fact, a theological and ethical exploration of food, if it also takes seriously the empirical data, raises further questions about the ways in which theological ethics draws on ideas of specialness or distinctiveness in order to establish hierarchies of embodiment. Before paying further attention to the questions raised by theological ethics' encounters with anthropology, a consideration of food sharing points to a wider issue: whether talking about *anthrop*ology is already too restrictive.

## The Common Table of Creation

Banner and others make the claim (which goes back to a reading of Levi-Strauss) that food sharing is not only universally human but distinctively human. Banner says, for example, that those people who are forced to live alone and "fall out of commensality . . . [are] joining our primate cousins as solitary eaters."[24] Comments like this—which are very far from unique to Banner's work—carry the implicit assumption that the values at the heart of ethics have to be distinctively and uniquely human. They thereby invite us to ask about the role of claims to *human* distinctiveness in theological ethics, particularly as theological ethicists attempt to use social anthropology.

The first problem with the implied claim that food sharing is something that sets us humans apart from other animals is that it is not accurate. There is an extensive literature on the complexities of food sharing with nonkin as well as with kin among nonhuman primates, and a smaller literature on food sharing among other nonhuman animals, such as vampire bats, wood ants, and members of the crow family. In much of this literature on food sharing, nobody even bothers to comment on the fact that the young of very many species need to be fed by their parents and cannot eat alone. Looking hard at food sharing makes us ask whether there is any prima facie reason why the ethics that learns from social anthropology should not also learn from ethology—and not merely to provide the term of contrast, the "bizarre" other that lets us see and condemn what we are *not*, but rather for the recognizable points of connection that show us what we *are*.[25] In sharing food, with nonkin as well as kin (but differently with each group), we are precisely *not* transcending our animal nature nor marking ourselves as qualitatively different from all the other animals; we are locating ourselves among the animals.

This recognition need not make the sharing of food, or any other behavior we have in common with other animals, any less significant for ethics. This is all the more true if, following the turn to practice, we have moved to reembody and recontextualize ethics, thereby escaping the rationalist straightjacket that restricts ethics to deliberately formulated rational choices on hard cases. It would be unfortunate—at the very least—if theological ethicists, following the turn to practice and trying to learn from social anthropology, proved to be interested only in the "added value" that being *anthropoi* supposedly gives us or only in evidence that would make *our* material and social embodiment look radically different from that of all the other animals. Once again, the challenge is to think theologically through, not in denial of, the conditions of our birth. And, here most apparently, the choice to recognize or to deny the conditions of our birth itself has significant ethical and practical implications.

A first indication of an approach to theological ethics arising from this recognition of food sharing as a creaturely—not just a human—phenomenon might arise from reflection on Psalm 104. Food appears in this psalm as a gift from God and an everyday need of all animals: "These all look to you to give them their food in due season; when you give to them, they gather it up" (Ps 104:27–28).[26]

In this picture, the human is conspicuously aligned with, rather than differentiated from, fellow creatures, frequently being mentioned with them in the same breath (as well as sharing the same breath, v. 30). Like the lions, the human has an everyday food routine: "The young lions roar for their prey, seeking their food from God. When the sun rises, they withdraw and lie down in their dens. People go out to work and to their labor until the evening" (vv. 21–23). And like (and alongside) the cattle, humans are directly dependent on seasonal plants: "You cause the grass to grow for the cattle, and plants for people to use" (v. 14). The nonhuman animals are, moreover, not eating alone. The young lions, to take the most obvious example, are not just fueling themselves but cooperating to "seek food from God." Humans and cattle, juxtaposed in this picture, are both eating together with their own kind *and* sharing space with each other.

From the point of view of an everyday ethics, the psalm invites reflection on the ecological implications of human food practices, on the ways in which food practices acknowledge creaturely dependence and interdependence, and on the difficulties of separating the biological and the social in food sharing and in particular of turning food into a basis for elevating the human above the animal. To come back to Jerome's terminology, a text like this can generate reflection on the many and interconnected "circumstances of birth" that shape what we eat and how we eat it. It both displays the contingency of those conditions and provides a caution against efforts to reshape them that are actually efforts to escape the condition of creatureliness that we share with other animals. As we shall see, while on the face of it the psalm seems merely descriptive—this is what humans do, this is what other animals do—the psalm read in a wider scriptural and theological context serves to redirect attention and the imagination in ways that in turn redirect ethical practice. It makes a difference, in practice, whether we imagine ourselves as the lords of a table of creation set out exclusively for us or as one group alongside many at a common feast.[27]

When the material from this chapter was presented at a conference—and the respondent, David Clough, focused on the section on nonhuman animals—the reaction from some in the audience of theological ethicists was striking.[28] Comments expressed deep resistance to the connection drawn between human food sharing and sociality with nonhuman animal behavior, taking the form of "but chimpanzees sharing food is not *the same* as humans sharing food" or "but humans *are different*." This was odd because there was no attempt, by me or by the respondent, to claim that humans were *just the same* as other animals in this or any other regard; that would be nonsensical. The assumption behind the comments seemed to be that there were only two options for many theological ethicists thinking about humans and animals—difference constructed as separation (with considerable investment in the maintenance of boundaries) or equivalence as denial of difference or particularity. It seems particularly challenging in the case of nonhuman animals to understand (even in theory) differences as relationships, boundaries as joining points, and the otherness of other ethical subjects as something that can be lived with.[29] The challenge is emotional and imaginative as much as cognitive; it has to do with how we have learned to inhabit our bodies. My suggestion is that Psalm 104—and other texts that place human and nonhuman animals alongside each other as recipients and sharers of food—helps to provoke the required movement of attention and imagination.

## Eating, Judging, and Reasoning: Solidarity and Difference in Food Sharing

Where does this movement lead us in the theological "ethics of everyday life"? To explore this further, I turn to the struggles over solidarity and difference taking place around shared tables in the nascent church communities of the New Testament, where new opportunities for joining—and for hierarchy-building, exclusion, and othering—were numerous; and I turn specifically to the epistle to the Romans.[30] In this context, we find further indications of how contingent circumstances of birth (different learned everyday ethics) can be transcended, not by escaping these conditions but by attentive encounter marked by generosity and vulnerability; we also see the effect that this has on the practice of ethics itself.

Theological presentations of Paul's texts on food, especially of Romans 14, have tended to downplay the significance of dietary difference—to assume that the direction of travel, as it were, is toward simply ignoring the learned and embodied habits of reasoning around food. After all, "the kingdom of God is not [about] food and drink" (Rom 14:17). The problem with reading Romans 14 simply as minimizing the significance of everyday food practices, however, is that within the text the disregard for food practices is the viewpoint of "the strong." It is the perspective of the people who think they have managed to transcend the circumstances of their birth and acquire a detached view of the rights and wrongs of the situation, the people who bring no vulnerabilities to the common table, the people who have solved all the ethical problems, to their own satisfaction at least. To adopt the perspective of the strong as normative appears to be in direct conflict with the basic patterns of reasoning elsewhere in the Pauline corpus about the formation of the Christian social body, which prioritizes the "weaker parts" and makes difference a basis of solidarity, not a barrier to it.

I argue, then, for a reading of Romans 14 that takes seriously the embodiment of different forms of ethical reasoning at the point of encounter between them. This text calls on its readers, first, to recognize the "reasonableness" of others' practice without being forced to pass judgment on it and in the context of a call to mutual obligation and responsibility. Food practices, ways of embodying and reproducing ethical judgments, in this text are reason-able and shareable around a common table.[31]

The first point that might strike the theological ethicist reading Romans 14 is the frequency of the language of judgment, which is generally given a negative inflection. In this text, judgment is a problematic enterprise. Condemnation or passing judgment (*diakriseis*) impedes the welcome of those who are weak in faith (14:1). Paul puts the sharp question, "Why do you [singular] pass judgment on your brother or sister?" (14:10) and makes the collective appeal, "Let us no longer pass judgment on one another" (14:13). The case against judging in this text proceeds on several fronts. First, there is an argument about the past (or the accomplished reality of the work of God in Christ)—God has received all these different groups, so they should not judge one another (14:3). Second, there is an argument about the eschatological future—it is wrong for brethren to judge one another, because all will stand before the judgment seat of God (14:10). Third, there is an argument about the lived present—judgment can damage or destroy the community or the individual, becoming a stumbling block (14:13).

This problematization of judgment takes us back—in the specific, concrete context of food sharing—to questions about how ethics is done. As I noted earlier, questions about judgment confront us at the joining point between different ethical practices and, indeed, at the joining point between theological ethics and social anthropology. Where and with what legitimacy does thick description pass over into normative claims and judgments? What is the point of doing ethics if no judgments are made? And if ethics has to do with judgment, how does it avoid turning into an illegitimate "passing judgment on one another"?

Lest it be thought that Romans 14 can get us nowhere with this, it is important to note that the collective appeal for "us" to stop passing judgment on one another in verse 13 moves directly into an appeal to "you" to judge in a particular way—to "make the judgment not to put stumbling blocks in the way of others."[32] Judging (evaluation, approbation, the application of norms) goes on in the community envisaged in Romans, but those who engage in judging cannot avoid material and contextual questions about how, by whom, and with what effect—including to whose detriment and to whose benefit—it is done. Judging becomes an everyday activity that does not sit above the community and its relationships but rather is drawn into the larger shared task of "walking in love" (14:15).

In order to take this further for theological ethics in relation to Romans 14, it is worth paying attention to the less frequent, but significant, use of the language of reasoning—the word family around *logos*. It appears in the first verse alongside the language of judgment—those weak in faith are to be welcomed but not for the purpose of passing judgment about *dialogismoi*, reasonings or notions. Starting by juxtaposing "passing judgment" with notions not attached to particular persons—perhaps ethical argument in the abstract—the text moves, not away from reasoning and judging but toward embodied reasoning. In the everyday ethics of table sharing in Romans 14, *logoi* are incarnate and contextual. Reasonings belong to particular people and have embodied histories; each person has to give an account (*logos*) about himself or herself (14:12), and a thing is not unclean for the one who has not reasoned it to be unclean (14:4). This particularity is not a problem; people are enjoined to be fully "convinced in their own minds" (14:5).

More than this, the center of the text juxtaposes the appearance of all before the judgment seat of God with the eschatological promise of the universal worship of God.[33] Every tongue—every body with voice—will confess or give praise to God (*exomologesetai*, 14:11). This is the context for giving account of oneself (14:12) and precedes the key text about the direction and purpose of judgment already discussed: let us stop judging one another, *but* "judge" not to put a stumbling block in front of a brother or sister. Particular embodied reasonings, and the encounters between them, are all linked directly to the eschatological praise of God uttered by "every tongue"— the telos of the common creaturely dependence on God expressed in Psalm 104. The joining of different practices culminates in shared praise rather than in uniformity or mutual condemnation.

In this context, the affirmation that "the kingdom of God is not food and drink" can be interpreted not as a dismissal of the everyday practices that form and re-form social life but rather as shifting the emphasis from possession to relationship—to "righteousness and peace and joy in the Holy Spirit" (14:17). This reading chimes with the repeated emphasis in Romans 14 on everyday mutual responsibility, care, and concern without and before passing judgment—attention to what causes the other to be injured or to stumble (14:15, 21). The challenge Paul confronts in Rome, and differently in Corinth, is the challenge of joining, of bringing together different learned food cultures in one social and commensal body, without taking the easy way out and saying that food practices do not really matter at all, and without stepping back from the critical interrogation, the judgment, of food practices based on exploitation.

This latter becomes particularly clear in the critique of eating practices in Corinth, where the rich go ahead and eat and the poor are left hungry (1 Cor 11:21), and where those who fail to see what is going on, who do not "discern the body" (*diakrineo*), are eating and drinking judgment on themselves. Judgment or discernment is required to recognize solidarity-in-difference and the course of action that will maintain it. Ethical judgment is pulled into everyday life and embodied reasonings, not mainly to reaffirm the way we already do things and not mainly to judge between my practices and another's but rather to perform the relationship between them in a way that moves toward "righteousness and peace and joy."

What other "everyday" food situations might be read through this lens? Looking at the "ethics" of food sharing in a variety of contexts reveals a number of examples of binding obligations that arise from one person or group's particular circumstances and that generate ethical calls on *others*. My obligations in relation to food do not, it seems, easily stay mine. I may need, as it were, to entrust my obligations to others in the sharing of food—to place myself in the hands of others and thereby to expose my vulnerability, not just as a hungry body but as a formed and embodied ethical subject. Particularly relevant here is the much-discussed context of hospitality. A guest arrives. Food must be shared, and the guest does not have a place in the established food-sharing system or a pre-allotted portion, so the guest's presence constitutes an open-ended obligation that the host cannot avoid. It is the guest who faces the ethical challenges—how to respect the host's vulnerability, how to ensure that the obligation does not put the host in danger.[34]

The trials of hospitality in a situation of food shortage indicate the complexity of the everyday ethics of eating. Consider, for example, the little piece of everyday ethics from extraordinary times (which are not so extraordinary, on a global scale) found in the extensive instructions issued to American GIs in Britain in 1942: "One thing to be careful about—if you are invited into a British home and the host exhorts you to 'eat up—there's plenty on the table,' go easy. It may be the family's rations for a whole week spread out to show their hospitality."[35]

The mirror-image instructions issued to the family would be the acronym that at least some Britons of my generation learned from their parents who grew up during rationing: FHB, "family hold back," because there might not be quite enough food to go around, and the guests *must* be fed. This situation entails the reciprocally gracious "covering of nakedness": the guest cares for the vulnerability of the host (by eating less) while pretending not to see that vulnerability, and the host throws herself on the mercy of the guest (by offering the best food) while pretending that it costs nothing. The whole situation is shot through with the possibility of cross-cultural misreadings that are the stuff of many traveler's tales, which are entertaining enough provided that nobody involved has actually gone to bed hungry, but it can never quite be free from that danger because actual bodies are involved. And this is before we have even considered the various other "circumstances of birth" that might affect the sharing and distribution of food around the table.

The point is not just that this is all very complicated but that there is some hope of working through it in practice, encountering the other *in practice* as an embodied ethical subject whose "circumstances of birth" are a call to me, not just a problem for her. There may be a range of vocabularies and concepts for describing this process. When a social anthropologist I know was undertaking fieldwork in the Pacific, she frequently had to tell people that she did not eat meat. She had been a vegetarian for many years, she had ethical objections to eating animals, and even if those objections had somehow disappeared, she had become physically accustomed to a diet without meat. Her normal way of explaining vegetarianism to her hosts was "it's my taboo." This was, apparently, an explanation that worked very well since it enabled the sharing of tables and the associated formation of relationships to carry on. It was also more informative than might at first appear. By saying that not eating meat was her taboo, she was conveying something like the following information: this was a serious restriction, not liable to sudden change on a whim; this was a restriction that fitted into a larger coherent pattern of obligations and relationships by which she was bound and by which her life was shaped and which others could in principle learn about; this was significant to her identity. In ethical terms, the terminology framed it primarily as a responsibility laid on *her* and distinctive to her, but it was also something with ethical implications for those who related to her—something that they were asked to recognize and respond to as part of what it meant to recognize and respond to her.

I am not claiming that sharing food with guests or strangers across different food systems and practices—and the associated set of processes, offering food, refusing food, distributing food—*inevitably* produces attentive encounter that forms and re-forms ethics. This is clear enough from the struggles that Paul, the Romans, and the Corinthians face. Theologically, the claim might be that good food sharing has a dynamic—embodied in Christ and empowered by the Holy Spirit—toward joining with the neighbor, honoring the obligations and vulnerabilities of others, receiving and sharing what belongs to each one. The food ethic that arises is not just "feeding the hungry" (from a distance) but "sharing *your bread* with the hungry" (Isa 58:7, my emphasis; c.f. Luke 3:11), acknowledging material solidarity and accepting vulnerability, recognizing boundaries as joining points. The earlier discussion of Psalm 104 suggests that this is an expansive dynamic that reaches out to the nonhuman creation as subjects of attentive encounter, not simply as objects of ethical action. And the link to the eschatological vision in the center of Romans 14 suggests that it finds its telos not only in peaceful coexistence but in shared and mutual joy. "Circumstances of birth" are transcended not by abandoning them but by their ceasing to be barriers to mutual understanding and shared discernment.

## "Good Food" and Ethical Conditions of Production

This may sound attractive, but where does it leave the actual practice of ethics, of reasoning and making judgments, about food or anything else? And what happens when the "differences" of food practice are not merely interesting cultural and ethical variations but—as, arguably, in the 1 Corinthians passage discussed above—indications of profound injustice and ethical failure? In my last main section, I take up a historical example of food sharing and food distribution to illustrate the difficulties of "joining" in the practice of ethics and the ways in which the ethicist's imagination and attention is not only shaped but also constrained by everyday practices and the interconnected systems to which they relate.

As I have already suggested, one of the moves that Michael Banner's work invites is an examination of the social relationships, structures, and imaginaries that produce the forms of ethics he judges to be problematic: the ethics of hard cases. Following the turn to anthropology and reading a little beyond Banner, we might think that ethics needs to attend to the ways in which its own social and institutional formation has produced a particular kind of ethical observer whose focus on certain issues, and inability to see other issues, is itself fraught with political and ethical dangers.

Following Alasdair MacIntyre and others, many of those who lament the collapse of ethics into "hard cases" attribute this collapse to the loss of meaningful participation in Christian and other communities shaped by shared narratives—a lack, perhaps, of "shared and ordered occasions in which our sociality is reaffirmed." Something like this analysis appears to inform Banner's project and his call for a return to "everyday ethics." However, following indications in the work of Katie Cannon, Ada María Isasi-Díaz, and others, I suggest that this might be a misrecognition of the problem.[36] What if the key problem is that ethics as a discipline became the province of people and institutions whose everyday lives were not troubled by the everyday troubles of late modernity? What if the "hard cases" of ethics are a systematic way of *not* attending closely to the everyday struggles of "hard lives"? And what if—just to be clear—this is not a conspiracy but is simply the way people who do ethics from certain institutional and social positions are inclined to think?

Food again offers particularly clear examples of how the institutional and social locations of ethicists shape not only the answers given to ethical questions but also how the questions are constructed. Everyone participates in, relies on, and is shaped by a food system, and this makes a difference to the food questions that we ask. Looking at a historical example of "doing food ethics" illustrates the point particularly starkly while posing sharp questions back to contemporary ethics.

*Round about a Pound a Week*, Maud Pember Reeves's 1913 study of East End family life, is quoted far more often by sociologists and social historians than by ethicists, but it offers fascinating case studies—with the benefit of hindsight—on how judgments about food (and many other subjects) are formed in and across different material contexts. Pember Reeves and her group of relatively wealthy social reformers narrate extended conversations with women living in relative poverty—conversations about household budgets, food purchases and food distribution, the shape of life in their contexts, its possibilities and constraints. One of the points at which Pember Reeves drops the careful scientific tone of her report and breaks out the anger—at least as far as sarcasm—is when she recalls "a course of eloquent and striking lectures delivered by an able medical man to an audience of West End charitable ladies," in which the audience was told that the best way to improve the lives of poor children would be "to walk through the East End streets with placards bearing the legend 'MILK is the proper food for babies.'"[37] Pember Reeves, though herself a

West End lady, was attentive enough to the voices and lived realities of working-class women to recognize the catastrophic failure this would be in a context where there was no reliable access to safe and appropriate milk and no spare money to obtain it, where reliance on the inadequate wage of the male breadwinner required that he be given priority in food distribution, and where "managing" to feed a family was more than what we would now regard as a full-time job.[38]

What was going on here in terms of the attention and imagination of ethics? It is clear from the records that at least some well-intentioned reformers simply never saw what Pember Reeves at least glimpsed, and their failure to see was systemic. They assumed that they as accredited experts had privileged access to all the relevant information.[39] They also assumed (and here I pick up another theme from Michael Banner's work) the institutional constraints of medical ethics—that the problem of infant nutrition, as encountered in hospitals and doctors' surgeries and all too often in mortuaries, was primarily a medical problem to which social or economic matters were at best peripheral. Here was a situation in which professional and institutional structures, in a context of class and gender injustice, worked together to reduce hard lives to hard cases, food practices to matters of individual choice, and people who did not "make the right choices"—here, mothers whose children received no milk—to rational and ethical failures, "bad mothers." I scarcely need to observe that this attitude to nutritional deficiencies among children raised in poverty, and their parents, has not gone away.

What alternative perspectives were available? *Round about a Pound a Week* still makes challenging reading, especially for those whose social location tends to put them in the position of the observer and the judge rather than the observed and the judged. It is easy to dismiss Pember Reeves's work as an only slightly more-enlightened version of middle-class do-gooding, a reformer or an ethicist using the voices and lives of the working classes as raw material for a study of "everyday life" without interrogating how her own everyday life is implicated in the situation. There is a tone of careful objectivity and distance, the voice of the researcher distanced from the (accented) voices of the observed. Parts of the report sound like the refusal or failure of joining that the young Willie Jennings—in an incident he recounts at the beginning of his book—identified in the well-intentioned white pastors who came to invite his family to church without bothering to find out which church they already attended.[40]

At other points, however, there are glimpses of how these sustained meetings and conversations might have shifted perceptions and practice or redirected attention and imagination. The practices of social solidarity, ethical and political reasoning, survival, and precarious flourishing of East End women and children emerge, piecemeal, in their own words—with food at the center of the story. The "researchers" learn not only how to fit what they find into a predetermined framework of evaluations and obligations but also what it means to operate within a different framework of evaluations and obligations shaped by material circumstances. They come to see clearly, for example, why the placards are an unethical way of doing good, why the judgments about poor people that underlie charitable giving are not only inaccurate in content but coming from the wrong place, and how the malnourished bodies of children in Lambeth are materially connected to the spaces in which the West End charitable ladies take tea.

One of the motivations behind the present collection, and behind the wider turn to practice that it represents, is the desire to stop theological ethicists acting like the doctor who tried to solve the problem of child malnutrition in Lambeth by sending in the placards. The participants in this project want theological ethics to be attentive to the complexities of, and the constraints on, everyday moral reasoning, and to be hesitant about assigning a problem to a particular subdisciplinary department (like "medical ethics"), especially if that is likely to mean systematic disregard for the lives that surround hard cases. I have already suggested that theological ethics should be attentive to its own conditions of production in order to understand why methodological problems might creep in.

How does this relate to discussions of food in contemporary ethics? Recent advocacy of "ethical eating" or "ethical consumption" has faced repeated accusations of elitism and classism. As the argument goes, "ethical" food products—organic, free range, fair trade—often are not only more expensive but also are marketed to middle-class consumers as part of a "lifestyle" package (building in assumptions about cultural preferences and educational background as well as income). As Josse Johnston and others have demonstrated through recent studies, the claim that "only middle-class people can afford to be ethical eaters" is misguided—and extremely problematic in eluding the ethical reflection and creativity of working-class and low-income consumers.[41] However, Johnston's studies also suggest that to focus the ethics of eating around "what is consumed" without paying attention to the processes surrounding consumption—where and how food is obtained, how and with whom food is shared—will tend systematically to privilege the wealthy consumer as an ethical subject. Johnston and colleagues heard from interviewees on low incomes about helping neighbors with food shopping, inviting isolated older people to their houses for dinner, or defending recent immigrants against racist criticisms of their food and eating practices. None of this, however, fitted into the "dominant ethical repertoire" (Johnston's expression) of questions and considerations that comes to the fore when people are asked about ethics and food.

Focusing on food sharing, I suggest, brings certain dimensions of everyday ethics into view with particular clarity. One is the embodied subject of ethics—the body not simply as an object of ethical claims but as the site of ethical judgment, imagination, and action. Pember Reeves (for all her faults as an observer) never forgets that the voices to which she attends come from bodies—chronically undernourished and exhausted bodies, habituated and located, emotionally connected, desiring and surviving bodies. "Circumstances of birth" form us as ethical subjects, and trying to ignore or denigrate one's own or others' "circumstances of birth" leads to bad reasoning. Gender, class, and race come to the fore in such an account of ethics. The key point is not just that gender, class, and race are structural features of everyday ethics but that they are relational constructions. These are the imagined and lived relations through which ethical bodies form *each other*, and they are marked by conflict and injustice that is exacerbated by failures to recognize material connection and interdependence, failures of attention and imagination. Ethical work in this context is done not by ignoring the differences altogether (which results in the Lambeth doctor's assumption that everybody is just like him and has the same range of choices), nor by reimagining the differences as the impermeable boundaries of distinct bodies, one group (one food culture or way of reasoning) set over against another.

Theological ethics, as the pieces in this book demonstrate, is moving away from an ethics of hard cases and discrete choices toward the everyday spaces and practices in which "sociality is reaffirmed, negotiated, enhanced and celebrated." In making this move, theological ethicists need to recognize the materiality and location of their own practices of reasoning and passing judgment as well as of the practices they describe and from which they draw their ethical claims. Theological everyday ethics takes place at the common table of creation, not at an observer's distance from it; in the middle of negotiations of solidarity and difference around a shared table; and toward the eschatological "giving account" that is also confession and praise.

## Coda: A Contemporary Site for Everyday Food Ethics

Where next for an everyday theological ethics of food sharing? To bring this discussion back to my own context and back to the ongoing project of theological ethics—and thus, among other things, to honor Michael Banner's approach to everyday ethics—I finish by proposing a possible contemporary site for reflection on some of these questions about food sharing, embodied relation, risk and vulnerability, and "circumstances of birth." The Real Junk Food Project, which began in Leeds and has now attained global reach, is a series of cafés that collect edible food that would otherwise go to waste, turn it into nutritious meals, and provide it to anyone who wants it on a "pay as you feel" basis. Payment is not limited to money and can include the offer of time or skills. The idea has spread rapidly, in part through the charismatic influence of the founder and an effective communications operation, and in some small part through the model's widespread appeal to churches, other faith communities, and existing community groups attempting to challenge and reform the food system.[42]

It is very tempting to accept uncritically an idealized version of what is going on here, which is why a good empirical study would help: the salvaging of thrown-away food to make shared meals could be read as a reclaiming of the meaning of food or as a resignification of food as primarily for sharing, not primarily for profit. To offer food to anyone who comes and to ask them to pay whatever they can is a considerable risk. In the experience of those who carry out the project, at least as they recount it in public, this risk-taking is met with a corresponding and unexpected generosity in most cases, and not necessarily of exactly the kind that is wanted or expected. Saying "pay as you feel" (where what is "paid"' does not have to be money) is a direct and culturally specific way of recognizing the recipients of the food as ethical subjects. It is also a way of making apparent the underlying material solidarity and shared vulnerability of those who serve the food and those who eat it, whatever their particular contexts and backgrounds. Moreover, the project is conceived as an intervention in local, national, and global food systems, but it consists of microscale realignments of food sharing, negotiated person to person.

The other important point is that the Real Junk Food Project is not a self-contained example of a perfect food-sharing system. It is an example not of the shared table completely "as it should be" but of food sharing as a work in progress—maybe best described as a project or an experiment rather than a "practice," existing temporarily at the boundaries between various food practices, including those of churches and places of worship as well as supermarkets, food banks, homes, and neighborhoods. By the founder's admission, it exists to put itself out of business; it takes an enormous amount of work to retrieve, check, and prepare waste food, so this is not a particularly efficient way of ensuring that everyone is fed. All of this, however, might help to enrich theological everyday ethics by focusing not only on long-sustained practices but at points of creative connection and innovation, intentionally temporary spaces and activities that draw on a range of social and ethical imaginaries to respond to local needs.

## Notes

1. Michael Banner, *The Ethics of Everyday Life: Moral Theology, Social Anthropology, and the Imagination of the Human* (Oxford: Oxford University Press, 2014), 123.

2. Banner, 123.

3. For example, on the obligation of sharing food and the iniquity of eating alone in medieval Europe, see Bridget Henisch, *Fast and Feast: Food in Medieval Society* (University Park, PA: Penn State University Press, 1976). On food sharing in urban Burkina Faso, see Liza Debevec, "To Share or Not to Share: Hierarchy in the Distribution of Family Meals in Urban Burkina Faso," *Anthropological Notebooks* 17, no. 3 (2011): 29–49. On food sharing in northern Siberia, see John Zilker et al., "Indigenous Siberians Solve Collective Action Problems through Sharing and Traditional Knowledge," *Sustainability Science* 11 (2016): 45–55.

4. As discussed, for example, in Maria A. Moisá, "The Giving of Leftovers in Medieval England," *Food and Foodways* 9, no. 2 (2001): 81–94.

5. Debevec, "To Share or Not," sees a tension between, on the one hand, the fact that children are taught not to eat alone but to "invite someone" and, on the other hand, the fact that adults fail to practice equal food distribution. As far as I can see, the tension arises more from the assumption that the anthropologist brings to her study, namely that "proper" sharing should be *equal* sharing; the families she studies do not share that assumption.

6. See Kathryn Tanner, "Theological Reflection and Christian Practices," in *Practicing Theology: Beliefs and Practices in Christian Life*, ed. Miroslav Volf and Dorothy C. Bass (Grand Rapids, MI: Eerdmans, 2002), 228–42. For a recent discussion and development of Tanner's approach, see Natalie Wigg-Stevenson, *Ethnographic Theology: An Inquiry into the Production of Theological Knowledge* (New York: Palgrave Macmillan, 2014), 24–30.

7. The turn toward ecclesiology and ethnography is presented in diverse voices—many of them raising critical questions that have given rise to ongoing discussion—in Pete Ward, ed., *Perspectives on Ecclesiology and Ethnography* (Grand Rapids, MI: Eerdmans, 2012).

8. On the significance of lay perspectives for understanding the contemporary work of theology, see Alistair I. McFadyen, "The Habitus of the Theologian," in *The Vocation of Theology Today: A Festschrift for David Ford*, ed. Tom Greggs, Rachel Muers, and Simeon Zahl (Eugene, OR: Wipf & Stock, 2013), 259–72.

9. I take the idea of "found" theological ethics from J. Ben Quash, *Found Theology: History, Imagination and the Holy Spirit* (London: Bloomsbury / T&T Clark, 2013).

10. A key example is Luke Bretherton, *Resurrecting Democracy: Faith, Citizenship and the Politics of a Common Life* (Cambridge: Cambridge University Press, 2013). See also the discussion in Rachel Muers with Thomas Britt, "Faithful Untidiness: Christian Social Action in a British City," *International Journal of Public Theology* 6, no. 2 (2012): 205–27.

11. "Joining" is a key concept in the work of Willie Jennings on undoing theological complicity in colonialism and racism, and my use of the term here is indebted to him. Jennings sees colonial resistance to "joining"—to nondominating encounter across embodied difference—rooted in a deficient theology and practice of embodiment. Willie James Jennings, *The Christian Imagination: Theology and the Origins of Race* (New Haven, CT: Yale University Press, 2010), 288–90.

12. For a discussion, following Bourdieu, Wacquant, and others, of how the practice of ethnography affects theological practice, see Christian Scharen, *Fieldwork in Theology* (Grand Rapids, MI: Baker, 2015); and Wigg-Stevenson, *Ethnographic Theology*, chap. 4.

13. See also Craig M. Gay, chapter 7 in this volume.

14. For a recent constructive example of how feminist attention to embodiment—encompassing vulnerability and fecundity—can challenge and reshape theological and anthropological imagination, see Tina Beattie, *Theology after Postmodernity* (Oxford: Oxford University Press, 2013), especially 364–87.

15. Jennings, *Christian Imagination*; see also J. Kameron Carter, *Race: A Theological Account* (New York: Oxford University Press, 2008).

16. An example from Banner is his critique—which I find very problematic on other grounds—of the widespread "modern" desire for a "child of one's own." See Banner, *Ethics of Everyday Life*, 35–81.

17. Jerome, *Against Jovinianus*, trans. W. H. Fremantle, G. Lewis, and W. G. Martley, in *Nicene and Post-Nicene Fathers, Second Series*, vol. 6, ed. Philip Schaff and Henry Wace (Buffalo, NY: Christian Literature Publishing, 1893), 2.7. See Rachel Muers and David Grumett, *Theology on the Menu: Asceticism, Meat and Christian Diet* (London: Routledge, 2010), 135–36.

18. Jerome, *Against Jovinianus* 2.7.

19. Jerome himself, I think, stays on the right side of this fault line in Christian anthropology and ethics. First, the specific context of his work is a critique of the taken-for-granted food practices in his own context and among people like him, so the target in a text like this is precisely *not* the far-off barbarian British but his neighbors, the supposedly civilized local elites who think they know what is good for them *and everyone else*—who have, in a different way, forgotten the circumstances of their birth. Jerome's text is similar in this respect to the "rhetorical sting operation" of Romans

1–2 described thus by Eugene Rogers—first evoking the response of disgust at "the other" and then using it to call into question a false construction of the self. See Eugene Rogers, *Sexuality and the Christian Body* (Oxford: Blackwell, 1999), 46.

20. See the discussion in Muers and Grumett, *Theology on the Menu*, 33–34.

21. Banner, *Ethics of Everyday Life*, 134.

22. For example, Stanley Hauerwas and Samuel Wells, eds., *Blackwell Companion to Christian Ethics* (Oxford: Blackwell, 2004), is structured around the Eucharist and, like Banner's work in this respect if no other, presents a direct challenge to decision-based models of ethics.

23. Siobhán Garrigan, *The Real Peace Process: Worship, Politics and the End of Sectarianism* (London: Routledge, 2010), 115–55.

24. Banner, *Ethics of Everyday Life*, 123.

25. For a comparative discussion from the perspective of evolutionary anthropology, see Adrian Jaeggi and Michael Gurven, "Natural Co-operators: Food Sharing in Humans and Other Primates," *Evolutionary Anthropology* 22, no. 4 (2013): 186–95. For a review discussion of food sharing in other species that is striking for its breadth of coverage ("from arthropods to apes"), see Jeffrey R. Stevens and Ian C. Gilby, "A Conceptual Framework for Nonkin Food Sharing: Timing and Currency of Benefits," *Animal Behaviour* 67 (2004): 603–14.

26. All biblical quotations are from the NRSV unless otherwise indicated.

27. Both possibilities are abundantly present within Christian theological tradition. For example, David Clough discusses the tensions within Luther's account of nonhuman creation, which is read both as a house furnished for humanity's use and as, at least in its unfallen state, a place in which human and nonhuman animals share a "common table." See David Clough, "The Anxiety of the Human Animal: Martin Luther on Non-human Animals and Human Animality," in *Creaturely Theology: On God, Humans and Other Animals*, ed. Celia Deane-Drummond and David Clough (London: SCM, 2009), 41–60.

28. I am very grateful to David Clough for his response and for the subsequent discussion.

29. On animals as subjects in religion, including in religious ethics, see Celia Deane-Drummond, Rebecca Artinian-Kaiser, and David L. Clough, eds., *Animals as Religious Subjects: Transdisciplinary Perspectives* (New York: Bloomsbury T&T Clark, 2013).

30. I take the terminology of "solidarity and difference" from David G. Horrell, *Solidarity and Difference: A Contemporary Reading of Paul's Ethics* (Edinburgh: T&T Clark, 2005).

31. What follows develops the argument of a short paper titled "Sharing Tables: The Challenge of Dietary Pluralism for Christian Communities," presented to a conference of the Christian Vegetarian Association UK in 2010; the original presentation is available at http://www.all-crea tures.org/articles/sharing.html.

32. This is my translation; English translations conceal the repetition of the verb *krineo* in verse 13, understandably because it is very hard to convey idiomatically.

33. The term is not etymologically linked, but the imagery is connected.

34. For discussions of the theological ethics of hospitality, see Christine D. Pohl, *Making Room: Recovering Hospitality as a Christian Tradition* (Grand Rapids, MI: Eerdmans, 1999); Luke Bretherton, *Hospitality as Holiness: Christian Witness Amid Moral Diversity* (Aldershot, UK: Ashgate, 2006), 126–46; and Elizabeth Newman, *Untamed Hospitality: Welcoming God and Other Strangers* (Grand Rapids, MI: Baker, 2007).

35. United States War Department, *Instructions for American Servicemen in Britain*, 1942 (Oxford: Bodleian Library, 2004), 40.

36. Katie Cannon, *Black Womanist Ethics* (New York: Oxford University Press, 1988); Ada María Isasi-Díaz, *En La Lucha / In the Struggle: Elaborating a Mujerista Theology* (Minneapolis, MN: Fortress, 1994). See especially Cannon's critical account of the exclusion of Black women's ethical reasoning from theological ethics in *Black Womanist Ethics*, 1–5. For more on Cannon and Isasi-Díaz in relation to everyday ethics, see also Thurston, chapter 2 in this volume.

37. Maud Pember Reeves, *Round about a Pound a Week* (1913; repr., London: Persephone Books, 2008), 90.

38. As Sebastien Rioux suggests in his article on pre-war food distribution that draws on Pember Reeves's work, women's undernourished bodies "reconciled the disjuncture between wage and household economies." Sebastien Rioux, "Capitalism and the Production of Uneven Bodies: Women, Motherhood and Food Distribution in Britain c. 1850–1941," *Transactions of the Institute of British Geographers* 40, no. 1 (2015): 1–14, at 3.

39. For an even more egregious example, see the transcript in Rioux, "Capitalism," 7, of part of the proceedings of the Inter-Departmental Committee on Physical Deterioration (1904).

40. Jennings, *Christian Imagination*, 1–4.

41. Josse Johnston, Michelle Szabo, and Alexandra Rodney, "Good Food, Good People: Understanding the Cultural Repertoire of Ethical Eating," *Journal of Consumer Culture* 11, no. 3 (2011): 293–318.

42. See The Real Junk Food Project, http://therealjunkfoodproject.org (accessed August 11, 2016).

# PART III
# EVERYDAY ETHICS

A FUTURE FOR MORAL THEOLOGY?

# 11

# THE TASKS OF CHRISTIAN ETHICS

═══════════

## THEOLOGY, ETHNOGRAPHY, AND THE CONUNDRUMS OF THE CULTURAL TURN

### LUKE BRETHERTON

IN THIS ESSAY I SITUATE a turn to ethnography in Christian ethics within a broader turn to culture, using this turn as a starting point for identifying and understanding the key tasks of Christian ethics. The catalyst and dialogue partner for my analysis is Michael Banner's book *The Ethics of Everyday Life*, a programmatic intervention in the field of Christian ethics in which ethnography, and social anthropology more broadly, is held up as a means of renewing the discipline. Through situating Banner's proposal within a wider Anglican tradition of moral and political reflection, one in which the work of Samuel Taylor Coleridge is key, I assess the strengths and weaknesses of Banner's proposal. While critical, I take Banner's account of the nature and form of Christian ethics to be right, particularly in the space it creates for ethnographic work to inform theological reflection on moral and political questions. But any turn to culture as a point of initiation for generating moral and political theology (and by extension the methods for analyzing culture) must address three conundrums that inevitably beset such a move. I address each of these in turn. The first conundrum is the tension between, on the one hand, the otherness of divine self-revelation given in Jesus Christ that challenges and represents a crisis to all our ways of knowing and being in the world, and, on the other hand, how history and culture are the crucibles of divine-human encounter. The second relates to the nature of social ontology and whether, east of Eden, conflict or harmony is the basic character of social, political, and economic relations. The last is the question of how to disidentify with and detach ourselves from the idolatrous structures and cultural processes that condition our ways of understanding and describing everyday practices related to such activities as learning, using technology, working, borrowing and lending, eating, and citizenship. Some means of disidentification is vital if we are to speak truthfully about ourselves, our neighbors, and the world we live in and thereby make fitting and faithful moral judgments. And each of these three conundrums must be addressed if, rather than simply accepting the terms and conditions of social anthropology as a field and ethnography as a method for analyzing culture, Christian ethics is to metabolize them in a theologically critical and alert way such that their use helps rather than hinders the core tasks of Christian ethics. Where appropriate, I use my own four-year ethnographic examination of community organizing as a case study for addressing these three conundrums in a constructive way.

## Coleridge, Anglican Theology, and the Cultural Turn

Michael Banner's book *The Ethics of Everyday Life* can be situated in a venerable tradition of Anglican moral and political thought, one in which Samuel Taylor Coleridge is a vital figure. It invokes culture as either a starting point or catalyst for further moral and political reflection rather than nature, Scripture, creedal confession, or philosophy. Within this tradition, natural law, doctrine, Scripture, and philosophy may well be vital elements in the subsequent development of a moral argument, but attention to expressions of and ways of imagining human life together is what initiates and provides the key reference point for moral and political reflection. Thomas Arnold and F. D. Maurice are two of the most prominent developers of Coleridge's ideas in the nineteenth century. In the contemporary context, we can trace the watermark of Coleridge's approach, particularly his emphasis on the role of culture and the imagination in shaping the good life, in those Anglican theologians who have made a move parallel to that of Banner, most notably Sarah Coakley, Kathryn Tanner, Elaine Graham, and Graham Ward. I will argue that the use of ethnographic methodologies in Christian ethics continues and expands this tradition.

Coleridge initiated a distinctive strand in the tradition of Anglican moral and political thought by rejecting a notion of natural law as that which can be excavated by reason alone. Rather, for Coleridge, creation was an open yet unfinished cosmos whose value is not objectively given but depends on our capacity to participate in it via symbolic processes of meaning-making. That is to say, the human self stands in an open, interpretive, and constantly evolving relationship to creation.[1] To orientate ourselves appropriately and participate faithfully, we need forms of observation and reasoning that do not lead us to step back from the world but enable us to discover with others how to participate in creation in ever richer ways.[2] For Coleridge, inattention to our actual forms of life through overly abstract kinds of reasoning renders us not only mere spectators but also spectral beings alienated from any determinate form of life. By contrast, close attention to, participation in, and open-hearted wonder about the world around us can generate imaginative visions for inhabiting creation in more nourishing, concrete, and profound ways.[3] The world as it is (i.e., as observed and participated in) can then be brought into conversation with and reimagined through the life, death, and resurrection of Jesus Christ.[4] As Banner puts it, "The imagination of Christ's life provides a rich and vibrant imaginary of a new social topography" through which we might discover what is fitting, right, and good.[5]

For both Coleridge and Banner, "culture"—which includes customary patterns of human speech, cooperative action, affective registers, and material expressions—is a site of simultaneous alienation from God and creation.[6] It is the crucible through which we struggle to attune ourselves to our status as creatures, neighbors, and redeemed sinners. On this approach, it is neither reason nor nature but culture that connects and divides humans from each other. What is sought is neither a change of mind nor a better approximation of a predetermined telos but a conversion of our imagination and a transformation of our practices and habits. On Banner's account, Christian moral thought should be both "therapeutic," helping us live as better creatures, and "evangelical," announcing new and good ways to live as those for whom Christ has died, Christ has risen, and Christ will come again.[7] Christian ethics stands at the cusp of the therapeutic, seeking to heal existing forms of life, and the evangelical, pointing to and imagining new ways of being alive in and through Christ. In a way that is consonant with Banner's book, Coleridge held that a humane culture must have an interplay between "permanence" (the tending of our inherited customs and traditions) and "progression" (innovation and development of new approaches).[8] That said, Coleridge and Banner, echoing Richard Hooker, see custom as able to embody tried and tested forms of practical reasoning, leading to a preference for what is already established rather than for innovation.[9]

In a gesture characteristic of much Anglican theology, it is "culture" (and/or history) rather than "nature" that forms the locus of Banner's inquiry. However, he does not posit a nature/culture binary.[10] Rather, the primary contrast to be kept in view is with natural law as an approach to moral theology. Natural law theories tend to conceptualize nature as having predetermined, protological ends that can be enumerated independently of any particular instantiation of, say, the family. They also tend to emphasize an intrinsic set of properties, universal laws, or rationally determined ends.[11] By contrast, an approach that makes a particular cultural historical form of life the beginning point and primary focus of moral reflection involves trying to describe and evaluate it within its own frame of reference and in relation to its conformity to Christ.[12] Whereas nature as a term tends to dehistoricize and mystify what is contingent and fallen, culture and history as terms make contingency, and thence revisability, a constitutive feature of all customary practices and forms of sociality. Such a view is not against a notion of nature per se but rather recognizes that our experience of nature is always already historical and cultural and thereby fallen and finite.[13] Such a view is in direct continuity with Coleridge's conception that to name nature requires poetic, historical, and cultural empathy and insight, not adherence to formal laws or speculative and abstract rationalizations.[14]

Banner draws on a painting by Stanley Spencer and other works of art to illustrate and exemplify the therapeutic and evangelical process of reflection he invites. Coleridge does this through his poetry, particularly the *Rime of the Ancient Mariner*, which is a parable of human attempts to instrumentalize what should properly lie beyond the realm of human control and consumption. The character and form of Coleridge's criticism of modernity in the poem is worth dwelling on as it illustrates a point that will be developed later in relation to a particular kind of orientation to modernity.

The *Rime* portrays seafaring as a means of participating in and navigating the ocean. But seafaring is also a means of transgressing that which is not given to humans as habitation and represents a limit to and space beyond human mastery. Along with Coleridge's "protest poems" and lectures such as "Lecture on the Slave Trade" (1795), the *Rime* is part of his attempt to critique and contest the emergence of consumer culture in eighteenth-century Britain, a culture built on slavery, imperial expansion, and the relentless commodification of nature. According to Thomas Pfau, the *Rime* does not protest this or that particular issue but rather the broader orientation to and way of imagining our place in creation.[15] For Coleridge, this orientation gave birth to modernity and its symptoms, such as commercialism, consumerism, and imperialism, which in turn gave rise to the Atlantic slave trade and industrial-scale extraction and destruction. Rather than seeking to cultivate our created being in pursuit of God-given ends and enable participation in creation in ways that hallow and cultivate it, the *Rime* portrays the modern condition as one of purposeless, spiritually empty curiosity driven by a desire to gratify our whims. This leads to our own alienation and the violent destruction of others. For Coleridge, what he calls "the spirit of commerce" is not a problem because it produces this or that instance of injustice. Rather, it is a problem because it inverts the moral order and makes the *libido dominandi* a point of virtue. In response, Coleridge sought ways to reimagine his cultural context through a trinitarian and Christological prism.[16] Whatever one makes of the form and content of his moral and political vision, we can see how Banner's understanding of Christian ethics echoes Coleridge's approach.[17] As Banner puts it, "The task of everyday Christian ethics is . . . to imagine, recount and thereby hopefully sustain the practice and enactment of human being after the measure of Christ's human being."[18] In the rest of this chapter, I explore how we should understand the tasks of Christian ethics and what role ethnography might play in undertaking them.[19]

## The Tasks of Christian Ethics

From the early twentieth century onward, Christian ethics has tended to focus on two dimensions of a single task, which, to use Banner's terms, has therapeutic and evangelical ends in view. The broader theological undertaking within which this task arises is the need to understand what it means to be "the church" in relationship to "the world" (church and world designating different orientations to and ways of receiving the gift of life). The work of the Christian ethicist is intimately bound up with his or her participation in the church and the world and the questions that arise at the interface between the two. The Christian ethicist is not a visitor on a research trip noting the strange flora and fauna of an exotic but alien terrain but rather a fellow worshipper and citizen sharing a common life with others on whom he or she depends and without which life and faith would not be possible. The contribution of the Christian ethicist to understanding church-world relations is twofold. First, the ethicist undertakes conceptual labor that clarifies and articulates ways of understanding what is going on in the context of a specific form of life or in relation to a particular problem, identifying the conditions and possibilities of judgments about this form of life or problem. Second, they offer normative prescriptions for how to live faithfully, hopefully, and lovingly in the midst of or in response to this form of life or problem. These prescriptions contribute to spelling out a Christian vision of human flourishing situated in and attentive to a particular context or area of concern.[20]

This twofold task entails assembling the intellectual resources through which we may, first, understand better what is going on (i.e., what we are doing when we speak and act together as moral and political animals) and, second, determine ways in which we might bear witness to what the healing and fulfillment of this form of life or area of concern might entail. The most common methods Christian ethicists deploy for undertaking this twofold task involves interpreting the Scriptures and their reception history, excavating the social and intellectual histories of the Christian tradition, and analyzing the "signs of the times" through engaging diverse philosophical frameworks, theoretical critiques, and forms of social scientific analysis. Sometimes this requires focusing on the everyday (e.g., how we grow our food, what counts as food, whom we should eat with) and sometimes this requires attention to the exceptional (e.g., defining abortion and whether it is licit).

However, we must pause at this point to consider Banner's claim that there is "no well-established practice of everyday ethics."[21] While this is true in the field of bioethics—Banner's thesis serving to open up this specific field in a generative way—it is patently not true and entirely contradicted by a swathe of both substantive proposals for Christian ethics and the cumulative work of ethicists across a wide range of topics. In terms of substantive approaches, the recovery of virtue ethics since the 1950s has, as a central concern, the social, economic, and political formation of the moral subject through everyday practices and habits.[22] This explicit focus on everyday practices of formation (e.g., bricklaying) was set over and against what Stanley Hauerwas called "quandary ethics."[23] Ethics, as a "wisdom-determined activity," requires being apprenticed into a particular form of life and way of seeing the world that enables one to make right judgments about how to act appropriately: virtue ethics is thereby constitutively concerned with the everyday. That said, the primary focus of Christian virtue ethicists such as Hauerwas was not the everyday but rather ecclesial practices, such as baptism and the Eucharist.

Like virtue ethics, but in a more determinate and focused way, a key feature of both Latinx and womanist Christian social ethics is the turn to the quotidian as a vital aspect of moral and political reflection, particularly when trying to discern what liberation for marginalized people might look like.[24] This is because the ordinary and everyday world is the site at which forms of domination, and the precarity and oppression they produce, are most acutely displayed. This is exemplified in Katie Cannon's seminal contribution to womanist ethics that made the work of the folklorist and anthropologist Zora Neale Hurston a key interlocutor in her turn to the ordinary and everyday as sites for generating moral wisdom and an emancipatory social ethics.[25] In terms of topics, focusing on the everyday is a definitional feature of the concerns contemporary Christian ethicists address. These include the treatment of the environment, and what we grow and how we eat; constructions of class, sexuality, gender, and kinship and thence the basic forms of human life together; the nature and form of citizenship; how to understand friendship as a moral relation; and what we buy and how we buy it via processes of consumerism.

The turn to ethnography by Banner and others can be read as simply intensifying a concern for the everyday already present within Christian ethics.[26] At one level, ethnography merely provides a more inductive, systematic, and contextually attuned method of asking the questions "What is going on?" and "What is to be done?" It does this through paying attention to, first, the somatic, affective, spatial, and temporal dimensions of moral and political discourses and judgments and, second, to the inevitable struggles and conflicts through which we come to be formed and tell the truth about our churches, our world, and our ourselves. But the turn to ethnography does not merely enhance what Christian ethicists have been doing for many years; it also adds something.

Ethnographic description is not the same as either theoretical critique or other forms of social scientific analysis. In a way that has parallels in womanist and Latinx social ethics, the body and being of the researcher is the primary research tool, and consequently, as a method it demands a higher degree of self-reflexivity. Where it differs from womanist and Latinx social ethics that do not draw on ethnographic methodologies is that such methods enable us to put under the microscope, with at least some degree of rigor, our intuitive and inevitable sympathies for our own context. Conversely, intellectual history and theoretical critique—the primary form Christian ethics takes in the modern period—are prone to bracket their own structural and historical location from the analysis and often sit so far above the fray that they forget they are also participants in that which they study. My claim is not that ethnography is necessary for doing good Christian ethics. It is rather that the addition of an ethnographic approach to Christian ethics *complements* other kinds of analysis, particularly as Christian ethics as a field of inquiry has become more professionalized, with many of its academic practitioners sequestered in universities and increasingly divorced from pastoral and other congregational and civic responsibilities. Ethnography can act as a poultice against abstraction, mystification, generalizations based on anecdote, the confusion of a worldly teleology for eschatology, and an amnesia that we are worshippers and citizens first and academics second.

As a methodology, ethnographic study helps address Coleridge's (and Banner's) core concern. It is, at least tacitly, committed to an epistemology in which knowledge of the world comes primarily through participation and apprenticeship and not through generalization and abstraction. It is thus more consonant with an incarnational understanding of truth: the truths of revelation are participative and relational events to be encountered, inhabited, and habituated into and not things or ideas to be possessed. Moreover, the accuracy of our apprehension of God's self-revelation in Jesus Christ is not, ultimately, assessed by whether we espouse this or that statement of faith but by the quality and depth of our love of God and neighbor.

Ethnography as a method is well suited to diagnosing and analyzing lived forms of belief and everyday practices that are mediated not only via texts but also by language in use, material exchanges, and a world of acoustic, visual, olfactory, and other physical affects. There is, however, a proper move from fieldwork to theology as a mode of theorization; this is part of the interplay of the descriptive and the normative.[27] Indeed, it is the move to constructive theology in reference to how to imagine new and good ways to live as those for whom Christ has died, Christ has risen, and Christ will come again that provides a normative point of reference for ethnographic evaluative description. Theology brings accountability beyond the emic and the immanent. That said, an ethnographically informed Christian ethics begins inductively, with broader conceptualizations emerging in an iterative and dialogical process that moves from the particular to the universal, not vice versa. In my own work on contemporary politics, for example, ethnography is a particularly fitting approach since politics, by nature, is about action in time. As action in time, politics involves questions of power (the ability to act) and historicity (the temporal and temporary nature of action). The unpredictable and unstable nature of political life directs attention away from universal principles and general historical patterns toward the peculiar features of singular events and institutions within particular historical contexts.

Ethnography as a method and social anthropology as a field are enormously helpful aids in identifying the kind of processes and practices through which contemporary moral and political judgments come to be.

This brings me to a broader point: political and moral judgments are discovered, not made. We do not impose meaning on the world by a voluntaristic act of will, as clunky distinctions between fact and value suppose. The universe is not a blank slate. Rather, we discover the world and its meanings and purposes through immersion in particular forms of what the anthropologist Tim Ingold calls a "meshwork": that is, the interlaced pathways, places, and events that form our lifeworld.[28] This lifeworld is one that creates us, and that we create, in an ongoing process. It is the water we swim in, which flows through us, and in which we flow. Our lifeworld, our judgments, and our visions of the good are mutually constitutive and coemergent.

Because ethnography can be a helpful aid in fulfilling the key tasks of Christian ethics, there is much that is appealing about Coleridge's and, by extension, Banner's cultural turn. But we must also consider some characteristic problems that attend any theological turn to culture and whether the use of ethnography exacerbates or mitigates these problems.

## Between Barth and Tillich

The first such problem is one Banner has addressed directly in his earlier work.[29] We may characterize this first conundrum as being caught between Barth and Tillich—that is, between, on the one hand, the otherness of divine self-revelation given in Jesus Christ that challenges and represents a crisis to all our ways of knowing and being in the world and, on the other hand, how materiality, history, and culture are the crucibles of divine-human encounter.[30] Strategies for coordinating Christ and culture abound. But in relation to the use of ethnographic methods, the polarization between Barth and Tillich has been addressed in specific ways. David Tracy offers one such influential account, advocating a critical correlation between "Christian texts" and "common human experience," with human experience being described through social scientific or other means.[31] Correlationist approaches like that pioneered by Tracy posit a relative autonomy between different modes of knowledge such as theology and social science, an autonomy that must then be correlated. On this account, ethnography is simply a means of delineating human experience that theology then reflects on. However, the complex and multifarious exchanges between theological and political, economic, or social categories makes implausible any such autonomy: Christian discourses and common human experience cannot be disentangled so clearly.

John Milbank's critique of social theory rejects correlationist approaches to co-ordinating Christ and culture and thus fuels a certain suspicion regarding the use of ethnography for constructive theological work. But Milbank's own approach must also be questioned. It is not sufficient to position theology as an independent sphere of knowledge that can disregard political and social theory or social scientific kinds of analysis as anti-theology. While a critique of anti-theological presuppositions and methodological atheism informing much social scientific work is necessary, we cannot simply depose it and reinstall theology on the throne. To borrow a phrase from Nicholas Healy, nontheological modes of analysis can be immanent without necessarily being immanentist.[32] Both Tracy and Milbank posit an inherent competition and conflict between modern social theory and social scientific analysis (and, by extension, ethnography) and theology, a conflict that must either be resolved by one side winning or a negotiated settlement arrived at through a process of mediation, compromise, or combination. Yet, as Catherine Pickstock has recently argued, theology, in all its forms, is inherently interdisciplinary: "It is not as if one first enthrones theology as a pre-linguistic pristine edifice, and then asks, how do I communicate this? Rather, its earliest formation, integrity and canonical bases presumed mediation by means of other discourses and bodies of learning. And theology must perforce have recourse to literary and linguistic forms, philosophical analysis, poetry, music and many other disciplines and idioms of expression, in order to express herself as herself."[33]

What Pickstock articulates unveils how both correlationist and competitive accounts of the relationship between theology and social science fail to reckon with the interpenetration of interpretations and the mutually constitutive nature of church and world. To parse and extend Hauerwas, if the world cannot know itself as the world without the church, the church cannot know itself as the church without the world. To be a "sister," "brother," or "citizen" requires conceptualizations of those terms in relation to actual sisters, brothers, and citizens and their histories and our encounter with each other as sisters and brothers in Christ and citizens of the kingdom of God.

Ethnography offers a disciplined way of paying attention to and excavating the intersection of ecclesial practices with social and political life. It thereby gives us a way to generate conceptualizations fully alive to the ways church and world are interdependent and mutually constitutive yet also not the same. Furthermore, it highlights the kinds of ad hoc and contingent commensurability between theology and other ways of naming and making judgments about different ways of being alive. The hope is that through such disciplined modes of listening to the church and/or the world, our conceptions of ourselves in relation to God and others can undergo a deepening moral conversion that enables our practical reasoning to be shriven and healed so that we may make increasingly just, wise, and faithful judgments and become more open to receiving and responding to the work of the Spirit among us.

The broader point to draw out for the relationship between ethnography and theology is that the church cannot be read as simply a microcosm of prior and wider social, political, or economic processes and structural forces: it has its own integrity. Yet neither can an analysis of the church be separated from how it is in a relationship of codetermination (and at times co-construction) with its political, social, and economic environment. What I mean by codetermination is illustrated by Charles Taylor's account of how secularity is the result not of external processes of modernization acting on belief and practice wherein the political environment determines the nature of belief and practice, nor of the internal logic of Christianity, but of how belief and unbelief are themselves constantly interacting and changing. Belief and unbelief codetermine and mutually constitute each other in an ongoing way.[34]

Let me illustrate all of this in relation to my own work. My second book, *Christianity and Contemporary Politics*, drew on the ethnographic work of others so as to avoid an essentialized and abstract conception of church-state relations and to attend to the ad hoc commensurability between "Christian" and "non-Christian" conceptions of the good. Subsequently, in *Resurrecting Democracy*, I extended and developed in a more in-depth and systematic way this inductive and ethnographic orientation. Through a four-year case study of a community organizing coalition in London, I was able to discern the interplay and intersection of notions of faithfulness and citizenship at work both in churches and in community organizing as a form of democratic politics. Central to any such exploration is a problem that ancient and modern political thought has wrestled with: namely, how to coordinate the sometimes conflicting obligations demanded by faithfulness to the polity and one's fellow citizens with faithfulness to God and one's fellow believers.

Part of what is at stake in both books is an attempt to move beyond overly materialist assumptions that dominate political theory and inherently construe theological discourses as epiphenomenal and therefore marginal to understanding political life. The arguments developed represent a form of what some call a "postsecular," "asecular," or "sociotheological" discourse, but which I call a "faithfully secular" one, wherein theological beliefs and ecclesial practices co-construct and are interwoven with other patterns of belief and practice so as to constitute a genuinely plural pattern of secularity that is open to multiple configurations of time and space. In this faithfully secular account, theological forms of analysis stand side by side with other modes and contribute to the form, coloring, and texture of the overall picture. This faithfully secular analysis is in keeping with developments in the contemporary study of "religion" and "secular" politics, which, once viewed as academically distinct areas of concern, are now seen as intertwined, both in theory and practice.[35] Jürgen

THE TASKS OF CHRISTIAN ETHICS  ·  181

Habermas is but one example of a contemporary philosopher who now recognizes the importance of religious categories for the development of generative political thought able to address central dilemmas of contemporary human existence. However, while "postsecular" philosophers often draw on theological ideas, they are not very interested in the lived experiences, practices, and communities of religious people.[36] And for all the recent emphasis on practice, a similar inattention plagues many theologians writing about politics.[37] Inattention to the actual embodiment and performance of religious beliefs and practices is deeply problematic, not least because it replicates an ideological marginalization of religion to the private, the internal, and the subjective and thereby replicates methodologically many of the false assumptions about the nature of religious belief and practice that underwrote the secularization thesis. My use of an ethnographic methodology and attention to theological discourses is an attempt to overcome the myopia about religious belief and practice that shapes much contemporary political thought, whether theological or not. Hence in the title *Resurrecting Democracy*, the term *resurrecting* is used in a deliberate play against expectations of what is considered "religious" and "political" language. The title instantiates what the book argues for, that is, a form of faithful secularity in which political and theological beliefs and practices are understood as coemergent, standing simultaneously in a mutually reparative and critical relation to each other.

As I worked on the book, I struggled with how to connect my interest in coming to normative judgments about what good democratic politics and faithful citizenship entail and the ethnographic research I was doing. I found particularly helpful the "extended case study" method developed by the sociologist Michael Burawoy. It has many parallels with the apprenticeship-based approach of Pierre Bourdieu and Loïc Wacquant. Like Bourdieu and Wacquant, Burawoy's method seeks to avoid, on the one hand, the positivism that reduces social science to a natural science model and, on the other hand, a reductive postmodernism that suppresses any scientific dimension at all, reducing social science to dialogue between insider and outsider aimed at mutual self-understanding without any attempt at explanation.[38] However, I found that the "extended case study" method more directly addressed my concerns related to the interaction of theory, fieldwork, and the formulation of normative judgments. Further lines of connection can be made between this approach and "phronetic social science" as developed by Bent Flyvbjerg and Matthew Desmond's conception of "relational ethnography."[39] The broader point to be made here is that not all ethnography is alike: it is not a monochromatic methodology, and some approaches are more amenable to theological engagement than others.

On this kind of approach, recourse to ethnographic methods is not done simply to describe practices and interpret their meanings. Rather, it sets the scene for constructive moral judgments based on practical reason. Theologically, such judgments are in the service of better (that is, more faithful, loving, and hopeful) ways of being alive. This is in keeping with how I formulated the twofold task of Christian ethics, which seeks not only to explain but also to generate moral judgments about what to do and how to do it. Of necessity, this requires dialogic encounter with practice, identifying the ways that preexisting moral judgments fail to connect with practice, and discovering the ways that practice challenges existing theological frames of reference. Flux and multiplicity become occasions for refinement and further specificity in Christian ethics as judgment on practice, whether that practice is of an everyday or exceptional nature. Such judgments are themselves contextual without becoming relativistic. They are part of the ongoing argument within a tradition about what is true, good, and beautiful (i.e., the nature and proper form of a flourishing life) that is itself caught between the otherness of divine self-revelation given in Jesus Christ and how history and culture are the crucibles of divine-human encounter.

## Temporality and the Nature of Social Ontology

The second problem that Christian ethics must consider in its turn to culture (and, by extension, ethnography) is the question of whether, east of Eden, conflict or harmony is the basic character of social, political, and economic relations. Here we are caught (sociologically) between Durkheim and Weber and (theologically) between James Cone and Desmond Tutu. Banner himself gives a definite answer: peace in the modern world is fugitive and is either "inserted" into a "world given to conflict and war and alienation" or snatched back from the "chaos."[40] In Banner's account, this chaotic world of conflict and alienation is most acutely represented by the instrumentalizing and technocratic culture of modern medicine, which he repeatedly contrasts with older, more "traditional" forms of life such as that of the Greek village studied by Juliet du Boulay.[41] Her book has a parallel framework: she poses her account of the Greek village as one that records a way of life on the cusp of dissolution by processes of modernization.

Banner echoes a large swathe of Anglican social thought as well as European sociology that posits a conflict between tradition and modernity. This opposition is exemplified in the work of Ferdinand Tönnies, particularly his distinction between *Gemeinschaft* and *Gesellschaft*.[42] On such an account, community is understood as either a static or inherited social formation that is subject to inevitable dissolution through processes of modernization such as industrialization and urbanization.[43] In ecclesial terms, the role of the church is to shore up or protect community from the depredations of modernity. Lurking behind the theological adoption of this particular stream of sociology are two assumptions. The first is a Neoplatonic view of an organic harmony and hierarchy of interests and ends ("the great chain of being") that modernity undermines and dissolves into a conflict of each against all. The second is a certain reading of Augustine. It is this latter view that underlies both Coleridge and Banner's approach. Modernity, with its technological prowess, commercial spirit, and will to power represents the antithesis of the city of God and incarnates the *libido dominandi* of the earthly city. But contrary to Augustine, for whom the *saeculum* was a field of wheat and tares, this modernity-critical stream of Augustinianism introduces a temporal division and, with it, a dangerous nostalgia that sacralizes the past and falsely demonizes the present, forgetting that the Spirit can make Christ present to all times and places.

On this kind of account, Christianity either becomes an endangered species to be protected on special reservations or weaponized in order to defend Western culture from internal collapse and external attack. As exemplified in the work of the Anglican political theorist and historian John Neville Figgis, there is a consistent move by twentieth-century European theologians to pose an Augustinian Christian moral vision as the last redoubt against a Nietzschean future of domination and depravity.[44] Joseph Ratzinger and John Milbank are but two prominent contemporary examples of such a stance.[45] For Ratzinger and Milbank, the fortunes of Christianity and the West rise and fall together, with Christianity called on to provide the moral and intellectual resources to prevent internal collapse and stave off external attack.

But Coleridge's cultural turn could also be taken to point in a different direction and be aligned with a more American stream of sociology exemplified in the work of George Herbert Mead, Robert Park, and Ernest Burgess. Park and Burgess were the founders of urban ethnography, and their philosophy was pragmatist and antipositivistic.[46] They saw community as an ongoing work of institution building and social interaction through which people form meaningful relationships and develop a collective sense of identity and place over time. Any such process involves both conflict and conciliation. The role of ethnography is to chart particular configurations of conflict and consensus, power and resistance. It was precisely this approach that directly informed the social and political vision of Saul Alinsky, the dean of community organizing, who was trained by Park and Burgess at the University of Chicago in the 1930s. Modernization can lead to new and better configurations of community as well as oppressive and decadent ones. Northern England artist L. S. Lowry's 1949 picture *A Football Match* exemplifies this vision: new and vibrant modes of sociality can emerge in the midst of modernity's dark satanic mills. But rather than being snatched or inserted into the picture, they are constitutive of it. The rules of the games that *Homo ludens* enjoys in modernity may be very different from those of ancient or medieval ones, but play still goes on. This would seem to be a truly Augustinian orientation, one that attempts to understand our social and political life as an order of love, albeit one disfigured and disordered by idolatrously loving the right things the wrong way.

Just and compassionate forms of life together and common objects of love in the earthly city must be discovered through processes of conflict and conciliation. Of necessity, if this process of discovery is to be faithful, it entails rendering ourselves vulnerable to God and neighbor. Strategies of invulnerability and keeping control are antimissiological; that is, they are a refusal to discover and bear witness to what the Spirit is doing among these people in this place by predetermining what Christianity looks like, overidentifying it with a previous cultural form. Such a move denies how loss, vulnerability, and lack of control are central to the experience of acting faithfully, lovingly, and hopefully with and for others. Indeed, as Rowan Williams argues, one of the most intense moments of divine presence and agency in human history is one in which "the sheer historical vulnerability of the human is most starkly shown, where unfinishedness, tension, the rejection of meaning and community are displayed in the figure of a man simultaneously denied voice and identity by the religious and political rationalities of his day."[47] The crucifixion is the condition and possibility of our conversion and movement into new kinds of relationship with God and neighbor. Yet this conversion demands that we orientate ourselves in a particular way to living in time and the experience of flux, change, and transition that is constitutive of being temporal creatures. A cultural turn should properly be a turn to reckon with our frailty, finitude, and fallenness and how becoming "church" is about discovering, with these people, in this place at this time, how unity in Christ amid our differences might be experienced and embraced. If the Spirit makes Christ present in all periods of history, albeit in different ways, then every historical era is a field of wheat and tares in which the work of Christ and the Spirit must be discerned and discovered. As Williams characterizes it in his reflections on Richard Hooker, this entails a "contemplative pragmatism" born out of discerning, in a particular historical context and out of a specific tradition of belief and practice, a pattern of wisdom "focused in and through the Word incarnate."[48] My claim is that ethnography can aid us in that process of pragmatic contemplation. What Christian ethicists *cannot* do is introduce a nostalgic division that poses the past as good and the present as intrinsically bad. But neither can we embrace the present as an unequivocal good or make crass judgments about who is and who is not on the "right side of history." Rather, we must find ways to identify with Christ and thereby disidentify with the idols and systems of domination with which we are always and already entangled.

## Disidentifying with Idolatry

This brings me to the last conundrum that needs to be addressed if Christian ethics is to foreground culture as a starting point: any *turn to* culture necessitates a paradoxical *turn away from* our culture so that we might disidentify with, and cease to invest in, the idolatrous structures and cultural processes that condition our ways of thinking about and describing the "everyday" practices such as learning, using technology, working, borrowing and spending, eating, and citizenship. Some means of detachment is vital if we are to speak truthfully about ourselves, our neighbors, and the world we live in and thereby make fitting and faithful moral judgments.

Here we are back to Barth, Tillich, and, we can add, Dietrich Bonhoeffer: three white European men who, each in his own way, tried to disidentify with the hegemonic structures and cultural processes of domination that conditioned them, and sought to develop trenchant, theologically driven critiques of such structures, which, in Bonhoeffer's case, executed him. In particular, Bonhoeffer's intellectual and personal journey from his bourgeois and nationalistic German milieu to Union Seminary, his immersion in the Harlem Renaissance, and his subsequent adoption of a confessional stance against Nazi Germany invites us to examine the intersection between our own structural location, the faithfulness of our witness, and the nature and focus of our theological reflection, research, and writing.[49]

Liberation theologies advocate a preferential option for the poor as a way of disidentifying with patterns of domination, realizing that theology is itself in bondage to social and political processes from which it needs liberation. A more recent proposal for addressing the need for liberation from our "mind-forged manacles" is Sarah Coakley's advocacy of contemplative prayer as a means of "unmastery."[50] Another, more "cataphatic" form of ascetic purgation and detachment is my own proposal for engagement in certain kinds of democratic politics.[51] What is in view in such proposals is how to take seriously the interrelationship between structural location, epistemology, and the need for the conversion of our moral reasoning. Such proposals are ways we might become "otherwise"; that is, becoming wise and insightful about those not like us (the other) in such a way that a fruitful common life might emerge between oneself and an other, whether at an interpersonal, intercommunal, or structural level. Becoming otherwise entails new patterns of being alive (embodied practices, structures of feeling, and ways of relating and remembering) that make possible a generative common life between friends, strangers, enemies, and the friendless. It thus involves conversion, the movement into another way of being alive so that "I" no longer interpret and experience the terms and conditions of our shared life together only in terms defined by my experience and history.[52] Part of becoming otherwise is disidentifying with and disinvesting in the structures and systems that unjustly privilege and insulate us from encountering and being shaped by others, particularly the poor and marginalized (the friendless), in ways we cannot control.

Ethnographic description and analysis might be conceived as a means of becoming otherwise for theologians.[53] At its best, what it produces is a kind of iconographic writing that summons us to contemplation, or open attention and reception of a lifeworld we did not make and do not control, in order to heal and convert our own forms of seeing, hearing, and talking about the world around us.[54] As a form of disciplined and active listening, ethnography thereby echoes Ambrose's exhortation: "The law says: 'Hear, O Israel, the Lord thy God.' It said not: 'Speak,' but 'Hear.' . . . Be silent therefore first of all, and hearken, that thou fail not in thy tongue."[55] For Ambrose, as for St. Paul, faith and the body of Christ come to be through an act of listening.

An ethnographic case study can be iconic because what it signifies can exceed its immediate representational conditions in such a way that it can germinate new ways of understanding other historical and contemporary contexts. As an icon pointing beyond itself, the particular is not subsumed within the universal, nor the part within the whole. Rather, an iconic case study invites and allows for a dynamic and imaginative interplay between its particularity and other contexts. The kind of iconic deployment of ethnography in relation to theory generation and the articulation of normative commitments that I am arguing for is in the spirit of Bruno Latour's call for criticism that moves beyond iconoclasm. Truth telling is not reducible to critique understood as exposing falsehoods. It can also entail bearing witness. And the form of the witness is not only that of the *testis* or "third party" who impartially observes and speaks out on behalf of another. There is also the testimony of the *superstes* (Latin) or *martyr* (Greek): the person who has lived through the events described and challenges others to come together with them to create something new or tend something of worth. The ideal critic, for Latour, is a kind of *superstes* who shows forth "arenas in which to gather" and offers constructive ways to care for and tend fragile matters of concern.[56]

As part of aiding theologians in becoming otherwise through beginning with disciplined forms of listening and contemplation, ethnographic modes can help identify how particular knowledge regimes, *habitus*, affective circuits, and structures of power are distorting or muting the legitimate claims of others.[57] Any analysis needs to face the reality of power relations and how certain histories and kinds of knowledge and experience are legitimized and others marginalized to the benefit of some and the detriment of others. At the same time, moral and political action must still be possible. In order to avoid overly abstract and all-encompassing analysis of power and identify spaces for judgments about what constitutes good and bad action among these people in this place, there is a need to focus on practices.[58] Without attention to the quotidian ways people are able to act in concert and form a *sensus communis* through public practices of speech and action, we have little to say other than wolves eat sheep, power corrupts, and the strong triumph over the weak. Overly deterministic accounts of unilateral, "command-obedience" conceptions of power and the domination of structural forces such as capitalism do not allow for the reality of the kinds of agency that is often observed through ethnographic research. Such agency embodied in practice can provide conditions for the emergence of "relational power." For Hannah Arendt, such relational power "corresponds to the human ability not just to act, but to act in concert. [Relational] power is never the property of an individual; it belongs to a group and remains in existence only so long as the group keeps together."[59] Through ends-oriented and conscious action in concert, the weak can resist the unilateral power of money and the state in order to establish goods in common. The early labor and civil rights movements, along with broad-based community organizing, are paradigmatic examples of such relational power in action, and all depended on forms of practice and habituation drawn from traditions of popular piety such as those found in Methodism, Black-led churches, and Roman Catholicism.[60] A relational view of power allows for human agency, something excluded from overly deterministic, reductionist, and materialistic views of the relationship between structure and agency. The kind of ethnographically informed investigation I am advocating focuses on the conditions and possibilities of agency, their outworking in political and social practices, the consequent generation of a common life, and the construction of ways to care for and cure the fragile patterns of sociality on which life itself depends—namely, relations of intimacy, care, and dependency that suffuse and undergird all aspects of our spiritual, ecological, political, social, and economic ways of being alive. Moreover, any account of politics as a moral enterprise depends on the reality of individual and collective agency, the comprehension of which requires nonreductive, nondeterministic, nonbinary, and imaginative portrayals of human life together.

## Conclusion

Recourse to ethnographic methods is made not simply in order to describe practices and interpret their meanings. Rather, Christian ethics can aid the formulation of constructive judgments about what is going on and what is to be done. As a discipline, it can utilize ethnographic modes of attention as a way of avoiding hasty abstractions and generalizations by listening closely and participating faithfully so as to make judgments based on practical reason. Such judgments are in the service of more faithful, hopeful, and loving action that nourishes forms of human flourishing. This kind of approach does not presume a coherent whole of which the rules or grammar can be uncovered through thick description. Christian ethics is not the explication and articulation of a preexisting set of meanings. Rather, it formulates judgments through dialogic encounter with practice. Flux and multiplicity become occasions for refinement and further specificity. For moral theologians, such judgments are contributions to and caught up within an ongoing argument about what it means in practice to bear faithful, hopeful, and loving witness to Jesus Christ in the power of the Spirit.

# Notes

1. Thomas Pfau, *Minding the Modern: Human Agency, Intellectual Traditions, and Responsible Knowledge* (Notre Dame, IN: University of Notre Dame Press, 2013), 489.

2. David P. Calleo notes that for Coleridge, "The besetting sin of radicals and reactionaries . . . was love of abstraction and oversimplification which generated 'partial' views of society and what it meant to be human. He singled out in particular the democratic Utopians, the Tory reactionaries, the English political economists [e.g., Bentham, Ricardo, and Malthus]." David P. Calleo, *Coleridge and the Idea of the Modern State* (New Haven, CT: Yale University Press, 1966), 9.

3. Alan Gregory, *Coleridge and the Conservative Imagination* (Macon, GA: Mercer University Press, 2003), 51–70. In some ways Coleridge is echoing Plato (in *Theaetetus*), who has Socrates say that philosophy begins in wonder.

4. Michael Banner, *The Ethics of Everyday Life: Moral Theology, Social Anthropology, and the Imagination of the Human* (Oxford: Oxford University Press, 2014), 3.

5. Banner, 209.

6. A definition of culture is notoriously hard to pin down. For a classic definition, see Raymond Williams, *Keywords: A Vocabulary of Culture and Society* (New York: Oxford University Press, 2015). In the field of Christian ethics, H. Richard Niebuhr made an influential distinction between culture and divine activity, on the one hand, and culture and nature, on the other. But these binaries blur and tend to collapse upon further reflection. For a more recent and increasingly influential discussion, see Kathryn Tanner, *Theories of Culture: A New Agenda for Theology* (Minneapolis, MN: Fortress Press, 1997). Tanner's analysis is drawn on by many as part of a turn to ethnography in Christian ethics.

7. Banner, *Ethics of Everyday Life*, 13–18.

8. What is in play for Coleridge is less a formal understanding of culture as an identifiable kind of phenomenon and, parallel to German notions of *Bildung*, a more humanistic sense of what is entailed in being a cultured person—that is, one who knows how to recognize what should be valued and thence preserved, and how to tend and care for it so that it flourishes and contributes to the common good. The cultured person knows how to appropriately cultivate, which means discerning what is fitting and finding the balance between continuity and change. Coleridge abhorred Jacobins and anti-Jacobins alike because both lacked the ability to tend to the world in such a way as to cultivate a humane culture. Jacobins so focus on progress that they destroy the soil out of which new life is cultivated, while anti-Jacobins reify tradition and custom to such an extent that they strangle or destroy any new life growing up in the soil.

9. Paul Avis notes that, for Hooker, "Custom is made up of the deposit of practical judgments and the ensuing practices that a society has inherited from its forebears. Custom is the product of the exercise of prudence by past ages and is therefore fundamentally reasonable." Avis also points out that for Hooker (and we might add for Coleridge and Banner), there should be a presumption as to the "integrity of custom" and a "bias toward tradition." See Paul Avis, *In Search of Authority: Anglican Theological Method from the Reformation to the Enlightenment* (London: T&T Clark, 2014), 120–21. On Burke and Coleridge's conservatism and the differences between them, see Gregory, *Coleridge and the Conservative Imagination*.

10. In many ways Coleridge anticipates the concerns of the "new materialists," such as Bruno Latour and Jane Bennett, who contest and disrupt distinctions between nature and culture, material and social, and human and nonhuman. And Coleridge's concern to avoid a Spinozist turn to monism and pantheism anticipates some of the key questions that confront theologians in any engagement with new materialist thought. For an overview of new materialist concerns, see William Connolly, "The 'New Materialism' and the Fragility of Things," *Millennium: Journal of International Studies* 41, no. 3 (2013): 399–412.

11. A contemporary instantiation of such an approach is that articulated by Germain Grisez and John Finnis. There are more contextually attuned approaches to natural law that are alert to issues of contingency. Jean Porter's work is one recent example.

12. In social scientific terms this could be characterized as the difference between nomothetic and idiographic approaches to the study of human life together.

13. For an exploration of this point directly in relation to Thomas Aquinas's conception of natural law, see Eugene Rogers, *Aquinas and the Supreme Court: Race, Gender, and Failure of Natural Law in Thomas's Biblical Commentaries* (Chichester, UK: Wiley-Blackwell, 2013).

14. Avis, *In Search of Authority*, 331–34.

15. Pfau, *Minding the Modern*, 454–67.

16. For an exploration of Coleridge's theological vision, see Colin E. Gunton, *The One, the Three and the Many: God, Creation, and the Culture of Modernity* (Cambridge: Cambridge University Press, 1993).

17. As set out in his *On the Constitution of the Church and State*, Coleridge sought development of a humane culture via proper attention to the interplay of "permanence" and "progression" guided by an educated "clerisy" who combine good sense (a sense of the whole, not just the parts) with a stake in and loyalty to the ongoing flourishing of a given culture, and who are prepared to defend it against revolutionary utopians (of left or right) and their final solutions and the emerging culture of mass consumerism. See Samuel Taylor Coleridge, *On the Constitution of Church and State: According to the Idea of Each* (London: Hurst, Chance, and Co., 1830).

18. Banner, *Ethics of Everyday Life*, 209.

19. What is missing is attention to the nonhuman. Culture seems to exist on top of or at one remove from "nature." Bruno Latour and other "new materialists" take society as a complex assemblage of human and nonhuman actors, not as an autonomous entity or realm that can be appealed to in order to explain why things are as they are, or that can be somehow changed apart from changing the way things are. As a result, the question of political or social change becomes a question of changing our relations not only to other humans but to the nonhuman as well.

20. Tacit here is H. Richard Niebuhr's admonition that the first question of Christian ethics is "What is going on?" See *The Responsible Self: An Essay in Christian Moral Philosophy* (New York: Harper and Row, 1963), 60–61. Although rather than "responsibility" being the primary value to be embodied, in my account, faith, hope, and love are the determinative dispositions to be cultivated.

21. Banner, *Ethics of Everyday Life*, 3.

22. For example, Alasdair MacIntyre argues that the very skills and virtues that make humans more than mere animal creatures (rational agency) emerge from quotidian and embodied practices of vulnerability and dependence. See *Dependent Rational Animals: Why Human Beings Need the Virtues* (London: Duckworth, 1999).

23. Stanley Hauerwas, *Vision and Virtue: Essays in Christian Ethical Reflection* (Notre Dame, IN: University of Notre Dame Press, 1981).

24. See, for example, Miguel De La Torre, *Doing Christian Ethics from the Margins* (Maryknoll, NY: Orbis, 2004), 72; Maria Pilar Aquino, "Theological Method in U.S. Latino/a Theology: Toward an Intercultural Theology for the Third Millennium," in *From the Heart of Our People: Latino/a Explorations in Catholic Systematic Theology*, ed. Orlando O. Espín and Miguel H. Díaz (Maryknoll, NY: Orbis, 1999), 6–48; and Ada María Isasi-Díaz, *Mujerista Theology* (Maryknoll, NY: Orbis, 1996), 66–72.

25. Katie Cannon, *Black Womanist Ethics* (Atlanta, GA: Scholars Press, 1988). See also Thurston, chapter 2 in this volume.

26. Banner does briefly note a vibrant stream of work that, like his, draws on ethnography to better address itself to the task of undertaking moral and political reflection in a theological key. See Banner, *Ethics of Everyday Life*, 3n3.

27. It is not the case that fieldwork does description and theory does normative evaluation and prescription. Theory can be descriptive, and any act of description is at the same time an evaluation of what is going on and carries, even if only tacitly, certain normative commitments.

28. Tim Ingold, "When ANT Meets SPIDER: Social Theory for Arthropods," in *Being Alive: Essays on Movement, Knowledge and Description* (London: Routledge, 2011), 89–97.

29. See especially Michael C. Banner, "Turning the World Upside Down—and Some Other

Tasks for Dogmatic Christian Ethics," in *Christian Ethics and Contemporary Moral Problems* (Cambridge: Cambridge University Press, 1999), 1–46.

30. I use Barth and Tillich not because they establish this polarity but because they are two of the most influential voices in modern Western Christian ethics to have taken up and developed these positions.

31. David Tracy, *Blessed Rage for Order: The New Pluralism in Theology* (Chicago: University of Chicago Press, 1996).

32. This distinction is drawn from a paper by Nicholas Healy titled "Playing Catch-Up to the Contemporary Social Imaginary: A Constructive Ecclesiology," Ecclesiology and Ethnography Conference, Fircroft College, University of Birmingham, January 4–6, 2011.

33. Catherine Pickstock, "The Confidence of Theology: Frontiers of Christianity in Britain Today," *ABC Religion and Ethics Online*, April 15, 2016, http://www.abc.net.au/religion/articles/2016/04/15/4444059.htm.

34. Charles Taylor, *A Secular Age* (Cambridge, MA: Harvard University Press, 2007).

35. For an overview of "postsecular" philosophical voices and the erasing of disciplinary boundaries between the study of religion and politics, see Ola Sigurdson, "Beyond Secularism? Towards a Post-Secular Political Theology," *Modern Theology* 26, no. 2 (2010): 177–96.

36. Sigurdson, 180.

37. See, for example, the work of Oliver O'Donovan, Stanley Hauerwas, John Milbank, and Jürgen Moltmann.

38. Michael Burawoy, *Ethnography Unbound: Power and Resistance in the Modern Metropolis* (Berkeley: University of California Press, 1991), 3.

39. Bent Flyvbjerg, *Making Social Science Matter: Why Social Inquiry Fails and How It Can Succeed Again*, trans. Steven Sampson (Cambridge: Cambridge University Press, 2001); Bent Flyvbjerg, Todd Landman, and Sanford Schram, eds., *Real Social Science: Applied Phronesis* (Cambridge: Cambridge University Press, 2012); Matthew Desmond, "Relational Ethnography," *Theory and Society* 43, no. 5 (2014): 547–79. Desmond explicitly situates his approach in dialogue with Burawoy's.

40. Banner, *Ethics of Everyday Life*, 208–9.

41. Juliet du Boulay, *Cosmos, Life and Liturgy in a Greek Orthodox Village* (Limni, Greece: Denise Harvey, 2009).

42. On the use of *community* in Anglican social thought and its links to the work of Tönnies, see Matthew Grimley, *Citizenship, Community and the Church of England: Liberal Anglican Theories of the State between the Wars* (Oxford: Clarendon Press, 2004), 1–4.

43. T. S. Eliot's "Choruses from The Rock" (1934) exemplifies this view.

44. John Neville Figgis states, "A cult of [Nietzsche], almost like a religion, has been proceeding. It is nearly twenty years ago since his danger and his charm became clear to me." *Will to Freedom; or the Gospel of Nietzsche and the Gospel of Christ* (New York: Charles Scribner's Son, 1917), 5.

45. In *Theology and Social Theory: Beyond Secular Reason* (Oxford: Blackwell, 2006), John Milbank introduces Augustine explicitly as the sole alternative to the Nietzschean politics of violent domination. In *Europe Today and Tomorrow: Addressing the Fundamental Issues* (San Francisco: Ignatius, 2007), Joseph Ratzinger identifies the fate of western Europe with the fate of Christianity.

46. Paul Atkinson, Amanda Coffey, Sara Delamont, John Lofland, and Lyn Lofland, eds. *Handbook of Ethnography*, rev. ed. (London: Sage, 2007), 19.

47. Rowan Williams, "Hegel and the Gods of Postmodernism," in *Wrestling with Angels: Conversations in Modern Theology*, ed. Mike Higton (Grand Rapids, MI: Eerdmans, 2007), 32.

48. Rowan Williams, *Anglican Identities* (Cambridge, MA: Cowley Publications, 2003), 38–39, 55–56.

49. Reggie Williams's work on Bonhoeffer's time in Harlem and his learning from figures in the Harlem Renaissance suggests that this encounter with a very different stream of Christianity and a very different experience led Bonhoeffer to disidentify with German bourgeois and nationalist values and identify more with Christ and, through Christ, with the persecuted and oppressed. On this

see Reggie Williams, *Bonhoeffer's Black Jesus: Harlem Renaissance Theology and an Ethic of Resistance* (Waco, TX: Baylor University Press, 2014).

50. Sarah Coakley, *God, Sexuality, and the Self: An Essay "On the Trinity"* (Cambridge: Cambridge University Press, 2013).

51. Luke Bretherton, *Christianity and Contemporary Politics: The Conditions and Possibilities of Faithful Witness* (Chichester, UK: Wiley-Blackwell, 2009).

52. The notion of becoming otherwise builds on a broad range of "other" orientated ethical reflection ranging from Judith Butler to Emmanuel Levinas and Jean-Luc Marion. A key concern of such reflection is the conception of the self as somehow autarchic, autonomous, and orientated toward securing itself and the world in terms established by itself, thereby refusing the call or claim of others and how the self is constituted through relations with others.

53. Aana Marie Vigen notes how ethnography for her involved a conversion to work with and learn from others not like her and inculcated a certain posture to the world and orientation to social transformation in her scholarship. See Christian Scharen and Aana Marie Vigen, *Ethnography as Christian Theology and Ethics* (London: Continuum, 2011), 7. It should be noted that the ethnographer has to have her or his own presuppositions challenged and unlearn what counts as common sense through the process of research. The ethnographer's "common-sense" assumptions often preconstruct in a problematic way what is taken to be an appropriate topic of inquiry. These assumptions are shaped not only by structural location but also by academic formation and field, which then shapes what constitutes legitimate foci and discursive frameworks of interpretation.

54. The idea of ethnographies as forms of iconographic writing draws on Coleridge's conception of history as both about the events in themselves and how any particular event can symbolize and represent more universal themes and "ideas" that spatially and temporally transcend their contexts, exceeding their immediate representational conditions in such a way that they can germinate other historical, symbolic, and semiotic configurations. This does not subsume the particular within the universal, or the part within the whole; rather, it allows for a dynamic interplay between them, an interplay in which imagination plays the part of mediator and reconciler, preventing the reduction of one to the other. On this, see Gregory, *Coleridge and the Conservative Imagination*, 112–18.

55. St. Ambrose, "On the Duties of the Clergy," in *Nicene and Post-Nicene Fathers*, Second Series, vol. 10, ed. Philip Schaff and Henry Wace, trans. H. De Romestein (Edinburgh: T&T Clark, 1989), 2. Ambrose explicitly links listening and "active silence" to faithful witness and the building up of the church.

56. Bruno Latour, "Why Has Critique Run Out of Steam? From Matters of Fact to Matters of Concern," *Critical Inquiry* 30, no. 2 (2004): 225–48, at 246.

57. On this, see Bent Flyvbjerg, *Rationality and Power: Democracy in Practice* (Chicago: University of Chicago Press, 1998).

58. The focus on practice can encompass both MacIntyre and Bourdieu's conception of practice. If MacIntyre brings into view conscious and ends-orientated forms of practice, Bourdieu's conception of *habitus* and practice renders visible and thence open to contestation prereflexive patterns of sociality and judgment-making.

59. Hannah Arendt, "On Violence," in *Crises of the Republic* (Orlando, FL: Harcourt Brace & Co., 1972), 143.

60. See Luke Bretherton, *Resurrecting Democracy: Faith, Citizenship, and the Politics of Common Life* (New York: Cambridge University Press, 2015), chap. 1.

# 12

# SACRAMENTAL ETHICS AND THE FUTURE OF MORAL THEOLOGY

## CHARLES MATHEWES

INSTEAD OF ENGAGING THE DETAILED PROGRAM of Banner's book, this chapter asks about the nature and purpose of the discipline of moral theology in light of it. For a work of moral theology, the book is quite theologically chaste and, for a programmatic work, remarkably austere. This signifies a sage Burkean prudence. Luckily, I do not have that virtue, so I will rush in where Banner fears to tread, offering some proposals for future formation and trying to connect them to social anthropology as well. To do that here, I will say something about where Banner's book might take us in years to come.

It is no criticism of *The Ethics of Everyday Life* to say the book is epoch-marking rather than epoch-making. It is a kind of capstone to the past few decades' methodological reflection in theological ethics and an exemplary text for what moral theology, once it has learned from those methodological reflections, can do. Banner's basic proposal to resituate theology in conversation with social anthropology rather than philosophy is a strikingly lucid way of articulating a move that many people have been struggling to accomplish since the 1970s. In this way Banner's book is not fundamentally an explorer but a pioneer settler, consolidating insights and systematizing them.

But the book is not essentially retrospective. Its prospective promise is what I find most interesting. Methodologically, it is the first major theological work in a long while to make self-conscious and unapologetic use of frankly secular social science. This is not the work of someone who takes his aim to be berating "secular reason" but instead to see what use he can make of this admittedly damaged thing. It is worth noting that historically the field of Christian ethics in the United States emerged in deep conversation with the social sciences in the late nineteenth and early twentieth centuries. The social sciences were a major presence in our field for scholars like H. Richard Niebuhr and James Gustafson. Indeed, I suspect the disappearance of serious engagement with social science is a consequence of the professionalization of the field that happened from the 1970s forward. I hope Banner's work heralds a willingness on the part of moral theologians and Christian ethicists to engage more seriously with such work in coming years.

Materially, the book seeks to cast a new and (what is to many of us) strange light on the shape of Christian moral life. In doing so it may disorient its readers a bit, but the disorientation serves its aim: to offer a fresh, vivid, and thick description of the moments of Christian life in a way that brings into view how that life means to sculpt creatures who not only confess that they are out of place in the world that we typically call home, but also *feel* and *act* out of place in that world. The orthogonality of this formation reveals something crucial about the orthogonality of the Gospel itself. As Flannery O'Connor is reputed to have put it, "And you shall know the truth, and the truth will make you odd."

## Banner's Theological and Philosophical Sources

Its method may be more sophisticated, self-conscious, and systematic, but in its matter we see much that we have seen, albeit more dimly, before. For Banner's work articulates a mode of moral theology that synthesizes two lines of scholarship that have both been quite foundational for Christian ethics and moral theology for the past few decades. Here the major players are Stanley Hauerwas (and, at some distance in several senses, Oliver O'Donovan) and, albeit a bit off center, Alasdair MacIntyre and, behind him, Elizabeth Anscombe. Understanding how this work relates to that scholarship may be useful.

The work of Stanley Hauerwas is one obvious influence, particularly Hauerwas's repeated essay-length assaults declaiming the need for the church first and foremost to be the church—to be the social ethic that some want it to profess—and for theology to be judged fundamentally by how well it enables this effort. What is it to "be the church"? Hauerwas focuses mostly on the church as an institution that builds character for its inhabitants, but it also aims at the proclamation of its message to the whole world. In a way you can say the churches have a catholic and an evangelical dynamism. The churches shape people to become fit for the weight of glory that will be their eschatological due in the kingdom of heaven, the republic of grace. They also train people to come to understand themselves (by being so shaped) as unable to stay complacent in their own sanctification, to be not so much obligated as compelled to communicate this shaping to other people and to carry their transfiguration out into the world, to announce it and invite others to understand themselves as sharing in it. Obviously these two foci are interrelated and manifest in multiple ways in different lives.

Negatively, Hauerwas's claim is a profoundly *anti-academic* move in theology, particularly in his American context: for his positive view implies that the primary audience of Christian theology ought not to be the academic community of scholars but the churches. This insistence, and the methodological and material implications that he takes to derive from it, have gotten him into no end of trouble with his colleagues, who read him to be insulting them. They are right, although his insults are typically on target. (Let me just say that contemporary higher education is a strange place for the center of Christian moral imagination to be located, but it is, and the churches and the theologians are both at fault for that.) But he is also critiqued, sometimes by the same people, for other and more interesting reasons. Hauerwas's endorsement of "the church" has been all too easy to take over by authoritative voices who wish to keep power at the cost of genuine requests or urgings from the faithful for a more Christian way of being in the church. Unfortunately, Hauerwas's own work has been rather easily co-opted by authoritative church structures and leaders. It is often read to authorize humans in positions of authority taking succor at the idea that the basic problem they must face is something called "liberalism," which is so vaguely described that it seems easy to affix to any claim for rights or legitimacy, and so they eagerly affix it to all such claims.[1] For all his discussion of pacifism and of standing up to the dominating powers, few actual ecclesiastical guerrillas find inspiration in reading Hauerwas's work. You may think this is a shame (I do), but it is hard to deny.

Banner's turn to social anthropology develops Hauerwas's strategy in a superficially more polite manner. This "turn" implies that the sterility of contemporary philosophical debate (even more professionalized and bureaucratized than academic theological discourse) is a Babylonian captivity for the Christian moral-theological imagination. Instead, we should look to social anthropology's attempts to scrutinize how distinct people in particular places and times are living out their moral imaginations and reshaping those imaginations in the wake of living them out. I agree with Banner on this. Although philosophy can still be quite handy, reforming moral theology on the lived attempt of actual particular people to understand and inhabit a distinctively Christian way of life may well help us to understand how theological discourse informs Christian practice and to do so in a way more clearly in dialogue with other disciplines in a mutually edifying manner.

The second influence on Banner's project is provided by Alasdair MacIntyre, although looming behind him in ways he occasionally acknowledges but his acolytes have overlooked is the prophetic essay "Modern Moral Philosophy," published by Elizabeth Anscombe in 1958. The core insight that Anscombe and MacIntyre give Banner is that there is no clear decision procedure or algorithm which can be taught and which will provide modern individuals with a satisfactory moral structure whereby to order their lives. Instead, we need to think hard about the microwork of moral formation, which will compel us to offer a morally articulate description of human psychology and anthropology, a description best couched for them in the idiom of virtue.[2]

Having learned from Hauerwas that Christian moral formation is the primary task of theological ethics, moral theologians like Banner learn from MacIntyre and Anscombe to scrutinize the micropractices of the Christian churches, in terms of virtue or some other low-to-the-ground language, and to pay better attention thereby to the details of human moral psychology and the "rough ground" of the cultural setting in which formation takes place. Much theological ethics inspired by this work is organized around one of two foci: some deal with a contemporary issue or theme from a surprising perspective;[3] others recover the thick description of some figure or movement from the past, near or far, as exemplary of something needing to be recovered.[4] Such projects have had some impact in bioethics, in political theology, and the ethics of war as well. And there have also been some small, halting attempts to speak about economic life or issues of gender, about sexual and marital ethics, or, in my context, the ethics of living in a deeply racist society and the dangers that it puts on Christian formation. Still, while some hot-button topics have been addressed, it seems to me that the larger cultural systems in which Christians live, move, and have their being have not been as fully and systematically engaged as they might be.[5] Here again Banner's book, by using social anthropology, makes definite advances on this front, most notably by looking at the textured surface of quotidian Christian life across a larger expanse of lived experience than pretty much anyone else heretofore has.[6] He tries to show us how practices of Christian life are orthogonal to the grain of everyday living in order to highlight both the knots of true difficulty in our common culture and the overall shape of the carvings that the carpenter is trying to make out of Christians. For example, his discussion of how Christian practices of baptism reconceive kinship by "troubling" natural kinship and his analysis of "long slow dwindling" that constitutes so much of dying in first-world late modernity help us rethink the whole shape of moral life.[7]

There is a larger methodological point to be made by work like this, and Banner's is a good text with which to make it. It is about the issue of religion in public. I have said that Hauerwas and others have perhaps bracketed the churches' vocation as evangelical institutions and not explicitly addressed at length how the churches should engage in public discussion and debate. The fair reply to this charge is that the evangel is best communicated by the *bodies* of the faithful. The best apologetics is a good dogmatics, so that public theological discourse "contributes" by being thoroughly and unapologetically Christian. Furthermore, in contemporary public life the best dogmatics is often a *moral* dogmatics, a form of practicing Christianity *more* primarily than first and foremost speaking about it.[8]

## The Benedict Option

Banner's form of engagement will help us think more complexly about the textured moral and spiritual terrain of late modernity, and this is needed because much of the work on offer today bespeaks a recoil from the darkness of this time, a stance against the self-images of the age. This recoil reflects a darker mood that has overtaken much of the Christian world in the West over these past few decades. Many think that the churches today face unprecedented dangers. For the past fifteen hundred years, the churches have by and large undertaken pedagogy in a pretty thoroughly Christian social context, one that existed in living memory, but now that era has ended.[9] If we understand "Christendom" to designate an intentional effort to shape and sustain a society on explicitly Christian terms, it is clear that Christendom is over. The status of religious beliefs—their legitimacy in public and the sincerity with which we try to organize our lives through them—is much more contested, and far more fragile and recognizably contingent, than they have ever been before, and there are no signs that the trend is being reversed. Our worlds are too religiously pluralistic, many are not identifiably religious at all, and it is no longer a public assumption that membership in some ecclesiastical association is a criterion for civilizational success today. In this way, our condition is very much like that of the late antique Roman Empire, the last age that possessed analogues to this pluralism and this skepticism.

In this context, how can the churches form Christians? Some propose a "Benedictine" strategy, which is especially popular among a growing subspecies of conservative white Christians in the United States. The "Benedict option" suggests that the larger culture is lost, and the church should turn inward to form itself for the coming dark ages. There is an autarkic vision implicit here, a proposal for retrenchment, a more vigorous reinstitutionalization of the church.[10]

We have been in, and all of us were trained under, a methodologically Benedictine age. But this strategy fails in two ways. First, it simply will not work. The church never forms souls in a vacuum, only in a dialectic with the surrounding culture. Sometimes those cultures are suffused with concern about *gloria* as in the Late Roman Empire, or with honor as in medieval chivalric social structures, or with the leisured culture of passion and dueling in early modern European court culture, or in the nineteenth and twentieth centuries with the rise of consumer culture, racism, and radical egalitarianism.[11] There are always multiple currents swirling in our social order, shaping human affect and thinking in multitudinous diverse ways. So, for example, much contemporary conservative Christianity partakes of consumerist identity politics, and it also often reinforces certain views on racial, sexual, and political matters in ways that are, at the least, arguably opposed to their doctrinal Christian commitments.[12] The churches are inevitably downstream from these cultural currents, and the ecclesial structures should be designed to amplify the Spirit's shaping of believers for their particular worlds. Churches should position their pedagogy to proclaim the good news, not only with their lips but in their lives, in a dialectic of perennial proclamation and temporally parochial formation, both to proclaim and to receive. And such positioning must attend not only to internal structure but also external context.

Second and more immediately, the "Benedict option" is mistaken, for there is no reason to despair utterly of the surrounding culture. The larger culture is not absolutely lost, either morally or as a vital context within which the Christian Gospel can be taught and preached.[13] The "end of Christendom" is an ambivalent phrase. If in one way Christendom is *over*, in another way it has been importantly, if albeit partially, *accomplished*. This is an old insight: the tradition of "aristocratic" critics of modern life—a tradition including de Tocqueville, Nietzsche, and Weber—all recognize the powerful moral impulse toward egalitarianism that lies at the heart of the modernizing process, and all of them root it, in different ways, in Christianity. And while their insight was lost for a while in the twentieth century, it has been rediscovered in recent decades. Thinkers like David Hollinger, Charles Taylor, Talal Asad, Michael Barnett, Webb Keane, and Didier Fassin have argued that our "secular age" is a distinctively *post-Christendom* secular age, and in some ways still if often unconsciously Christian, even as that revolution has self-consciously tried to leave some of those resources behind, becoming potentially more unrooted, more "hydroponic," as it were, in the process. We are living in the midst of a huge moral revolution, and it is deeply informed by Christianity.[14]

Consider the presumptive universalism of our moral ideals, the concept of the individual, the tension between our public and our private lives. Or ask, What does it mean to find transcendent value palpably present in the immanent or to recognize that the supple contingencies of our flesh can host the absolute value of the spirit? These are concepts and questions intelligible to us only because for almost two thousand years the strata of Western intellectual thought were compressed by the weight of Christian doctrine. As a consequence, even the most "secular" among us would be unintelligible to an ancient pagan, while a member of an ancient Christian church would find much common ground with an atheist. Even as the explosion of egalitarian movements in the past four or five hundred years has itself become an engine of de-Christianization in some ways, it also reflects a quite radical institutionalization of deep Christian logics in other ways. In very many ways, we live in a world far more deeply akin to some construals of the kingdom of God than was the case even a few hundred years ago.

Am I saying that we do not live in a secular age? Not at all. But the nature of this secular age is far more complicated, and far more complicatedly related to Christianity, than declinists will allow. (In this I am siding with Charles Taylor over Alasdair MacIntyre.) I say this not to reinforce any smug Eusebian triumphalism or naive secular progressivism that lets us slouch back into a comfortable despair of culture or smug confidence that history is on our side. My aim is the opposite: to make us *think harder* about the concrete reality of our situation, and thereby, as Philip Lorish suggests in chapter 8, pay better attention to the ambiguities inherent in our setting. Neither optimism nor despair are compatible with the virtue of hope: the details of our situation may change, but the basic problem of the human, the human heart at war with its God and itself (in that order), will not be solved by any immanent force but will be transfiguratively solved by God at the eschaton. In the meantime, our world will stay typological and ironic. And that is the context that needs to be understood.

Social anthropologists are doing some of the best work on these issues right now. They have become freshly attuned to the complexity of our situation, and the rise of the "anthropology of Christianity" in particular makes for fascinating reading for theologians interested in the complexities of our lives. But Christian theology has resources as well. Think only of theologians like Augustine, who lived through the analogous transition into "Christendom," or Kierkegaard, who worried endlessly about the fate of *true* Christian faith amid the kitschy dross of Christendom. Banner's book helps us see how this anthropological literature can inform where we should go from here. It positions us well to do better than we have done before.

## The Francis Option

I propose that we refuse the Benedictine strategy and instead situate Banner's proposal within the context of another strategy, what we can call the Franciscan option. This one takes its focus on certain themes that the current pope has seemingly drawn from the saint, particularly a focus on radical dispossession and an overall vision of evangelism, of seeking others, as an activity to be pursued with one's whole being.

This vision believes that *God* will take care of the church, no need to be anxious about that. Formation is institutionally fugitive in any event. Instead, preach the Gospel fearlessly, in multiple forms of "preaching," and look hopefully in the world for signs of God's work and partners to advance that work and to converse with about how best to understand that work. This is the key difference, for I do *not* see a lot of effort at seeking allies or conversation partners among the Benedictines.

The Franciscan option would certainly affirm the Benedictine insistence on strong internal inculturation and explicit spiritual pedagogy, alongside a serious boundary-marking practice (albeit one less paranoid than the Benedictines urge). But it embeds that formation in a larger awareness of the church *for* the world, not just the church *in* the world. Because of this, it situates its own boundary-marking strategy within a larger project of church mission and (I would argue) accommodates more readily the idea of a range of possible ways to be "Christianly engaged" in the world.

This strategy begins from a different judgment than the Benedict option's despair of the world: the surrounding culture is clueless, not hostile, and the churches are most fundamentally threatened by internal lassitude rather than external enemies. There was no golden age of Christian faith; each era has its own challenges, and even Christendom needed its Kierkegaard. So the right solution is not to retreat but to engage, to undertake a conversionist strategy that will effect a true conversion of the heart *within* and without the churches.[15]

This will involve a different sort of rhetoric of speaking on public matters. It is not that the Benedictine strategy did not speak about these matters, but it spoke about them in fairly nonconversational ways. Figures like Hauerwas and Milbank are known more for denunciation than conversation. More institutionally, John Paul II's basic attitude toward human rights was less a matter of engaging seriously with rights activists or thinkers and more often a matter of appropriating that language for his church's own tactical ends. Similarly, his defense of reason was often more polemical than conversational, just as Benedict's defense of love in *Deus Caritas Est* was also more disappointingly declamatory than dialogical.

How might such a "Franciscan" program relate to the ethics of everyday life? Below I identify two large issues that people today confront in the quotidian details of their everyday lives. Both of them need many micropractices, and many forms of discipline, to inhabit. I speak of our culture's understanding of *agency* and its perplexities about *pluralism*. Both are part of "everyday life" for all of us. We are confronted as never before with the question of how we are to exercise our agency in a context in which talk about our agency has valorized it, indeed *over*valorized it, as never before. While this is obviously an immediate existential issue for our own personal lives, it has also recently become an issue for the fate of the globe in terms of the problem of the Anthropocene, the problem of how we are to understand and manage our action on the planet as a whole. Second, we are confronted today with the question of genuine pluralism, of how to live not just nearby but in genuine relation, perhaps something akin to communion, with those who do not act like us, speak like us, think like us, believe like us. This too has more personal and more political valences.

## Agency

First is the contemporary confusion around the character of human agency—how to understand the human person's capacities for action, individually and collectively, and how to understand the way the human navigates their course of life in the world. In many ways, the expansion of agency, across more and more of humanity and within more and more of our individual existences, is an unquestionably good thing. Yet it comes with challenges. Our typical picture of agency implies a fairly individualistic and consumeristic context, which presents distinct challenges to right Christian moral formation and good human life. We are also vexed by certain confusions about agency that are revealed by the fact that inhabitants of our culture typically operate with two intuitions about human agency today. The first is a Promethean intuition: we recognize that our agency has expanded exponentially in the past several centuries, in part because political egalitarianism encourages all people to imagine they make all their own decisions. We now realize we can alter the ecosystem and our own DNA, and we conceive of ourselves as fundamentally agential forces who can effectively conceptualize and realize almost any reality we can imagine—so much so that we increasingly fear not the resistances to our agency but the way in which that agency may succeed *too well*, provoking "unintended consequences" of the sort considered so richly by contemporary anxieties about "risk."[16] The second and contradictory intuition is more chthonic: our very extension of knowledge and power has led us to realize the profound truths of historicism and cultural relativism as well as given us a greater awareness of the deep psychological and biological factors that constitute what we call our "selves." On this front, we grow anxious that our entire agency is taken away from us, by our genes or our ancestors, and so question the whole logic of agency and responsibility itself. As my old teacher Jean Elshtain once put it, "We no longer believe in sin, we believe in syndromes."

Our wider culture schizophrenically oscillates between affirmations of these two intuitions, in hubristic proclamations at our utterly unconditioned power and bleak gloom at our enslavement to our DNA, our psyches, or our history. This oscillation compels our vision of our own capacities to swing wildly between antic mania and paralytic despair.

In this setting, a more traditional Christian account of agency—one of the many accounts that are possible—may need to be taught with great intentionality. But if it can be done, it can be a powerful witness to an alternative and more coherent—or at least less schizophrenic—picture of agency. For Christians reject the Promethean fantasy of humans as ex nihilo actors, whose action, to be free, must be unsponsored, unsolicited, or unresponsive to anything outside of itself. To them, it seems remarkably blind to the context, validity, and conditionality of all human agency—to the fact that humans are created, contextualized within and responsive to the primordial divinity ordering the cosmos.[17] Yet Christians also affirm that while they are, in Martin Luther's phrase, "more acted upon than acting," humans can still participate in, or dissent from, that dynamic creative power to which they inevitably relate and on which they inescapably rely, and that creative power that acts on them acts to make them free. Christians have multiple ways of affirming the two aspects of this proposal, but it is quite clear that both sides are part of the basic grammar of agency that is part of the Christian tradition.

Such a Christian exposition of agency, paired with a visible, indeed vivid, inhabitation of it, could contribute significantly, and broadly "evangelically," to contemporary cultural debates about agency. It could do so in two ways. First, by exhibiting a truly deep picture of agency in a particular religious and cultural idiom, Christians may help others advance their self-understanding. Eric Gregory's account of humanitarianism in chapter 6 or Rachel Muers's discussion of eating in chapter 10, for example, may bespeak a way to use reflections to think about what it means to be a creature of God in a way that may provoke resonances for those outside the Christian faith. Such Christian interventions are far from alone in doing this as a contribution to public culture, of course; many people are offering analogous contributions, or at least trying to do so. Certainly, other religious traditions do this. But some of the most interesting work on questions of agency and freedom has been done by anthropologists studying the "anthropology of ethics." And it is no accident that this work has often focused on forms of inculturation into serious religious traditions, such as Laidlaw on virtue or Robbins on how Christians are taught to "become sinners."[18]

Second, such an account could directly address the specifically political anxieties about freedom that have emerged in this era of the Anthropocene, identifying what is good and worthy of cultivation in these movements while protecting against their excesses. In particular, it may be able to address what Charles Taylor and others have called the "moral revolution" and what Didier Fassin has called the contemporary political theology of "humanitarian reason."[19] Both of these are significant ongoing topics in anthropological inquiry. In so engaging the moral revolution, Christians and analogous others can be what Taylor calls this era's "loyal opposition."[20] Their suspicions about the ultimate adequacy of any wholly this-worldly approach to human life will encourage them repeatedly to challenge modernity's immanent frame, warning all of its tendency toward self-consuming excesses, chastening the apocalyptic energies, and urging it to become paradoxically more properly *worldly*. But they will still work with others on many fronts and recognize and affirm the core goods that these movements attempt to pursue, however imperfectly Christians judge those attempts to be.

For example, consider the Christian practice of confession—both the communal public confession in church services and the more intimate and less general practice of confession with a confessor.[21] Such practices of confession teach Christians to reflect on their lives as retrospectively revealing the presence of God in the moments that compose their life story—as present in chastisement of misbegotten action or consolation in grief, as conversation partner in moments of exultant joy or realized gratitude, as simply visible in the ordinary warp and weft of everyday experience. This practice is not simply one of settling accounts with God; it is an attempt to cultivate an ever-deeper awareness of God's presence in human action at all times.

Furthermore, this is not simply an *extrinsic* presence, as if God were simply beside the person doing the confessing; for believers, God's presence is far more intimately involved in their agency than that. Part of what the practice of confession does is thank God for the continual providential guidance, even involvement, in the everyday activities of human agency. A practice of this sort, deliberately and intelligently reflected on, would provide a wealth of possible insights for reconsidering how we talk about human action in the world and the nature of proper human freedom and autonomy. It would certainly offer a vivid alternative to more anodyne and simplistic notions of autonomy that seem to have completely occupied public discussions of freedom and agency these days.

## Pluralism

A similar conundrum can be discerned vis-à-vis Christianity's engagement with another great issue in the coming decades, the challenge of genuine pluralism. How can theology speak civically? That is, how can Christians be unapologetically themselves yet remain dialogically open to others with different beliefs? Most pointedly, how might one, as Philip Lorish put it in chapter 8, come to judgment—how can we articulate a normative view, with as full and self-conscious as possible a confession of one's own parochial location, and a nondefensive invitation to others to scrutinize critically the presuppositions implicit in my judgment, all while *still* affirming that this judgment that I have made, with my complications and commitments and perspective, nonetheless is not merely an expression of my subjective preferences or opinions but understands itself as tracking something true about the reality we all share and seeks to be held accountable to our collective and individual confrontations with that reality in order better to track it?

It is clear that many people today doubt the possibility of genuinely living together in community of some real sort amid conditions of radical difference. But it is equally clear that just such a fate is and will be ours for the foreseeable future, whether we like it or not. Social and demographic realities make the cultural enjambments of such pluralism increasingly inescapable, and so people of profoundly different views will be forced to find ways to manage to live together genuinely, not just in political community but also (if human history is any predictor) in more intimate spheres such as marriage and family life. That seems one of the larger projects of coming decades, perhaps centuries. Once again, conflicting intuitions—authentic impulses toward a defensive self-protection and a genuine reaching out—exist alongside one another. Can we find a suitable language to describe this?

It seems to me that even our current political perplexities partake of this paranoia of the other and the question of who can be a true member of our communities.

That is certainly the case in the United States, and from what I can tell, elsewhere in the world things seem not much better. Obviously the churches cannot simply step in at present and address these immediate political problems in the way they need addressing right now.[22] But the churches' long-term boring into the hard boards of our souls may well effect some modest change over the long run. For this is a long-term problem: this issue first came into widespread view, in our societies, as a question of secularism, of how religious and nonreligious people can collaborate and cohabit. But its more basic frame is as the problem of pluralism, as it is clear we will not be living in a secular world in the foreseeable future but rather an increasingly diverse religious one, both globally and locally.

It may help us to recognize more fully than we heretofore have done that "pluralism," ambitiously understood, is a very difficult task indeed. It asks us to behave in a way that our species has never yet managed to master. In other words, the myth of the Tower of Babel is misleading: the best evolutionary evidence suggests that humans started out not from a coherent unity that then splintered, but something like the reverse.[23] We often talk as if humanity had an original unity, but in fact we were always already diverse in the deep past and have been, over millennia, moving ever closer together, reducing our diversity as we coordinate across old cultural borders. For most of our species' history we have lived in intimate kin groups of around three hundred people, and each of these groups, it seems, had its own slightly different language, culture, and way of living, with each group as best as we can see keeping well clear of others. Not even language was unitary: multiple groups of *Homo sapiens* developed the capacity for sophisticated language at roughly the same time. It is only since the agricultural revolution, around eleven thousand years ago, that we have been combining together in ever-larger configurations, sharing common languages, common social structures, common beliefs. Most of this time, we have handled the diversity of human beliefs by pursuing our lives in relative separateness from one another. That condition is increasingly compromised, not just by technologies of communication, travel, and trade but also by the ideological expansion of universalizing forces such as the Abrahamic religions that have forced us to find such separations more akin to apartheid than a judicious respect.

How might Christian discourse and Christian communities help address this problem? Admittedly, Christians have not exactly been models of charitable welcome when it comes to dealing with deep differences. Neither in the deep past nor today, if polling data can be trusted, do many Christians manage to combine the deep particularistic convictions appropriate to their faith with a welcoming and engaging attitude toward those who do not share those convictions.[24] Yet this must be seen as a failure of profound dimensions for Christians, who have great resources to recognize and make theologically interesting the reality of difference among people, and even within people, in our world.

Happily, the conundrum of pluralism has been one of the largest areas of interest in the so-called anthropology of Christianity since its beginnings. Major works in this movement, such as Susan Friend Harding's *Book of Jerry Falwell*, Tanya Luhrmann's *When God Talks Back*, and most recently and interestingly for me, Matthew Engelke's *God's Agents*, explore how Christian communities understand themselves to be acting in a richly pluralistic setting and provide very useful conceptual and thematic insights for theological work (such as Engelke's discussion of "ambience" as a feature of public religion in a complicatedly secular [or pluralistic] space).[25]

On the other side, as in the earlier discussions of agency, theological discussions of "religion in public" may be useful to anthropological inquiry. After all, much of the anthropology of morality and of Christianity is precisely attempting to get beyond a now-recognized problem in earlier anthropological inquiry, namely, that it did not actually manage pluralism very well itself. For example, it had failed genuinely to engage what Harding calls "the morally repugnant other" of lived Christianity, preferring instead to exoticize their objects of study.[26] (That's one major reason why the anthropologists of Christianity, and of morality, undertook their projects in the first place.) In contrast, theologians have been engaged, for quite some time, in debates about the nature of pluralism that have led them to relatively well-developed modes of argument and analysis about these issues. The past few centuries have made Christians particularly self-conscious about their own parochialism, in a way that others might learn from, even if they manifest different kinds of pluralism than religious pluralism. I am not saying Christianity has *all* the answers, but it may help us work toward a solution. Theologians, for example, are richly informed about complicated questions regarding the rhetorics of public engagement—the degree to which you "translate" a particularistic language of faith, with all its semantic idiosyncrasies and hermeneutic prickliness, into a register less foreign to those who do not share that faith, and the degree to which the refusal to translate may itself convey more meaning via showing the semiotic indigestibility of the categories or symbols within the audience's current conceptual frame.[27]

How might such a renewed engagement with pluralism proceed in Christian thought? It is not as if Christians lack all resources for constructive thinking about this. After all, Augustine's world had its share of quite radical difference, and it was the father of the afflicted boy who said to Jesus, tears in his eyes, "Lord I believe! Help thou my unbelief" (Mk 9:24). Closer to our own age, an exchange between Felix Frankfurter and Reinhold Niebuhr nicely captures this: after hearing Niebuhr give a sermon, Frankfurter, a lifelong atheist, said, "Reinie, may a believing unbeliever thank you for your sermon?" Niebuhr replied, "May an unbelieving believer thank you for appreciating it?"[28] Pluralism is in this way simply a synecdoche for living in a complicated world that provokes in our complicated hearts a deep ambivalence. The complexity of our lived condition on the ground reveals far more interesting terrain for engagement than we typically allow ourselves to recognize. And this is definitely the case as regards the fraught issue of pluralism: Christians can engage this debate about pluralism as one manifestation of the fundamental Christian story of the self who seeks out the other, who knows the self in a new way; the self seeks out others to be surprised by them, to *not* "know already" who they are and what they offer—in short, to see the world as something other, and something more, than a wilderness of mirrors. This is another way of learning to live a life in an overall shape of gratitude, a gratitude that blossoms into joy and praise. And this joy is itself a gift that is received, not a state or condition that we ourselves achieve or accomplish. So in terms of this large issue of pluralism, the churches need to teach their members what can be called broadly "passive" virtues, virtues of being more acted on than acting, virtues of reception, waiting, forbearance, gratitude, joy.

## Theology and Anthropology in Conversation

What will we need for this theological program—this "Franciscan strategy"—to happen? A number of things. Most basically, theological minds willing to do it. But it would help those minds if there were a kind of genre and idiom of writing that could better deliver the kind of pedagogical training of which I am speaking here.[29] We would benefit from a theological idiom lucidly in continuity and communion with the kerygmatic heritage of the churches yet also capable of articulating that heritage in contemporary terms for the everyday lives of typical believers.

Such a process of articulation will undoubtedly repeat some of the steps of Banner's book: first, exploiting the knowledge we have gained in secular genres (such as the social sciences) about human beings, our world, and the modes of inquiry (such as ethnography) that enable such knowledge; second, critically apprehending that knowledge when it comes (as it often does come) inflected with a covert normative orientation inhospitable to, and possibly actively corrosive of, the churches' self-understanding and proclamation; and third, metabolizing that knowledge into the churches' self-understanding and proclamation in order to enflesh that message as densely in our textured everyday life as possible. As I imagine it, this idiom bears no small resemblance to a kind of moral ethnography. But it is hardly the exclusive province of anthropology, of course; there are multiple disciplinary genres from which this theological idiom can borrow. We just happen to be in an era in which much of the best work is done in and through ethnographic studies.

This sort of theological idiom might be of use to anthropologists as well, particularly since these themes are close to the center of much discussion in anthropology today. Disciplined theological reflection may well offer insights not only into the discrete topics of the nature of human agency and virtue, affect and disposition, and the character of cognitive affirmation and affective commitment. It may also offer useful illumination about the overall themes of self- and community-formation in a scholarly register sufficiently different from anthropology to highlight a discrete set of problematics that their own "native" lens might readily overlook.

Fruitful exchange between these genres of inquiry may be made easier because they share an understanding of what they are trying to do. Both resist an anxiously exclusive criteriological emphasis on a scholastic accountability to texts and linguistically articulated arguments and on the effectively esoteric exegetical knowledge owned by the guardians of those canonical philosophical and theological traditions. Or rather more directly, they refuse to focus on impressing other professors. Instead, they choose to be more engaged by events and phenomena in the world, to which they try intentionally and self-consciously to hold themselves accountable. Of course, neither of these genres of inquiry denies their relation to a canonical collection of texts and arguments: "theory," in the sense of self-conscious traditions of rigorous and lucid intellectual inquiry, clearly plays a role in the disciplines of history, anthropology, sociology, and the like. But both of these genres of inquiry insist that, along with criteria derived from texts and dialectics, their own projects are also accountable to the deliverances of *lived reality* and to multiple kinds of "judges" of what lived reality has delivered in the way of judgments.[30] So I agree. This may resonate with Luke Bretherton's argument in chapter 11 that ethnography produces a higher degree of self-reflexivity; I also suggest it may well do that in moral theologians, but one thing it cannot help but produce is a greater attention to realities *outside* the self, which I also think is a very good thing for a discipline as self-involved as ours.

I trust that other academic theologians will not mishear what I am saying. Our textual spelunking, in our own solipsistic research as well as in our all-too-often solipsistic teaching, can continue as placidly as before, and the theurgic rituals of bibliodolatry that we enact in our seminars will go on, same as they ever were. I am not inviting anyone to mock the noise of our solemn scholarly assemblies (well, maybe a little). Mine is merely a request to *expand* the shape of legitimate theological inquiry, not to replace one kind with another.

Indeed, this is not a new addition at all, but rather a recovery. For in a way I am asking for a return to the kind of "theological journalism" that many theologians used to practice in media articles, other public interventions, and even in sermons. Several generations ago, before the Babylonian captivity of theology by the academy had been fully accomplished (in the United States, say, before the 1970s), theological minds such as Abraham Heschel, Reinhold Niebuhr, and John Courtney Murray wrote for a nonacademic public in a much wider way than they do now. It would be good, I think, to get back to that (for those minds as well as for that public). An openness to the kind of topics, and the kind of investigations, that anthropology holds before us may well induce us to reacquaint ourselves with those older modes of writing.[31]

This gets, at last, to why I included in my title a call for a "sacramental ethics." By this I mean an ethics that sees the shape of life itself, in all its granular actions, as semiotic, as being real—gaining its moral determination and specification—"here," but only having that determinate reality here on loan, as it were, gaining that determination only by anticipating an eschatological confirmation. And the kind of theological writing for which I am calling here would try to help its audience discern the ways that the events of the present day are so semiotic and so theologically freighted. It would do so by highlighting how the acts and events it describes are themselves intelligible only in light of our larger projects, our remembered pasts and expected futures, our histories and hopes. As sacramental, an ethics so described would be constituted by eschatological anticipations and thus by participation in a larger and deeper mystery that is not immediately and palpably present today. Furthermore, our actions are thus semiotic here, not only in their constitution but in their communication; that is to say, their status as semiotic is revealed in their being evangelical. In their being "meaningful" they bear witness to the story that makes their sense apprehensible, thus inviting people to contemplate that sense as well. Finally, this ethic is sacramental also in how it reveals the world itself to be sacramental. The world is not an exhaustively profane place; it bears theological significances that it itself cannot explain or even recognize. When the world gives up the world and becomes simply creation, when it stops presenting itself as the totality of reality and admits it is the consequence of a direct and purposeful act of a loving agent, then the world appears in a new light. And the only way that light can become perceptible to us is through the transfiguration of the everyday—through, as it were, our everyday ethics.

## Conclusion

One aim of this volume is to develop moral frameworks and theological narratives for the everyday practices, institutions, and daily activities that shape our character and moral decisions. I take it as granted that the kind of interdisciplinary work that Michael Banner's excellent book undertakes, and the insights it gleans from anthropology for moral theology, are exemplary for all our work. What I have done here is suggest several new fronts that have opened up for me in the wake of reading this work and the literatures to which this work directs us.

To those who work in those literatures and are not theologians, I can only say that the kind of inquiries you are undertaking, on the cultural conditions of agency, the nature of ethical prohibitions and proscriptions, and the question of the ontological reality of cultural norms, are conversations that moral theologians and Christian ethicists have been having for some time now. I suspect there is much more to say in conversation between the two sets of scholars; I hope this volume can help to open up those conversations and does not end them.

To those theologians who are wondering what to take away, I have tried to propose one new strategy that will keep us in rich conversation with those scholarly disciplines on which Banner and the contributors to this volume have so fruitfully drawn. I also hope this strategy will allow us to engage them on their terms and in reference to their own questions, highlighting resources and insights that are more than just data for them but also perhaps collegial contributions for us.

And to all with ears to hear, I hope you will join me in being grateful for the gifts Michael Banner has given us thereby.

## Notes

1. This is nicely brought out in Jeffrey Stout's critique of Hauerwas in *Democracy and Tradition* (Princeton: Princeton University Press, 2004), 140–61.

2. A few visionaries tried to talk about such things before MacIntyre had made his and Anscombe's point properly felt (I think of W. H. Vanstone, Josef Pieper, and even Abraham Heschel), but few listened.

3. William T. Cavanaugh's *Torture and Eucharist: Theology, Politics, and the Body* (Cambridge, MA: Wiley-Blackwell, 2008) is one excellent example. Joshua Hordern's *Political Affections: Civic Participation and Moral Theology* (Oxford: Oxford University Press, 2013); and Jennifer Herdt's *Putting on Virtue: The Legacy of the Splendid Vices* (Chicago: University of Chicago Press, 2008) are other, albeit more abstract, examples.

4. A great deal of work on Augustine and politics, or Thomas and the moral life, runs along these lines. See Paul Kolbet, *Augustine and the Cure of Souls* (Notre Dame, IN: University of Notre Dame Press, 2009); Jennifer McBride, *The Church for the World: A Theology of Public Witness* (New York: Oxford University Press, 2012); or Sarah Azaransky, *The Dream Is Freedom: Pauli Murray and American Democratic Faith* (New York: Oxford University Press, 2011).

5. David Matzko-McCarthy's work is an exception here; see his *The Good Life: Genuine Christianity for the Middle Class* (Grand Rapids, MI: Brazos, 2004).

6. I note that some philosophers tried to make such a move in their field—see Michelle Moody-Adams, *Fieldwork in Familiar Places* (Cambridge, MA: Harvard University Press, 1997)—but it ended up going nowhere.

7. Michael Banner, *The Ethics of Everyday Life: Moral Theology, Social Anthropology, and the Imagination of the Human* (Oxford: Oxford University Press, 2014), 41, 116.

8. Note, however, that practicing Christianity organically involves speaking. My point here is simply that the discourse must be organically rooted in action and cannot be propounded authentically apart from it. I suspect that Banner and I share a common conviction that a Kierkegaardian ironism must necessarily inflect such "public confessions" in our world for them to be at all honest.

9. Callum Brown, *The Death of Christian Britain: Understanding Secularisation, 1800–2000* (London: Routledge, 2001); Molly Worthen, *Apostles of Reason: The Crisis of Authority in American Evangelicalism* (New York: Oxford University Press, 2013).

10. Rod Dreher, "The Benedict Option," *American Conservative*, December 12, 2013, http://www.theamericanconservative.com/articles/benedict-option/. The idea has been most vigorously debated in the pages, and on the websites, of the journals *First Things* and *American Conservative*.

11. Éric Rebillard, *Christians and Their Many Identities in Late Antiquity* (Ithaca, NY: Cornell University Press, 2012); Kate Cooper, *The Fall of the Roman Household* (Cambridge: Cambridge University Press, 2007); Peter Brown, *Power and Persuasion in Late Antiquity: Towards a Christian Empire* (Madison: University of Wisconsin Press, 1992); Peter Brown, *Through the Eye of a Needle: Wealth, the Fall of Rome, and the Making of Christianity in the West, 350–550 AD* (Princeton,

NJ: Princeton University Press, 2012); Conrad Leyser, *Authority and Asceticism from Augustine to Gregory the Great* (Oxford: Oxford University Press, 2000). For another powerful example of a theologian working in a particular and complicated context, see Angela Dienhart Hancock, *Karl Barth's Emergency Homiletic, 1932–1933: A Summons to Prophetic Witness at the Dawn of the Third Reich* (Grand Rapids, MI: Eerdmans, 2013).

12. See, e.g., Bethany Moreton, *To Serve God and Wal-Mart: The Making of Christian Free Enterprise* (Cambridge, MA: Harvard University Press, 2009); and Linda Kinz, *Between Jesus and the Market: The Emotions That Matter in Right-Wing America* (Durham, NC: Duke University Press, 1997).

13. Stout, *Democracy and Tradition*. For a reasonably sympathetic critique of Ratzinger's writings on the secular, see James Gerard McEvoy, *Leaving Christendom for Good: Church–World Dialogue in a Secular Age* (Lanham, MD: Lexington Books, 2014), esp. 143–58.

14. Charles Taylor, *A Secular Age* (Cambridge, MA: Harvard University Press, 2007); Didier Fassin, *Humanitarian Reason: A Moral History of the Present* (Berkeley: University of California Press, 2012); Webb Keane, *Ethical Life: Its Natural and Social Histories* (Princeton, NJ: Princeton University Press, 2015); David Hollinger, *After Cloven Tongues of Fire: Protestant Liberalism in Modern American History* (Princeton, NJ: Princeton University Press, 2013); Talal Asad, *Formations of the Secular: Christianity, Islam, Modernity* (Stanford, CA: Stanford University Press, 2003); Michael Barnett, *Empire of Humanity: A History of Humanitarianism* (Ithaca, NY: Cornell University Press, 2011).

15. In terms of theological motivations, this is inspired less by a protectionist vision of theology such as one might find in Lindbeck's *Nature of Doctrine* or Hauerwas's writings, and more by Kathryn Tanner's work, especially her still underappreciated work *Theories of Culture: A New Agenda for Theology* (Minneapolis, MN: Augsburg Fortress, 1997). Some tentative steps toward such an ecclesiology in a Roman Catholic context are sketched out in Charles Taylor, José Casanova, and George F. McLean, eds., *Church and People: Disjunctions in a Secular Age* (Washington, DC: Council for Research in Values and Philosophy, 2012).

16. Ulrich Beck, *Risk Society: Towards a New Modernity* (London: Sage, 1992); Anthony Giddens, *Runaway World: How Globalization Is Reshaping Our Lives* (London: Profile, 1999).

17. Marcel Lieberman, *Commitment, Value, and Moral Realism* (New York: Cambridge University Press, 1998); Judith Butler, *Giving an Account of Oneself* (New York: Fordham University Press, 2005); Eric Santner, *On The Psychotheology of Everyday Life: Reflections on Freud and Rosenzweig* (Chicago: University of Chicago Press, 2001).

18. James Laidlaw, *The Subject of Virtue: An Anthropology of Ethics and Freedom* (Cambridge: Cambridge University Press, 2013); Joel Robbins, *Becoming Sinners: Christianity and Moral Torment in Papua New Guinea* (Berkeley: University of California Press, 2004). See also James Faubion, *An Anthropology of Ethics* (Cambridge: Cambridge University Press, 2011).

19. See Taylor, *Secular Age*, and Fassin, *Humanitarian Reason*.

20. Taylor, *Secular Age*, 745. See also Fassin, *Humanitarian Reason*; and Keane, *Ethical Life*.

21. There are less formal versions of such a practice of confession as well, in terms of regular practices of personal prayer or small-group discussion, although such informal structures are less vivid than the formal ones.

22. Although I note the Argentinian Pope Francis seems to be the last person in Europe truly to believe in the idea of Europe itself; see his Charlemagne Prize speech: "Pope Francis' Vision for the Refounding of Europe: Text of Charlemagne Speech Awards Address," *Catholic Voices Comment*, May 6, 2016, https://cvcomment.org/2016/05/06/pope-francis-vision-for-the-refounding-of-europe-text-of-charlemagne-speech-award-address/.

23. My claims in this paragraph are inspired by Yuval Harari, *Sapiens: A Brief History of Humankind* (London: Harvil Secker, 2014), esp. 21, 44–45.

24. For one recent example, see "Republicans Prefer Blunt Talk about Islamic Extremism, Democrats Favor Caution," *Pew Research Center*, February 3, 2016, http://www.pewforum.org/2016/02/03/republicans-prefer-blunt-talk-about-islamic-extremism-democrats-favor-caution/.

25. See Susan Friend Harding, *The Book of Jerry Falwell: Fundamentalist Language and Politics* (Princeton, NJ: Princeton University Press, 2001); T. M. Luhrmann, *When God Talks Back:*

*Understanding the American Evangelical Relationship with God* (New York: Knopf, 2012); and Matthew Engelke, *God's Agents: Biblical Publicity in Contemporary England* (Berkeley: University of California Press, 2013).

26. Susan Harding, "Representing Fundamentalism: The Problem of the Repugnant Cultural Other," *Social Research* 58, no. 2 (1991): 373–93.

27. See Michael Barnes, *Interreligious Learning: Dialogue, Spirituality and the Christian Imagination* (New York: Cambridge University Press, 2012); and Francis Clooney, *Comparative Theology: Deep Learning across Religious Borders* (Cambridge, MA: Wiley-Blackwell, 2010). For two proposals that raise interesting questions about this, see Catherine Cornille, *The Im-possibility of Interreligious Dialogue* (New York: Crossroad, 2008); and Hugh Nicholson, *Comparative Theology and the Problem of Religious Rivalry* (New York: Oxford University Press, 2011). For a more traditional "public theology" project that may have some resonances with this proposal, see Elaine Graham, *Between a Rock and Hard Place: Public Theology in a Post-Secular Age* (London: SCM Press, 2013).

28. Arthur M. Schlesinger, *A Life in the Twentieth Century* (Boston: Houghton Mifflin, 2000), 513.

29. An ironic but not cynical idiom; academics are better at cynicism than irony. This is a problem.

30. This accountability may be necessarily formulated in ways initially more indeterminate than the more standard-issue textual and argumentative criteria whereby we typically assess academic proposals, but it is perhaps a more profound form of accountability in part *just because* of that initial indeterminacy, which after all is due to the existential complexity of the potential challenges.

31. So understood, furthermore, both this kind of theological discourse and the findings of social anthropology can serve as a useful counterweight to a scholastic narrowing in higher scholarship that we all ought to resist. This is a general complaint about the increasingly self-referential discourse of academic scholarship, especially its resistance to direct attention to reality.

# 13

# CONFESSIONS OF A MODERATELY (UN)REPENTANT SINNER

<hr>

## MICHAEL BANNER

O CCASIONALLY I HAVE FOUND MYSELF losing concentration (I am ashamed to admit) during those sometimes overlong commendations with which, by tradition, visiting speakers are introduced at university seminars. When I come to, so to speak, I am often excited to hear that the lecturer has the most exemplary pedigree to address the topic in hand, qualifications second to none, and an incomparable reputation for learning, lucidity, and logic. You will imagine my deep disappointment when I discover, as I sometimes do as the commendation winds its weary way to a conclusion, that I am due to give the lecture.

I had a similar but equal and opposite experience at the conference to discuss the themes raised by *The Ethics of Everyday Life*.[1] Occasionally, I am again ashamed to admit, I found myself losing concentration during the more solemn presentations, only to hear (upon coming to) a clear, compelling, and rousing denunciation of the sins of such and such a commentator. With a shared sense of indignation, I would mentally "hear, hear!" the condemnation, audibly "tut tut" at the utter wrongheadedness of the offender, and join the wave of affront rolling round the room—only to discover that the most egregious sinner, whose offenses I was so ready to deprecate, was me. (Others were good enough to broach their criticisms somewhat more indirectly, and in accordance with the conventions of academic politeness, whereby a gaping hole in an argument is a "slight difficulty which deserves further work," a complete lack of evidence for a claim offers the author the opportunity to "widen the material" on which he or she has drawn, and blatant illogicality is an "unusual and unexpected turn in the argument.")

Of course, other contributors (happily as I would see it) were set a task that allowed them to ignore my sins, supposing they found them. These contributors (whose essays appear in part II) had been asked to take up my book's central and most important contention—that Christian ethics would be a better discipline if it learned to engage carefully and critically with social anthropology—and apply it to topics that I had not touched on or were at least not central to the discussions in my book. Thus, essays appear on education, eating, humanitarian aid, technology, work, and spending and borrowing within our modern economy. Given the claim of my book that Christian ethics would speak more therapeutically, and more evangelically, insofar as it learns to understand the world with the assistance of social anthropology, I naturally welcome these attempts to extend, elaborate, refine, and test the claim. And there are other topics from everyday life, such as shopping, having children, and keeping pets (to name just three), to which I wish I, or others, could give attention since, as I believe, Christian reflection on the everyday world would be more serious and effective just insofar as it addressed these topics with the insights it might glean from social anthropology.

Of course, as well as being grateful for these attempts to advance the book's main thesis, an author really should be grateful for any attention of any kind, even critical. Hume claimed (somewhat melodramatically) that his *Treatise* fell "still born from the press." These days academics are so busy writing books that they rarely find time to read any, so nearly every title shares that fate. But even while being grateful for attention, it rather behooves an author to express something more than mere gratitude, especially when his sins and wickedness are said to be, as the Book of Common Prayer has it, manifold.

As I did at the conference where many of these chapters were first presented, let me offer a confession first—not least, of course, because I hope that, as in courts of law both human and divine, this is reckoned to count in favor of the accused. My confession is just that, in *The Ethics of Everyday Life*, in which there is quite a lot going on, I did not with proper care and attention distinguish two claims that I now wish to make about social anthropology and its relationship to Christian ethics. These two claims are as follows.

First, Christian ethics, as a normative intervention into contemporary moral life, must understand the context into which it speaks, especially those modes of life it is inclined to speak either for or against. It is only as it comprehends (by means of social anthropology among other resources) the world it addresses that Christian ethics, as proposing a conception of what it is to be human, can speak effectively, neither busily condemning merely imagined evils nor commending what we might call mere dreams of humanity. It is for this reason that I cannot accept the probably kindly meant seeming agreement with my book that says yes, social anthropology is quite an interesting discipline, and we should attend to it—but only as we might attend to history, novels, or whatever. History and novels may bring all sorts of things to the table, but the discovery of the realities of our current context also requires the lens of social anthropology, and not merely as one among many. Social anthropology describes (although fallibly) not possibly imagined social worlds nor even remembered ones but rather the social worlds made and lived here and now. Imagined and remembered worlds may, of course, have things to teach us, as my own occasional turns to painting and history presuppose. But just insofar as social anthropology attends to the lived realities of everyday life, it has a privileged claim to the attention of the ethicist, Christian or otherwise.

Second, however, Christian ethics must make a turn to social anthropology not only for the sake of grasping its context and the lived reality of different modes of human being but also for the sake of grasping its very own content. I want to suggest that Christian ethics must be comprehended ethnographically just because it is constructed, so to speak, through embodied social forms. This is not to deny the existence of norms that govern their construction, norms that may be given to Christian theology on theological terms alone, but it is to say that because the form of Christian life emerges just as the world is engaged on Christian terms, knowledge of true human being can never be solely knowledge of those norms. For example, many Christians have thought of themselves as living out the Christian life through an imaginative engagement with, and an outworking of, the life of Christ—they have taken Christian ethics to be expressed in trying to bring Christ's life to a practical realization in their own everyday lives. But if this is a valid mode of Christian ethics (and it would be difficult to imagine from what vantage point its validity could be denied), then knowledge of Christian life is knowledge of the form these lives have taken—knowledge of the life of the saints, if you like. Or to put it more abstractly, Christian ethics is discovered and emerges in practice, and it is known ethnographically through knowledge of this practice.

I think that in *The Ethics of Everyday Life* I failed to mark this distinction with sufficient clarity and therefore failed to make the case for engagement with social anthropology as it should be made. Had I made that distinction more adequately, I would have been more robust in insisting on a new direction for moral theology.

This confession is not, of course, the sort of confession that those who found serious fault with my book were necessarily looking for. From that perspective, it will seem more like a determination to go on sinning yet more forcefully. As I turn to the more critical comments of the contributors, I welcome the chance to clarify or improve the statement of my thesis but feel no compelling reason to abandon it.

I do now regret, however, ever having used the expression "the Christian imagination" without putting in disclaimers, since to a number of ears (and the number is more than two) the phrase is obviously very troubling as denying the diversity of Christian life and thought.[2] Thus, in chapter 1, Molly Farneth rightly points out that "the Christian imagination" of Christ's suffering, for example, has taken different forms and has been used to very different moral ends. Quite so, and in the chapter that touches on suffering, I tell in very compressed form part of the story of what I would term (nonpejoratively) the invention of Christ's suffering—and to tell that story is just to begin to point to the many different imaginings of Christ's life and death. (Very early on, I make a similar point of stressing the very many imaginings of Christ's life, not just his suffering, which have been rendered in paint, music, song, theatre, prayer, liturgy, and so on and so on.) I used the phrase "the Christian imagination" as I might use the phrase "the medieval diet," and it would come as absolutely no surprise to me that the medieval diet was highly varied, differentiated by class and perhaps gender too, and indeed, the subject of some fierce dispute at the time as to what constitutes a good diet. That being so, however, I will, for fear of misunderstanding, endeavor to speak here and in the future of Christian imaginations—and medieval diets.

Another worry is not that I deny that there are different Christian imaginations of this and that, but that I provide no explicit account of the means of adjudicating between those different accounts. I agree with that claim, but since the decision not to provide such an account was indeed a decision and no mere oversight, I obviously think this is just an observation and does not need to appear on the charge sheet. The decision was, in fact, both practical and, in a certain sense, principled. Practically, the concern of the book is to demonstrate the fruitfulness of an engagement between Christian moral thought and social anthropology—that is, to bring conceptions of the human imagined within Christian life into conversation with those conceived and described within social anthropology. But, of course, I have advanced not all but some conceptions from within theology—that is, as I have tried to show how the engagement might improve our reflections on various topics, I have made choices. Thus, I have taken, for example, the institution of godparenthood (itself highly varied and contested, of course) as providing a normative lens through which to look at other conceptions of parenthood. It is not, however, the concern of the book specifically to elucidate those choices but rather to demonstrate the power of an engagement with a neglected but crucial partner in conversation. Had I attempted to elucidate and fully defend those choices, and done so at length in a systematic way, I guess I would have written (yet another book) on methodology in Christian ethics—naturally enough, the sort of books that academics tend to expect and favor. But in this book, I wanted to establish the fruitfulness of the engagement between moral theology and social anthropology, not to set out all the rules that might identify the moral theology which is doing the engaging on any particular issue as the right moral theology.

Lurking in those practical considerations, however, is a possibly elusive hint at an underlying principle, which is just that I think method in theology is better displayed than described. That is to say, our arguments to normative conclusions are just that, arguments, and if they are good arguments, they are typically subtle and nuanced, drawing on many different sources and considerations and holding very many different considerations rather delicately in balance. There is no reason to proscribe abstract treatments of methodology, but then again, it is by no means clear to me that Christian ethics cannot just get on with its business without laying out the terms on which it does so in advance. A proper response to any normative claim from within Christianity about suffering, death, old age, or whatever, which is taken to be mistaken, is to suggest the point of which it has failed to take account, deal with adequately, or whatever it might be rather than to insist the claimant set out (at length presumably) a prolegomenon to any ethic that will be entitled to call itself Christian (as Kant might have it).

The charge that I do not account for my normative theological choices according to some explicit methodology is true enough—I just do not think it matters for the project I had in hand in the book (or possibly at all). There is a criticism, however, that Luke Bretherton appears to advance (and that I have heard from others) which is related but rather more fundamental: that I do not make any normative theological choices at all, because I simply come cap in hand to social anthropology to learn how the world goes and then accept it, devoid of any critical means of judging "culture."

Bretherton declares that he "take[s] Banner's account of the nature and form of Christian ethics to be right," which is a generous and encouraging start (and I am very glad to receive it from someone who has thought carefully about the issues that concern us both). But I find myself perplexed when he goes on to make his further criticism about my cap-in-handedness given that each and every chapter of my book involves me in doing just what he says I fail to do. To take some examples, in chapter 2 I bring Augustine's reflection on the reality of Joseph's fatherhood of Jesus Christ to bear on our thinking about the use of assisted reproductive technologies. In chapter 5 I repudiate as wrongheaded the terms on which the current debate about the elderly is conducted, and in chapter 6 I contest the description of mourning practices provided by certain anthropologists. That does not seem terribly cap in hand to me. So I wonder why Bretherton is so concerned to disagree with me? The explanation for this misadventure may lie in Bretherton's being possessed of a typology for Anglican theology. The trouble with typologies is just, of course, that once you have one, the world needs chopping up in accordance with it. I feel I have been thusly chopped, although I do not want to complain too much since naturally I may find myself in some very good company. Brian Brock brings a different typology to the task of trying to fathom my method and meaning, and fortunately, it seems in no way procrustean.

Given the distinction I stated above in order to clarify (so I hope) what I was trying to do in *The Ethics of Everyday Life*, it will be clear why I particularly welcome Stephanie Mota Thurston's contribution to this collection. She discusses work over the last three decades within the womanist and *mujerista* traditions that identifies everyday lives lived in particular communities as authoritative expressions of ethical wisdom. I confess my prior ignorance of many of the writers she discusses, from whom I am sure I have much to learn.

I do wonder, however, whether the existence of this, as Thurston terms it, "marginal" strand within Christian moral theology should cause me to retract my pessimistic appraisal of contemporary Christian ethics. Other contributors point to this or that paper or book as insisting, long before I did, that moral theology needs an anthropological turn, contending that there has been something of a shift in the discipline away from engagement with philosophy and toward engagement with the social sciences in general, and social anthropology in particular—and thus that my pessimism is somewhat overstated.

One of the distinct pleasures of pessimism is the pleasure one can take in being wrong (not a pleasure, I find, that is very generally enjoyed). In this case, however, I find that the pleasure, which I would dearly love to experience, is postponed by the thought that, although my insistence on the importance of an anthropological turn may not be original (and originality is not, in my view, a high virtue in Christian ethics), it remains timely just because so much ethics seems to go on regardless of the need for such a turn. The example that recurs in my book concerns the abject miscomprehension of the parents at Alder Hey, and not just by hospital administrators and medical professionals but by the wider field of bioethics, within which, as far as I read it, no distinct and clear Christian voice was sounded maintaining the possible moral integrity or wisdom of the parental attitudes. In other words, the ethical world of the Alder Hey parents was not comprehended because, even though we have (allegedly) been making an anthropological turn for a good while now, the discipline really does not seem to have taken that to heart. And I could provide plenty of other examples of the ethnographic poverty of many discussions in many fields. That a splendid paper insisting on the significance of social anthropology for ethics was read at the National Academy of this or that many years ago may well be true; it is just that, as far as I can tell, not many people have noticed.

The discipline of moral theology or Christian ethics, or however we name it, has just not come to terms with the case for attending to social anthropology, no matter that the case is not brand new. Even though it is not concerned with the nature of moral theology, Robert Orsi's challenge to the practice of history (developed in *The Madonna of 115th Street*, or more specifically, in the three prefaces to the three editions of that work[3]) poses a challenge to moral theology that is still pertinent.

The crux of Orsi's argument is expressed in his repudiation of the concept or category of "popular religion" in favor of the concept or category of "lived religion" (borrowing a term that he credits to David Hall[4]). But lest this should seem a mere change of nomenclature, the designation *popular religion* not only named a field, says Orsi, but effectively served to proscribe it. More specifically, a central claim of the third edition is that "Religious theory played a key role in defining and policing the borders between acceptable and unacceptable religion and thus in shaping the inner worlds of modern persons."[5] That is to say, religious theory, with its category of "popular religion," positioned what Orsi now terms *lived religion* as beyond the pale, fit neither to be studied nor for that matter practiced. "The designation *popular religion* served to seal off certain expressions of religious life from an unspecified but obviously normative 'religion' (without the qualifier *popular*)."[6] There was, in other words, some serious boundary work going on here, which rendered "some practices and perspectives as essential to a particular religious and cultural world and others marginal."[7]

But boundary work of this kind is plainly not accidental. It is neither innocent nor uninterested, as it might be if it were simply a matter of tidy-mindedness and no more—as is, say, sorting knives and forks into different compartments in a cutlery drawer. In the boundary work Orsi describes, our interests are affected, even if they are not consciously consulted. Now Orsi is not very specific, and certainly not dogmatic, in specifying what interests have produced the boundary he describes (the boundary that discounts the devotion to the Madonna of 115th Street referred to in his title as a fit subject of study and an acceptable form of religious life). He does think, however, that although these boundaries may "present themselves as matters of academic or professional limits or standards," they "clearly involve much bigger existential and ethical dilemmas."[8] That is to say, then, that the marking and policing of these boundaries involves the taking of positions that "have to do with the nature of historical knowledge, with the relationships between ethnography and historiography, between present and past, and between everyday life and academic knowledge and protocols, with the relative usefulness of text and practice as historical sources, with the appropriate position of the scholar of religion to his or her subject, and with the gendering of knowledge."[9]

Whatever motivates the taking of these positions, what is clear is that only as we overcome the constraints of the category and concept of "popular religion," with its negative connotations and value judgments, can we actually attend to and take seriously "lived religion." As Orsi puts it,

> The study of lived religion explores how religion is shaped by and shapes the ways family life is organized, for instance; how the dead are buried, children disciplined, the past and future imagined, moral boundaries established and challenged, homes constructed, maintained, and destroyed, the gods and spirits worshipped and importuned, and so on. Religion is [thus] approached in its place within a more broadly conceived and described life-world, the domain of everyday existence, practical activity, and shared understandings, with all its crises, surprises, satisfactions, frustrations, joys, desires, hopes, fears, and limitations.[10]

It will be clear immediately, I think, how Orsi's interest in making "lived religion" the subject of historical attention (rather than an academically defined "religion") resonates with the interest of *The Ethics of Everyday Life* in attending to "lived ethics" or "everyday ethics" (rather than the idealized ethical schema of so much moral philosophy and moral theology). My suggestion is that moral theology has very typically been framed by an undeclared and unacknowledged distinction between ethics and popular ethics, or between ethics and lived ethics as we might put it. I suspect, however, that for the most part we have not even bothered to refer to popular ethics and certainly did not pause for long enough to wonder what it is or how it works. We never troubled to describe it. At best—or at worst, I should say—we probably imagined it. The creation and policing of this unacknowledged boundary is not accidental but rather the work of a set of preferences or interests. Whatever these interests may be (and the tradition to which Thurston refers us would name patriarchy as one), they have produced an account of ethics, or a way of conceiving it, that replicates many of those boundaries to which Orsi points in his critique of the practice of history. Plainly, my ill-advised talk of *the* Christian imagination may have suggested an attempt to confine and constrain the range of what is counted as Christian in a similar way.

In other ways, *The Ethics of Everyday Life*, so I suggest, indicates at various places some of the lines that have been drawn in specifying the subject. Within Christian ethics, these lines privilege written texts above all else as the proper source for study in moral theology, particularly abstract treatments of the subject over more practical treatments—thus Thomas on the natural law over Benedict's Rule, for sure, but just as certainly either of those over the paintings of Rembrandt or the slave songs of America, or over the lives of the "saints" who fashion their Christian lives among the trials and tribulations of their existences. But the boundaries and lines relate not only to the nature of the sources that are preferred and permitted but also to what is deemed important or even fit subject matter for ethics. Thus, Christian ethics (as a formal discipline), so I would say, has typically taken an interest in what it deems significant (and male) over what it has deemed less significant (and female)—thus political ethics and the ethics of war, for example, over the ethics of childbearing, caring, or mourning.

*The Ethics of Everyday Life* is, I believe, aware of a distinction between ethics as a subject of study and ethics as a lived practice, for that is what its turn to social anthropology and its promotion of "everyday ethics" is all about. But it is by no means as clear or insistent as it should be that the proper practice of Christian ethics (still) requires an overcoming of moral theology just as necessarily as it requires the overcoming of moral philosophy.

We need to fashion an ethics that is concerned to fathom and describe real ethical lives rather than the phantom lives we have tended to conjure up, either for praise or blame. So let me conclude by again citing Orsi's concern for the "ongoing efforts of men and women to make sense of, to live more or less well within, and to represent and communicate their worlds, [in] work that goes on in endless rounds of conversation, reflection, discussion, imagination, practice, gesture and ritual."[11] Christian ethics needs to attend to this work and to take it seriously. It needs to have the humility and patience to engage ethical lives attentively and openly, with a willingness to allow these lived ethical worlds to disclose themselves to us. And it needs the skills of the anthropologist for this patient listening since ethnography can, like history in Orsi's words, "teach us something new about ourselves, about the limits of our imaginings and ways of knowing, and even of our particular and distinctive ways of being human."[12]

## Notes

1. Michael Banner, *The Ethics of Everyday Life: Moral Theology, Social Anthropology, and the Imagination of the Human* (Oxford: Oxford University Press, 2014). Several chapters in the current volume began as presentations at the May 2016 conference "Everyday Ethics: A Future for Moral Theology" at The McDonald Centre for Theology, Ethics, and Public Life at the University of Oxford.

2. See Farneth, chapter 1; Thurston, chapter 2; and Herdt, chapter 5.

3. Robert Orsi, *The Madonna of 115th Street: Faith and Community in Italian Harlem, 1880–1950*, 3rd ed. (New Haven, CT: Yale University Press, 2010).

4. David D. Hall, *Lived Religion in America: Toward a History of Practice* (Princeton, NJ: Princeton University Press, 1997).

5. Orsi, *Madonna of 115th Street*, xiv.

6. Orsi, xxxii.

7. Orsi, xxxiii.

8. Orsi, xxxi.

9. Orsi, xxx.

10. Orsi, xxxii.

11. Orsi, xliv.

12. Orsi, xlv.

# APPENDIX

---

## EVERYDAY ETHICS: A BIBLIOGRAPHIC ESSAY

### Patrick McKearney

Until recently, a bibliographic review of the relationship between social anthropology and moral theology would have been very short indeed. In this chapter, I identify two trends that have made a conversation between these disciplines unlikely and I highlight changes that have prompted a more constructive interdisciplinary dialogue between social anthropology and moral theology. To illustrate tensions and alternatives, I consider two themes—suffering and tragedy—that illuminate different kinds of connections between different positions in theology and anthropology. Along the way, I identify some of the most important texts and authors working in each area and the central questions that emerge in this exchange. Ultimately, I hope this bibliographic essay highlights relevant resources for scholars, students, and citizens interested in exploring further research in this burgeoning field.

## Trends

Two trends have hindered the interdisciplinary exchange between social anthropology and moral theology. The first is each discipline's tendency to studiously ignore the other. Anthropologists have long been averse to studying explicitly the ethical lives of their informants (Lambek 2000; Faubion 2001; Laidlaw 2002; Mahmood 2004) and to taking seriously normative religious frameworks in general (Asad 1983; Robbins 2006), particularly Christian ones (Cannell 2005; Harding 1991).

### Critiques of Anthropology's Lack of Focus on Ethics

- Lambek, Michael. "The Anthropology of Religion and the Quarrel between Poetry and Philosophy." *Current Anthropology* 41, no. 3 (2000): 309–20.
- Faubion, James D. "Toward an Anthropology of Ethics: Foucault and the Pedagogies of Autopoiesis." *Representations* 74, no. 1 (2001): 83–104.

- Laidlaw, James. "For an Anthropology of Ethics and Freedom." *The Journal of the Royal Anthropological Institute* 8, no. 2 (2002): 311–32.
- Mahmood, Saba. "The Subject of Freedom." In *Politics of Piety: The Islamic Revival and the Feminist Subject*. Princeton, NJ: Princeton University Press, 2004.

## Critiques of Anthropology's Approach to Religion and Christianity

- Asad, Talal. "Anthropological Conceptions of Religion: Reflections on Geertz." *Man* 18, no. 2 (1983): 237–59.
- Harding, Susan. "Representing Fundamentalism: The Problem of the Repugnant Cultural Other." *Social Research* 58, no. 2 (1991): 373–93.
- Cannell, Fenella. "The Christianity of Anthropology." *Journal of the Royal Anthropological Institute* 11, no. 2 (2005): 335–56.
- Robbins, Joel. "Anthropology and Theology: An Awkward Relationship?" *Anthropological Quarterly* 79, no. 2 (2006): 285–94.

Meanwhile, moral theology—in part because of its association with philosophical ethics (Banner 2014, 18–22)—has traditionally suffered from a lack of engagement with how people actually practice ethics in their social lives.

## Critiques of Moral Theology

- Cannon, Katie G. *Katie's Canon: Womanism and the Soul of the Black Community*. New York: Continuum, 1995.
- Isasi-Díaz, Ada María. *Mujerista Theology: A Theology for the Twenty-First Century*. Maryknoll, NY: Orbis, 1996.
- Hauerwas, Stanley. *With the Grain of the Universe: The Church's Witness and Natural Theology*. Grand Rapids, MI: Brazos Press, 2001.
- Scharen, Christian, and Aana Marie Vigen, eds. *Ethnography as Christian Theology and Ethics*. London: Continuum, 2011.
- Banner, Michael. Introduction to *The Ethics of Everyday Life: Moral Theology, Social Anthropology, and the Imagination of the Human*. Oxford: Oxford University Press, 2014.
- De La Torre, Miguel A. *Doing Christian Ethics from the Margins*, 2nd ed. Maryknoll, NY: Orbis, 2014.

## Critiques of Philosophical Ethics

- Anscombe, G. E. M. "Modern Moral Philosophy." *Philosophy* 33, no. 124 (1958): 1–19.
- MacIntyre, Alasdair. *After Virtue: A Study in Moral Theory*. Notre Dame, IN: University of Notre Dame Press, 1981.

- Williams, Bernard. *Ethics and the Limits of Philosophy*. Cambridge, MA: Harvard University Press, 1985.
- Pincoffs, Edmund. *Quandaries and Virtues: Against Reductivism in Ethics*. Lawrence: University of Kansas Press, 1986.

The second trend is the recurrence of a significant, fraught, and remarkably similar divide *within* both disciplines between more engaged and more detached ways of conceiving the purpose of academic work. In anthropology this has manifested as the distinction between what we might term *activist* versus *culturalist* or *intellectualist* ways of tackling the question of normativity (Fassin 2008, 2012; McKearney 2016; Stoczkowski 2008). I define activists as those who see the point of anthropology as being to stand in solidarity with, attest to the suffering of, and / or politically represent the marginalized (Biehl 2005; Scheper-Hughes 1995). I regard as intellectualists those who are more wary of direct normative engagement—seeing the point of anthropology as helping us understand how, in general, cultural differences shape us and, more specifically, how they affect our particular understandings of morality and ethics (D'Andrade 1995; Robbins 2013).

### Intellectualism and Activism in Anthropology

- Clifford, James, and George E. Marcus, eds. *Writing Culture: The Poetics and Politics of Ethnography*. Berkeley: University of California Press, 1986.
- D'Andrade, Roy. "Moral Models in Anthropology." *Current Anthropology* 36, no. 3 (1995): 399–408.
- Scheper-Hughes, Nancy. "The Primacy of the Ethical: Propositions for a Militant Anthropology." *Current Anthropology* 36, no. 3 (1995): 409–40.
- Biehl, João. *Vita: Life in a Zone of Social Abandonment*. Berkeley: University of California Press, 2005.
- Fassin, Didier. "Beyond Good and Evil? Questioning the Anthropological Discomfort with Morals." *Anthropological Theory* 8, no. 4 (2008): 333–44.
- Stoczkowski, Wiktor. "The 'Fourth Aim' of Anthropology: Between Knowledge and Ethics." *Anthropological Theory* 8, no. 4 (2008): 345–56.
- Fassin, Didier. Introduction to *A Companion to Moral Anthropology*. Edited by Didier Fassin. Chichester, UK: John Wiley & Sons, 2012.
- Robbins, Joel. "Beyond the Suffering Subject: Toward an Anthropology of the Good." *Journal of the Royal Anthropological Institute* 19, no. 3 (2013): 447–62.
- McKearney, Patrick. "The Genre of Judgment." *Journal of Religious Ethics* 44, no. 3 (2016): 544–73.

In religious studies and religious ethics, a similar divide exists (Lewis 2011). But in many theological debates, this fault line manifests slightly differently. In these circles, the question is not whether theology can or should be normative; most take it as read that their academic pursuit necessarily is, and should be, directly engaged in shaping the ethical life of the reader. As a result, the division between intellectualist and activist projects expresses itself as different ways of configuring the relationship between doctrinal and empirical material (Coakley 2012). On the one hand, there are practical or pastoral theologians who have long been drawing on social scientific studies of contemporary moral and ecclesial situations in order to reflect on how to navigate them (Ballard and Pritchard 1996; Browning 1990; Healy 2000; Swinton and Mowat 2006). In this tradition, doctrine tends to take a backseat: it is either not referred to much at all, introduced in an ad hoc manner, or directly challenged with the empirical material.

On the other hand, there are those more doctrinal theologians who are suspicious of this approach (e.g., Milbank 1993; Webster 2012). These scholars tend to reject the idea that theology is worth doing only inasmuch as it is useful according to contemporary criteria. Instead, the point of theology, as they see it, is to provide a way to reflect in a more fundamental way on the categories we employ in our relation to the world. Theology, on this view, should not be measured by how realistic it is or how closely it fits the concerns of those who read it. Instead, theology should challenge our idea of what the "real" is and actively shape—rather than just respond to—our ethical concerns. This tradition's wariness of empirical approaches to theological material was most neatly and provocatively expressed by John Milbank as he ended one of the chapters of *Theology and Social Theory* by arguing that "If the analysis given in this chapter is correct, the sociology of religion should come to an end" (1993, 139).

## Practical and Doctrinal Theology

- Browning, Don S. *A Fundamental Practical Theology: Descriptive and Strategic Proposals*. Minneapolis, MN: Fortress Press, 1990.
- Milbank, John. *Theology and Social Theory: Beyond Secular Reason*. Oxford: Blackwell, 1993.
- Ballard, Paul, and John Pritchard. *Practical Theology in Action: Christian Thinking in the Service of Church and Society*. London: SPCK, 1996.
- Healy, Nicholas M. *Church, World and the Christian Life: Practical-Prophetic Ecclesiology*. Cambridge: Cambridge University Press, 2000.
- Swinton, John, and Harriet Mowat. *Practical Theology and Qualitative Research*. London: SCM Press, 2006.
- Lewis, Thomas. "On the Role of Normativity in Religious Studies." In *The Cambridge Companion to Religious Studies*, edited by Robert A. Orsi, 168–85. Cambridge: Cambridge University Press, 2011.

- Coakley, Sarah. "Ministry Is Not Easier than Theology." *Faith and Leadership*, October 22, 2012. www.faithandleadership.com/multimedia/sarah-coakley -ministry-not-easier-theology.
- Webster, John. "'In the Society of God': Some Principles of Ecclesiology." In *Perspectives on Ecclesiology and Ethnography*, edited by Pete Ward, 200–222. Grand Rapids, MI: Eerdmans, 2012.

This state of affairs did not stop interested scholars of either discipline from venturing into the other. So there have been many great anthropological works that engage with normative religious traditions (e.g., Douglas 1966; Evans-Pritchard 1956; see also Larsen 2014), and many anti-intellectualist activist projects within anthropology also rely, even if only implicitly, on existing normative philosophical frameworks for their points to have any cogency (e.g., Scheper-Hughes 1995). Similarly, the practical theologians cited above have long been interested in the empirical findings of social science, and even Milbank's more intellectualist project (e.g., 1995, 1997) has been well served by his use of the work of Marcel Mauss (1954) and René Girard (1972).

## Intellectualist Cross-Fertilization

- Mauss, Marcel. *The Gift: The Form and Reason for Exchange in Archaic Societies.* London: Cohen & West, 1954.
- Evans-Pritchard, E. E. *Nuer Religion.* Oxford: Clarendon Press, 1956.
- Douglas, Mary. *Purity and Danger: An Analysis of Concepts of Pollution and Taboo.* New York: Praeger, 1966.
- Girard, René. *Violence and the Sacred.* London: Bloomsbury Academic, 1972.
- Milbank, John. "Can Morality Be Christian?" *Studies in Christian Ethics* 8, no. 1 (1995): 45–59.
- Milbank, John. *The Word Made Strange: Theology, Language, Culture.* Cambridge, MA: Blackwell Publishers, 1997.
- Larsen, Timothy. *The Slain God: Anthropologists and the Christian Faith.* Oxford: Oxford University Press, 2014.

But these works were either pulled off by individual brilliance or relied on only sporadic engagement with other disciplines, leading to some uses of philosophy, theology, and social anthropology that may well have horrified those from the other side had they known about them. I am not at all sure, for instance, that anthropologists would think highly of empirical work in practical theology, nor what religious ethicists or moral philosophers would have made of any anthropological ethical proposals up until this point.

## Changes

In recent years, this situation has changed quite dramatically. Movements within both anthropology and moral theology have pushed these disciplines toward a genuine and fruitful engagement with the other that takes the other discipline as having something serious to teach it. Within anthropology, these movements are the anthropology of Christianity and the anthropology of ethics—both largely culturalist projects that have forged intellectually rigorous ways for a wider range of anthropologists to take normative religious and philosophical traditions a great deal more seriously than was possible before.

### Reforms within the Anthropology of Religion and the Dawn of the Anthropology of Christianity

- Asad, Talal. *The Idea of an Anthropology of Islam*. Center for Contemporary Arab Studies, Georgetown University, Washington, DC, 1986.
- Lambek, Michael. "The Anthropology of Religion and the Quarrel between Poetry and Philosophy." *Current Anthropology* 41, no. 3 (2000): 309–20.
- Robbins, Joel. "What Is a Christian? Notes toward an Anthropology of Christianity." *Religion* 33, no. 3 (2003): 191–99.
- Robbins, Joel. *Becoming Sinners: Christianity and Moral Torment in a Papua New Guinea Society*. Berkeley: University of California Press, 2004.
- Cannell, Fenella, ed. *The Anthropology of Christianity*. Durham, NC: Duke University Press, 2006.
- Keane, Webb. *Christian Moderns: Freedom and Fetish in the Mission Encounter*. Berkeley: University of California Press, 2007.

### The Emergence of the Anthropology of Ethics

- Mahmood, Saba. *Politics of Piety: The Islamic Revival and the Feminist Subject*. Princeton, NJ: Princeton University Press, 2004.
- Hirschkind, Charles. *The Ethical Soundscape: Cassette Sermons and Islamic Counterpublics*. New York: Columbia University Press, 2006.
- Zigon, Jarrett. *Morality: An Anthropological Perspective*. New York: BERG, 2008.
- Lambek, Michael, ed. *Ordinary Ethics: Anthropology, Language, and Action*. New York: Fordham University Press, 2010.
- Faubion, James D. *An Anthropology of Ethics*. Cambridge: Cambridge University Press, 2011.
- Fassin, Didier, ed. *A Companion to Moral Anthropology*. Chichester, UK: John Wiley & Sons, 2012.

- Laidlaw, James. *The Subject of Virtue: An Anthropology of Ethics and Freedom.* Cambridge: Cambridge University Press, 2013.
- Mattingly, Cheryl. *Moral Laboratories: Family Peril and the Struggle for a Good Life.* Berkeley: University of California Press, 2014.
- Keane, Webb. *Ethical Life: Its Natural and Social Histories.* Princeton, NJ: Princeton University Press, 2015.
- Lambek, Michael, Veena Das, Webb Keane, and Didier Fassin. *Four Lectures on Ethics: Anthropological Perspectives.* Chicago: HAU Books, 2015.
- Lambek, Michael. *The Ethical Condition: Essays on Action, Person, and Value.* Chicago: University of Chicago Press, 2015.

Within theological ethics, the impetus for engagement with anthropology has come from both sides of the intellectualist/activist divide. Practical theology's traditional emphasis on empirical material has developed into a more systematic engagement with ethnographic methods.

## The Ethnography and Ecclesiology Movement

- Fulkerson, Mary McClintock. *Places of Redemption: Theology for a Worldly Church.* Oxford: Oxford University Press, 2007.
- Scharen, Christian, and Aana Marie Vigen, eds. *Ethnography as Christian Theology and Ethics.* New York: Continuum, 2011.
- Scharen, Christian B., ed. *Explorations in Ecclesiology and Ethnography.* Grand Rapids, MI: Eerdmans, 2012.
- Ward, Pete, ed. *Perspectives on Ecclesiology and Ethnography.* Grand Rapids, MI: Eerdmans, 2012.

This has coincided with a growing tendency within more intellectualist scholarly traditions, and paralleled by ordinary language (e.g., Austin 1964) and neo-Aristotelian philosophy (e.g., MacIntyre 1998; Williams 1993; Lear 2006), to reflect theologically on artistic, historical, liturgical, and literary phenomena.

## Description in Moral Philosophy and Theology

- Austin, J. L. "A Plea for Excuses." In *Essays in Philosophical Psychology,* edited by Donald F. Gustafson, 1–29. Garden City, NY: Anchor Books, 1964.
- Hauerwas, Stanley. *The Peaceable Kingdom: A Primer in Christian Ethics.* Notre Dame, IN: University of Notre Dame Press, 1983.
- Williams, Bernard. *Shame and Necessity.* Berkeley: University of California Press, 1993.
- MacIntyre, Alasdair. *A Short History of Ethics: A History of Moral Philosophy from the Homeric Age to the Twentieth Century.* London: Routledge, 1998.

- Hauerwas, Stanley, and Samuel Wells, eds. *The Blackwell Companion to Christian Ethics*. Chichester, UK: Wiley-Blackwell, 2006.
- Lear, Jonathan. *Radical Hope: Ethics in the Face of Cultural Devastation*. Cambridge, MA: Harvard University Press, 2006.
- Ford, David F. *Christian Wisdom: Desiring God and Learning in Love*. Cambridge: Cambridge University Press, 2007.
- Banner, Michael. *Christian Ethics: A Brief History*. Chichester, UK: John Wiley & Sons, 2009.
- Quash, Ben. *Found Theology: History, Imagination and the Holy Spirit*. London: Bloomsbury T&T Clark, 2013.

This movement has experimented more recently with the possibility of reflecting theologically and ethically by recourse to anthropological and sociological descriptions more specifically (Isasi-Díaz 1993; Adams and Elliott 2000; Frederick 2003; Floyd-Thomas 2006; Stout 2010; Snarr 2011; Bretherton 2012; Coakley 2013; Bretherton 2015).

*Sociological and Anthropological Description in Theology and Religious Ethics*

- Isasi-Díaz, Ada María. *En La Lucha / In the Struggle: A Hispanic Women's Liberation Theology*. Minneapolis, MN: Fortress Press, 1993.
- Adams, Nicholas, and Charles Elliott. "Ethnography Is Dogmatics: Making Description Central to Systematic Theology." *Scottish Journal of Theology* 53, no. 3 (Autumn 2000): 339–64.
- Frederick, Marla F. *Between Sundays: Black Women and Everyday Struggles of Faith*. Berkeley: University of California Press, 2003.
- Floyd-Thomas, Stacey M. *Mining the Motherlode: Methods in Womanist Ethics*. Cleveland, OH: Pilgrim Press, 2006.
- Stout, Jeffrey. *Blessed Are the Organized: Grassroots Democracy in America*. Princeton, NJ: Princeton University Press, 2010.
- Snarr, C. Melissa. *All You That Labor: Religion and Ethics in the Living Wage Movement*. New York: New York University Press, 2011.
- Bretherton, Luke. "Coming to Judgment: Methodological Reflections on the Relationship between Ecclesiology, Ethnography and Political Theory." *Modern Theology* 28, no. 2 (2012): 167–96.
- Coakley, Sarah. *God, Sexuality, and the Self: An Essay "On the Trinity."* Cambridge: Cambridge University Press, 2013.
- Bretherton, Luke. *Resurrecting Democracy: Faith, Citizenship, and the Politics of a Common Life*. Cambridge: Cambridge University Press, 2015.

One of the striking things about these movements within theology, anthropology, and religious ethics is the way in which they have begun to challenge not simply the opposition *between* but also the traditional divides *within* the disciplines. There is still an important difference between the ethnography and ecclesiology movement and the movement toward drawing on anthropological studies as part of doctrinal reflection on ethics. But these two projects stand in a much more interesting relationship to each other—as well as to questions about normativity and the role of doctrine—than the previous practical and doctrinal camps did. Similarly, while the impetus for change has come largely from the intellectualist side in anthropology, the increasing involvement of this scholarly project with normative religious traditions and serious ethical questions has forced these intellectualists into a more exciting and sophisticated engagement with questions about normativity.

All of this has produced the happy situation in which a bibliographic review of the relationship between anthropology and moral theology must struggle not so much to scrabble together a few disconnected threads but, as the above bibliographies attest, to select carefully from the many works. However, the abundance of material does not necessarily make it easy for students and experts in either discipline to navigate this dialogue. I hope that the bibliographies above already help with that task. But there is still more that can be said because the difficulty is not just knowing what is happening elsewhere but also finding a way to draw the connections between alternative conversations and those one is involved in.

The difficulty of this task often leaves scholars in one discipline being drawn to a particular approach in another that well suits their own objectives, without realizing the implications of their choice—or that they have even made one at all. This is an inevitable part of the early stages of such interchange, but it runs the risk of turning an aspiration for dialogue into just a monologue that uses the words of another. To maintain the possibility of a genuinely interdisciplinary conversation between theology and anthropology, in which both sides will be challenged in surprising ways as they go forward, it is essential to understand the debates that have formed the various positions within each discipline—and the relationship between these diverse standpoints and those one occupies in one's own field. As a way to respond to this difficulty, in what remains I want to take two themes—suffering and tragedy—as ways to draw different kinds of connections between different positions in theology and anthropology.

## Suffering

In this section, I outline the contours of the considerable debate that has surrounded the topic of suffering within anthropology. In the course of doing so, I draw connections between the various positions within this debate and analogous ones that have been staked out by theologians in other conversations. My aim in doing so is to encourage interested theologians not simply to borrow one of the anthropological perspectives in isolation but rather to incorporate and draw on this anthropological conversation as they arrive at their own stance. My argument is that a greater understanding of this debate will enable theologians to use anthropology more subtly, to render their own positions more explicit, and, in doing so, to deepen and enrich their disagreements with each other.

I begin with the most explicit collaborative connection that has so far been forged between an anthropological project and a theological one.[1] Christian Scharen and Aana Marie Vigen's (2011, 48–50) *Ethnography as Christian Theology and Christian Ethics* marks itself as clearly in opposition to the kind of intellectualist project that Milbank (1993) pursues; instead it signals its trajectory toward a more activist form of theological work that uses the practice of ethnography to achieve its ends. To ground their project in dialogue with anthropology, Scharen and Vigen turn to re-nowned anthropologist João Biehl (2005).[2] For those outside of anthropology, it is worth asking, Why Biehl?

Some context to Biehl's project will be helpful here. As far back as the 1980s, Scheper-Hughes (1995) had argued that intellectualist descriptions and analyses were distancing anthropologists from the plight of those they worked with. These worries were echoed by those outside of anthropology who argued that, far from helping us respond to humanitarian crises, mass-media images of suffering were producing "moral fatigue, exhaustion of empathy, and political despair" (Sontag 2004, 71). A number of anthropologists took up these moral concerns with vigor and came to argue that ethnography had the capacity to remedy this situation. They sought a way to produce a kind of anthropology that would have a deeper affective and moral impact on those who read it (Kleinman, Das, and Lock 1997; Das et al. 2001; Biehl, Good, and Kleinman 2007).

Biehl's (2005) debut ethnographic monograph *Vita* in many ways marks the cul-mination of this project. It narrates the story of how Biehl came to know and offer his help to Caterina, a woman who has been classified as having some kind of psy-chological disorder. Biehl argues, however, that the force with which this classifica-tion has been applied to Caterina represents simply one more way in which she has been betrayed by the Brazilian state, medical establishment, and her family, to the point that she is now consigned to a corrupt and degenerate shell of a care home. Biehl's representation of Caterina's plight through distressing narrative and com-pelling photography cannot fail to move. It constitutes a "finely tuned aesthetic of misery" that fully embodies the kind of affective description that these reforming anthropologists hoped would play such a vital role in responding to contemporary crises (Csordas 2007, p. 2009).

*The Anthropology of Suffering*

- Scheper-Hughes, Nancy. "The Primacy of the Ethical: Propositions for a Militant Anthropology." *Current Anthropology* 36, no. 3 (1995): 409–40.
- Kleinman, Arthur, Veena Das, and Margaret Lock, eds. *Social Suffering*. Berkeley: University of California Press, 1997.
- Das, Veena, Arthur Kleinman, Margaret Lock, Mamphela Ramphele, and Pamela Reynolds, eds. *Remaking a World: Violence, Social Suffering, and Recovery*. Berkeley: University of California Press, 2001.
- Sontag, Susan. *Regarding the Pain of Others*. London: Penguin, 2004.
- Biehl, João. *Vita: Life in a Zone of Social Abandonment*. Berkeley: University of California Press, 2005.
- Biehl, João, Byron Good, and Arthur Kleinman, eds. *Subjectivity: Ethnographic Investigations*. Berkeley: University of California Press, 2007.
- Csordas, T. J. "Vita: Life in a Zone of Social Abandonment. João Biehl." *American Ethnologist* 34, no. 2 (May 2007): 2009–12.

This is why Scharen and Vigen chose Biehl: because he has been arguing for the ascendancy, within anthropology, of the kind of direct engagement with the "poor" that Scharen and Vigen advocate for in a theological setting. It was a very astute choice, too. Biehl not only shares their scholarly aspirations but has, it is widely agreed, realized them to a greater degree than most anthropologists. Biehl's book won enormous admiration and with it a significant number of followers for his kind of anthropology of suffering. As they seek to reform theology to take more seriously the plight of those who, as they see it, are left out of theological analyses of the church and of ethics, Scharen and Vigen could not have chosen a better anthropologist to draw on.

If I were to end the story there, I could simply hail a successful cross-fertilization between anthropology and theology. But the success of Biehl's book is not the only story that can be told about it. If Biehl's ability to fulfill his purposes has rarely been questioned within anthropology, the purposes themselves have been subject to greater scrutiny. So now I turn to the anthropological concerns that have been raised about Biehl's work—and go on to draw attention to some similarities between the kind of intellectual tradition that leveled criticisms at Biehl's anthropological project and analogous strands of contemporary theology.

One of the most high-profile criticisms of Biehl's work comes in Joel Robbins's (2013) article that contrasts this kind of activist anthropology of suffering with more traditional anthropological aims of depicting cultural difference. Robbins argues that a culturalist approach has typically been animated not by a conviction to remedy ills so much as a hope of finding a better way of living "out there." While he does not advocate an unreconstructed return to this objective, Robbins argues that focusing purely on suffering, as Biehl does, carries with it significant dangers. In particular, he contends that the objective of sharing in the trauma of distant others through empathetic engagement with them encourages us to ignore cultural differences (see also Fassin and Rechtman 2009; Fassin 2011). In particular, he contends that a stronger sense of cultural difference allows us to portray others not just as victims of hegemonic structural processes but rather as agents pursuing particular kinds of moral good. He thus argues for an "anthropology of the good" that would at least sit alongside, and perhaps encompass, an anthropology of suffering.

To exemplify what he is arguing for, it is worth turning our attention briefly to Sophie Day's (2010) narration of the life journeys of sex workers in London (see also Day 2007). Day describes how young sex workers are highly aware of the moral importance, in a British context, of the distinction between love and money: genuine relationships, in this moral imagination, have nothing to do with financial transactions and are, indeed, corrupted by them. When they start sex work, these young women maintain this moral stance absolutely—distinguishing carefully between their contractual relationships and their really affectionate ones. But, Day relates, as they get older they see that their careful moral work goes unnoticed and that their simple involvement in sex work renders them morally impure in the eyes of many. As a result, through activism and forming affectionate relationships that straddle the supposedly inviolable boundary between these ethical categories, they eventually come to critique the justice of a dichotomy that renders their lives subject to so much moral condemnation.

It is one of the virtues of Day's ethnographic account that she relates the stories of these women with considerable humanity, giving us an insight into their remarkable courage in the face of difficulty. But Day's narration does not stop there. Instead of simply portraying their suffering at the hands of wider forces, Day also gives a strong sense of how these women make sense of these difficulties and try to construct ethical lives in the midst of them. Her attention to the detail of their ethical aspirations—the ways in which these women come to aspire to particular and unexpected moral goods—is the key here. Had Day's story simply stopped with a more generic story of hardship, emphasizing the difficulty of the situation these women find themselves in, she would have missed some of the most important and surprising aspects of their engagement with ethical life.

Robbins's proposal of an anthropology of the good, as exemplified in work like Day's, has generated a great deal of controversy among those he categorized as working on the anthropology of suffering (e.g., Biehl et al. 2015). To many anthropologists, however, Robbins diplomatically pulled some of the most significant punches. Those sympathetic to Robbins's argument, but wanting to go further, would argue that the problem with the anthropology of suffering is not simply that it narrows our anthropological focus but that it can actively distort it (see, for instance, the re-sponses appended to Scheper-Hughes [1995]). It leads us to imagine ourselves as the benevolent, empathetic saviors of those we work with rather than as people need-ing to understand the complex situations we encounter. The job of anthropology, on this alternative account, is not to rush into the kind of moralism the anthropol-ogy of suffering responds to and propagates. Instead, anthropology's task should be to challenge, by attention to the fine details of cultural difference, this readiness to pursue and impose universalistic moral projects without reflection on them. Part of the "point of anthropology," as Robbins puts it, is "to challenge our own versions of the real" (2013, 458).

## Anthropological Debate and Alternatives

- Day, Sophie. *On the Game: Women and Sex Work*. London: Pluto Press, 2007.
- Fassin, Didier, and Richard Rechtman. *The Empire of Trauma: An Inquiry into the Condition of Victimhood*. Princeton, NJ: Princeton University Press, 2009.
- Day, Sophie. "Ethics between Public and Private: Sex Workers' Relationships in London." In *Ordinary Ethics: Anthropology, Language, and Action*, edited by Michael Lambek, 292–309. New York: Fordham University Press, 2010.
- Fassin, Didier. *Humanitarian Reason: A Moral History of the Present*. Berkeley: University of California Press, 2011.
- Robbins, Joel. "Beyond the Suffering Subject: Toward an Anthropology of the Good." *Journal of the Royal Anthropological Institute* 19, no. 3 (2013): 447–62.
- Biehl, João, Naisargi N. Dave, Anne Alison, C. Han, L. Cohen, and Angela Garcia. "What We Talk about When We Talk about Suffering." Presented at the 2015 Annual Meeting of the American Anthropological Association, Denver, 2015.

It is here that I see routes back into conversations within theological ethics. Scharen and Vigen (following the precedent of Scheper-Hughes and Biehl) sometimes por-tray the theological alternative to their approach as a cold, detached, and unempa-thetic type of intellectualist pursuit. But this is not the only way to articulate those approaches to moral theology that focus their energies into reflection over activ-ism. Consider, for instance, a recent set of lectures on empathy by Rowan Williams (2015a, 2015b), who argues that conceiving of empathy as an erasure of difference between self and other (such as that Robbins identified in Biehl's focus on shared suf-fering and a lack of concern for cultural difference) is morally troubling. As Williams asserts, sympathy, so construed, covers over the need for complex political and moral negotiation of our difference; thus, it can lead to an unhealthy absorption in the life of another and a failure to recognize them *as* an *other*.

234 • PATRICK MCKEARNEY

In an earlier essay called "The Judgment of the World," Williams (2000 [1989]) offers a constructive proposal for how we might conceive of appropriately responding to the other. In doing so, I see him as articulating a theological version of Robbins's intellectualist project in anthropology. Williams sees good intellectual work and good ethical engagement as characterized by a "contemplative hesitation" before the other that neither rushes into identification nor hangs back from involvement completely. Instead, this process involves mutual transformation wherein each party is reconfigured in unpredictable ways by the other. It is not that they simply learn new bits of ethical information to process but rather that their whole frame of ethical reference is challenged.

This gives us another way to articulate Robbins's critique of Biehl. Robbins's argument gestures toward the conclusion that Biehl's moral aims are unaffected by the particular situation at hand. Neither Biehl's encounter with Caterina nor the complex sociopolitical situation in Brazil directly transforms his existing understanding of right or wrong. Instead, the ethnography simply adds affective weight to his existing understanding of the world. Williams allows us to describe Robbins's perspective, by contrast, as a more contemplative than activist way to engage with others—one open to what *they* might have to teach *us*.

This is the alternative vision of ethnographic engagement that Luke Bretherton offers to us in his (2012) article "Coming to Judgment." He draws on another strand of the intellectualist tradition within anthropology—as exemplified, in this case, by the work of Timothy Jenkins (1994, 1999)—to describe fieldwork as a complicated process of apprenticeship, discernment, and negotiation. Bretherton uses this mode of anthropological engagement to approach his own theological-ethnographic work rather differently from how Scharen and Vigen approach theirs. Rather than witnessing to suffering, Bretherton contemplatively attends to a particular attempt to practice the "good" in the form of community organizing. He argues that doing ethnography in this mode trains one in vital theological virtues—a kind of reflective judgment that neither detaches from conversation nor rushes in to impose its prefabricated conceptual and moral project.

## Theological Debate and Alternatives

- Jenkins, Timothy. "Fieldwork and the Perception of Everyday Life." *Man* 29, no. 2 (June 1994): 433–55.
- Jenkins, Timothy. *Religion in English Everyday Life: An Ethnographic Approach.* New York: Berghahn Books, 1999.
- Williams, Rowan. *On Christian Theology.* Oxford: Wiley-Blackwell, 2000.
- Bretherton, Luke. "Coming to Judgment: Methodological Reflections on

the Relationship between Ecclesiology, Ethnography and Political Theory."
*Modern Theology* 28, no. 2 (April 2012): 167–96.

- Williams, Rowan. "Myself as Stranger: Empathy and Loss." Given at the Tanner
  Lectures on Human Value, Cambridge, MA, Harvard University, 2015a.
- Williams, Rowan. "The Other as Myself: Empathy and Power." Given at the
  Tanner Lectures on Human Value. Cambridge, MA, Harvard University, 2015b.

Here, then, around the relationship between intellectual work and the suffering of
the distressed, we begin to see two contrasting ways in which anthropology and theology might be practiced and related to each other. I hope to have shown that the
difference between Scharen and Vigen's theological project, on the one hand, and
Bretherton's, on the other, correlates with the type of anthropology they employ.
And I hope that presenting this situation challenges any sense that there is any one
way for theology to engage with anthropology, or for ethics to become ethnographic.

But, similarly, I hope that this presentation does not encourage a further divide
between different approaches. My argument is that within both anthropology and
theology there are significant disagreements about the role normativity should play
in academic work that are animated by a commitment to intellectualism or activism.
My purpose has been to make clear some of what has remained implicit so far in
these conversations. The aim has been to clarify the positions being staked out, and
their implications, so that the disagreement between them might be acknowledged,
deepened, and, in time, made more complex. But part of what is so promising about
the recent movement toward anthropology within theology—to which Bretherton,
Scharen, and Vigen have contributed much—is the development of a more complicated middle ground between the previously well-defined borders of practical and
doctrinal approaches to ethics. In the next and final section, I go on to suggest that
attention to tragedy rather than suffering will enable this middle ground to develop
in and between anthropology and theology even further.

## Tragedy

In this section I argue that, by translating the focus on suffering into one on tragedy,
the distinctions between activism and intellectualism become helpfully complicated.
For instance, although many of the anthropological authors cited in the previous section have opposed answers to questions about suffering, they might be said to share
a similar project: to reform anthropology's attention to tragedy. Scheper-Hughes
(1995), for instance, criticized much anthropology for filtering out the nastier aspects
of social life, the ways in which sometimes things go wrong and people do wrong

in horrific ways. But Scheper-Hughes has herself been criticized (see the responses to that same article) for losing a sense of any specifically *moral* tragedy—the ways in which life presents complex ethical choices rather than the stark either-or, good/evil decisions she portrays.

Similarly, Biehl (2005) might be said to be bringing tragedy properly to the fore. But his search for a shared communion in trauma might also be said to be imposing a particular and potentially inappropriate understanding of tragedy on a complex social picture (Robbins 2013). Likewise, Robbins's intellectualist approach could be said to either ignore tragedy altogether or argue for a culturalist understanding of it—that is, contending that things can go wrong in multiple ways and that not everyone will agree on what tragedy consists of. Laidlaw (2013, 138–78) has also criticized Mahmood (2004) for ignoring the ways in which ethical projects are open to multiple forms of moral failure. But Das (2014) has criticized him, in turn, for overintellectualizing such agonizing ethical situations.

The intellectualist and activist positions on this front can be seen as different ways to reform anthropology's traditional inattention to tragedy. The more activist approach of Scheper-Hughes (1995), Biehl (2005, 2012), and Das (2014) focuses on the precarity of human existence. These authors emphasize the vicissitudes of such basic conditions of participating in ethics as being alive, having political freedom, and staying sane. Our dependence on these factors makes our subjectivity and our life highly vulnerable to external forces.

By contrast, the intellectualist approach of Robbins (2004, 2007, 2013), Laidlaw (2013, 2014), Mattingly (2013; 2014, 33–58, 80–121), Zigon (2007), Lambek (2010), and Faubion (2011) works toward foregrounding another manifestation of tragedy in ethical life: the presence of value conflicts and the ways people negotiate them. Essential to the work of all these more culturalist authors is a sense that ethics always involves a reflective relationship to difficult choices, easy scripts for which are not provided by one's culture.[3] Their diverse work can be regarded as various attempts to find a position that holds together both the fact that social forces decisively influence our moral lives and that this fact does not mean morality is simply a matter of social reproduction. Instead, as Laidlaw puts it, ethics always involves a degree of agonism (2013, 108).

*Debates about Tragedy in Anthropology*

- Robbins, Joel. "Between Reproduction and Freedom: Morality, Value, and Radical Cultural Change." *Ethnos* 73, no. 3 (2007): 293–314.
- Zigon, Jarrett. "Moral Breakdown and the Ethical Demand." *Anthropological Theory* 7, no. 2 (2007): 130–50.

- Biehl, João. "Care and Disregard." In *A Companion to Moral Anthropology*, edited by Didier Fassin, 242–63. Chichester, UK: John Wiley & Sons, 2012.
- Mattingly, Cheryl. "Moral Selves and Moral Scenes: Narrative Experiments in Everyday Life." *Ethnos* 78, no. 3 (2013): 301–27.
- Das, Veena. "Ethics, the Householder's Dilemma, and the Difficulty of Reality." *HAU: Journal of Ethnographic Theory* 4, no. 1 (2014): 487–95.
- Laidlaw, James. "Significant Differences." *HAU: Journal of Ethnographic Theory* 4, no. 1 (2014): 497–506.

But while this intellectualist perspective on value conflict represents a decisive contrast to the activist anthropological focus on suffering, at a philosophical level the two approaches to tragedy are more easily reconcilable. So, for instance, philosophers such as Martha Nussbaum (1986), Bernard Williams (1981), and Jonathan Lear (1995, 2006) have done much to attend simultaneously to human dependency in ways that Biehl might endorse and to value conflict in just the kind of ways that Laidlaw would encourage. Indeed, for theologians, it is far from obvious that, out of this relatively unified philosophical emphasis on tragedy and vulnerability, one should end up with the radically different academic traditions that anthropology tends to splinter into (e.g., Mathewes 1990).

## Tragedy in Philosophy

- Williams, Bernard. *Moral Luck: Philosophical Papers, 1973–1980*. Cambridge: Cambridge University Press, 1981.
- Nussbaum, Martha C. *The Fragility of Goodness: Luck and Ethics in Greek Tragedy and Philosophy*. Cambridge: Cambridge University Press, 1986.
- Mathewes, Charles. "The Rebirth of Tragedy." *Anglican Theological Review* 79, no. 2 (1990): 253–61.
- Lear, Jonathan. "Testing the Limits: The Place of Tragedy in Aristotle's Ethics." In *Aristotle and Moral Realism*, edited by Robert Heinaman, 61–84. London: UCL Press, 1995.

As a result, the category of tragedy allows us to focus our energies not on maintaining the divisions between existing camps within theology and anthropology but rather on finding scholarly work that innovatively brings both of these perspectives on tragedy together in productive ways. Rebecca Lester's *Jesus in Our Wombs* (2005) is a good example of this. Her ethnographic monograph follows a series of women as they become nuns in a Mexican religious order. Lester traces their journey from their initial explorations of their vocation, through their entry into the convent, and into the spiritual practices they encounter, internalize, and cultivate within it. There is much that is commendable in the ethnography, but the point I want to make here is quite specifically about Lester's portrayal of the process of discerning whether one is called to be a nun through realizing one's "brokenness."

The institution demands that novice nuns reflect on whether they truly have a vocation to be there by considering their own inadequacies. This process is emotionally demanding on the novices as they contemplate their own sinfulness and try to decide whether their long-held aspiration for life in the convent is really from God or an illusion they need to abandon. Because so many novices do come through this process to become nuns, it would be easy to read this supposedly fraught reflection as really just another example of effective socialization and enculturation processes—far from being affected by individual agency or chance, the process actually reliably turns ordinary people into nuns.

But Lester's sensitivity to the ethical aspect of her informants' lives leads her to see that discerning one's vocation in this way is the major individual and communal moral labor of all of the stages of formation within the convent up until taking perpetual vows—and one that is absolutely fraught with risk. When the postulants successfully inculcate a sense of their own brokenness, weakness, and inadequacy before Christ, they are paradoxically exposing themselves to the thought that they really might not have a vocation at all as well as realizing a major step on the road to convincing themselves and the elder nuns that they do in fact have such a vocation. Not everyone gets past this point—the convent is not a perfectly self-reproducing social organism but rather an ongoing ethical improvisation. By resisting viewing this process of formation in brokenness as either an inauthentic performance or a form of authoritarian indoctrination, Lester gives a picture of her informants as both open to value conflicts *and* ethically fragile at the same time.

Authors as diverse as Day (whose work I described in the previous section), Scheper-Hughes (1993), Anand Pandian (2009), and Omri Elisha (2011) achieve something analogous. Veena Das's (e.g., 2007) research on violence in India and Mattingly's work with poor, single, Black mothers of disabled and/or terminally ill children represent similar achievements of integration between these perspectives (e.g., Mattingly 2010, 2014). These authors manage to combine attention to the way their informants pursue specific cultural goods (and the value conflicts these various goods produce) with a heightened sense of the very real, painful, and often humanly imposed material limits to their ability to do so.

## Examples of Tragic Writing in Anthropology

- Scheper-Hughes, Nancy. *Death without Weeping: The Violence of Everyday Life in Brazil.* Berkeley: University of California Press, 1993.

- Lester, Rebecca. *Jesus in Our Wombs: Embodying Modernity in a Mexican Convent.* Berkeley: University of California Press, 2005.
- Das, Veena. *Life and Words: Violence and the Descent into the Ordinary.* Berkeley: University of California Press, 2007.
- Pandian, Anand. *Crooked Stalks: Cultivating Virtue in South India.* Durham, NC: Duke University Press, 2009.
- Mattingly, Cheryl. *The Paradox of Hope: Journeys through a Clinical Borderland.* Berkeley: University of California Press, 2010.
- Elisha, Omri. *Moral Ambition: Mobilization and Social Outreach in Evangelical Megachurches.* Berkeley: University of California Press, 2011.

Some contemporary philosophers (e.g., Lear 2006; Nussbaum 1986) and a number of theological authors have pulled off a similar feat (see also Surin 1989; Taylor and Waller 2011). Take, for instance, Stanley Hauerwas's more descriptive writing in *Suffering Presence* (1986), in which he articulates the multiple goods pursued by the American medical profession, the conflicts that arise between them, and the damage this does to vulnerable human beings. In doing so, he combines a sense of universal vulnerability with a culturally specific understanding of how things go wrong. Williams's (2002) *The Body's Grace* also reaches such heights as it explores how the lack of attention to difficulty, complication, and tragedy in various approaches to sexual ethics renders them impoverished descriptions of reality and poor ethical guides. Banner (2014), especially in his discussions of the Alder Hey scandal and the sensibility of mourning, takes us there often as well.

## Tragedy in Theology

- Hauerwas, Stanley. *Suffering Presence: Theological Reflections on Medicine, the Mentally Handicapped and the Church.* Notre Dame, IN: University of Notre Dame Press, 1986.
- Surin, Kenneth, ed. *Christ, Ethics and Tragedy: Essays in Honour of Donald MacKinnon.* Cambridge: Cambridge University Press, 1989.
- Williams, Rowan. "The Body's Grace." In *Theology and Sexuality: Classic and Contemporary Readings,* edited by Eugene F. Rogers, 309–21. Oxford: Blackwell, 2002.
- Taylor, Kevin, and Giles Waller, eds. *Christian Theology and Tragedy: Theologians, Tragic Literature, and Tragic Theory.* Surrey, UK: Ashgate, 2011.

The inability of much previous anthropological, philosophical, and theological work to combine both of these perspectives on tragedy suggests that it is no easy task. But the fact that those works that have already achieved a measure of success in this task have proven so provocative and engaging to both sides of the intellectualist/activist divide indicates that it is a search well worth continuing. There is something about a careful attention to the force and varieties of human limitation that is ethically rich in ways that can speak across theoretical and disciplinary fault lines and, in doing so, prompt a much more complicated kind of ethical discussion that challenges both poles of the debate. My suggestion would be that future work in anthropology and theology might follow the lead of these works by trying less to distinguish than to combine these two ways to focus on human vulnerability—or any other area of ethics. At stake in this enterprise is what is at stake more generally in this book's efforts to deepen conversations between theology and anthropology: learning how to speak with greater humility, integrity, and depth about the ethics of everyday lives.

## Notes

1. My discussion here owes much to Michael Banner's work on suffering. I hope, though, to expose more systematically the relationship between theological and anthropological positions than his subtle interweaving of the two aims at. See Michael Banner, *The Ethics of Everyday Life: Moral Theology, Social Anthropology, and the Imagination of the Human* (Oxford: Oxford University Press, 2014).

2. Not only is his work hailed as an example of good anthropology that many of the authors in the volume attempt to replicate, but he also directly adds his anthropological seal of approval to the book on the blurb.

3. For important differences, see James Laidlaw, *The Subject of Virtue: An Anthropology of Ethics and Freedom* (Cambridge: Cambridge University Press, 2013), 124–34; James Laidlaw, "Significant Differences," *HAU: Journal of Ethnographic Theory* 4, no. 1 (2014): 497–506; and Cheryl Mattingly, "Moral Selves and Moral Scenes: Narrative Experiments in Everyday Life," *Ethnos* 78, no. 3 (2013): 301–27.

# CONTRIBUTORS

**Michael Banner** is dean, fellow, and director of studies in Theology and Religious Studies at Trinity College at the University of Cambridge. He held previous appointments at the University of Oxford, King's College London, and Edinburgh University. He was chair of the Committee of Enquiry for the Ministry of Agriculture, the CJD Incidents Panel at the Department of Health, the Home Office's Animal Procedures Committee, and the Shell Panel on Animal Testing. He was also as a member of the Royal Commission on Environmental Pollution and the Human Tissue Authority. He currently serves on the Ministry of Defence's Advisory Committee on Less Lethal Weapons. He is the author of *Christian Ethics and Contemporary Moral Problems*, *Christian Ethics: A Brief History*, and *The Ethics of Everyday Life: Moral Theology, Social Anthropology, and the Imagination of the Human*.

**Luke Bretherton** is professor of theological ethics and senior fellow of the Kenan Institute for Ethics at Duke University. Previously he was reader in Theology and Politics at King's College London. Alongside numerous journal articles and contributions to edited volumes, he is the author of *Hospitality as Holiness: Christian Witness amid Moral Diversity*; *Christianity & Contemporary Politics: The Conditions and Possibilities of Faithful Witness*, winner of the 2013 Michael Ramsey Prize for Theological Writing; *Resurrecting Democracy: Faith, Citizenship and the Politics of a Common Life*; and, most recently, *Christ and the Common Life: Political Theology and the Case for Democracy*. He also writes in the media (including *The Guardian*, *The Times*, the *Washington Post*, and *ABC Religion and Ethics*) on topics related to faith and politics.

**Brian Brock** is professor of moral and practical theology in the School of Divinity, History, and Philosophy at the University of Aberdeen. Along with numerous articles and edited volumes in moral theology, he is the author of *Christian Ethics in a Technological Age*, *Singing the Ethos of God: On the Place of Christian Ethics in Scripture*, and *Wondrously Wounded: Theology, Disability and the Body of Christ*. He is the managing editor of the *Journal of Disability and Religion*.

**Morgan Clarke** is associate professor of social anthropology at the University of Oxford and fellow of Keble College. His research focuses on the anthropology of religion, ethics, law, and medicine, with a special interest in Islam in the Middle East. He is the author of *Islam and New Kinship: Reproductive Technology and the Shariah in Lebanon* and *Islam and Law in Lebanon: Sharia within and without the State*.

**Molly Farneth** is assistant professor of religion at Haverford College. She is the author of *Hegel's Social Ethics: Religion, Conflict, and Rituals of Reconciliation*. Her research focuses on religious and philosophical ethics, ritual studies, feminist and gender studies, and the relationship between religion and politics. She is currently working on a book on the political significance of ritual.

**Craig M. Gay** is professor of interdisciplinary studies at Regent College in Vancouver, British Columbia. He is the author of *With Liberty and Justice for Whom?*; *The Way of the (Modern) World: Or, Why It's Tempting to Live as if God Doesn't Exist*; *Cash Values: The Value of Money, the Nature of Worth*; and *Dialogue, Catalogue & Monologue: Personal, Impersonal and Depersonalizing Ways to Use Words*. His latest book is titled *Modern Technology and the Human Future: A Christian Appraisal*.

**Eric Gregory** is professor of religion and chair of the Council of the Humanities at Princeton University. He is the author of *Politics and the Order of Love: An Augustinian Ethic of Democratic Citizenship*. He has published widely on Christian ethics, political theology, and the role of religion in public life. He is currently finishing a book titled *The In-Gathering of Strangers: Global Justice and Political Theology*.

**Jennifer A. Herdt** is Gilbert L. Stark Professor of Christian Ethics at Yale University Divinity School. The author of *Putting on Virtue: The Legacy of the Splendid Vices* and *Religion and Faction in Hume's Moral Philosophy*, she has served as guest editor for special issues of the *Journal of Religious Ethics* and the *Journal of Medieval and Early Modern Studies* and serves on the editorial boards of the *Journal of Religious Ethics* and *Studies in Christian Ethics*. Her most recent book is *Forming Humanity: Redeeming the German Bildung Tradition*.

**Michael Lamb** is assistant professor of politics, ethics, and interdisciplinary humanities and director of the Program for Leadership and Character at Wake Forest University. He is also a research fellow with the Oxford Character Project. He has published articles on the virtue of hope, the ethics of climate change communication, and the thought of Aristotle, Augustine, and Aquinas. He is currently finishing a book titled *A Commonwealth of Hope: Reimagining Augustine's Political Thought*.

**Philip Lorish** is a fellow of the Institute for Advanced Studies in Culture at the University of Virginia and director for Cultural Research at Praxis Labs. He holds a PhD in theology, ethics, and culture from the University of Virginia, an MPhil in Christian ethics from the University of Oxford, and a BA in philosophy from Furman University. He is currently working on a book on the future of work, *Our Permanent Problem: Work and Meaning in the 21st Century*.

**Charles Mathewes** is Carolyn M. Barbour Professor of Religious Studies at the University of Virginia. He is the author of *Evil and the Augustinian Tradition*, *A Theology* *of Public Life*, *Understanding Religious Ethics*, and *The Republic of Grace: Augustinian Thoughts for Dark Times*. He is also a senior editor of *Comparative Religious Ethics: The Major Works*. He is currently finishing a book on the future of political theology.

**Patrick McKearney** is a research associate and affiliated lecturer at the Max Planck Cambridge Centre for Ethics, Economy and Social Change, in the Department of Social Anthropology at the University of Cambridge. He holds a PhD in social anthropology and two degrees in theology and religious studies. His research explores the moral lives of people with mental disabilities in care settings, religious and secular, in the United Kingdom and India. He has published in *The Journal of Religious Ethics*, *City & Society*, *The Cambridge Journal of Anthropology*, and *The Journal of Disability and Religion*.

**Rachel Muers** is professor of theology at the University of Leeds. Among many articles and books, she is the author of *Living for the Future: Theological Ethics for Coming Generations* and *Keeping God's Silence: Towards a Theological Ethics of Communication*, co-author of *Theology on the Menu: Asceticism, Meat, and Christian Diet*, and co-editor of *Eating and Believing: Interdisciplinary Perspectives on Vegetarianism and Theology*.

**Stephanie Mota Thurston** is a PhD candidate at Princeton Theological Seminary and holds an MAR in ethics from Yale and a BA in religious studies and politics from Scripps College. At Princeton Seminary, she oversees the Certificate of Theology and Ministry's inside-outside prison cohort and is the director of the Center for Theology, Women, and Gender. Her dissertation research uses ethnographic methods to explore practices of civic formation in public schools. She is particularly interested in how young people form civic habits and identities amid a diversity of racial, ethnic, linguistic, and religious identities.

**Justin Welby** is the 105th archbishop of Canterbury. Previously he spent eleven years as an executive in the oil industry. Among his many positions in the Church of England, he served as dean of Liverpool and bishop of Durham before being installed as archbishop of Canterbury. A member of the House of Lords and the Parliamentary Commission on Banking Standards, he is the author of *Can Companies Sin? "Whether", "How" and "Who" in Company Accountability*.

**Brian A. Williams** is dean of the Templeton Honors College and assistant professor of ethics and liberal studies at Eastern University. He previously served as departmental lecturer in theology and Christian ethics at the University of Oxford. He holds a DPhil and MPhil in Christian ethics from the University of Oxford, where he was a Clarendon Scholar, and a ThM and MA in systematic theology from Regent College, Vancouver. He is the author of *The Potter's Rib: Mentoring for Pastoral Formation* and is currently finishing a book on the theology and practice of education in Hugh of St. Victor, Philip Melanchthon, and John Henry Newman.

# INDEX